Healthy People in Unhealthy Places

Healthy People in Unhealthy Places

Stress and Fitness at Work

KENNETH R. PELLETIER

A MERLOYD LAWRENCE BOOK
Delta/Seymour Lawrence

A MERLOYD LAWRENCE BOOK
Delta/Seymour Lawrence Edition
Published by
Dell Publishing Co., Inc.
1 Dag Hammarskjold Plaza
New York, New York 10017

Reprinted by arrangement with Delacorte Press/Seymour Lawrence
Printed in the United States of America

First Delta printing — March 1985

Published by arrangement with
Robert Briggs Associates,
San Francisco

Acknowledgments

Increasingly, the year 2000 A.D. is coming to mark a point of profound transformation in the life of every individual aboard spaceship Earth. One of the most striking characteristics of our planet's growing population is that more people are attaining extreme longevity than at any other time in history. In the United States alone, the number of people living well beyond 65 years of age will more than double from 25 million in 1980 to over 55 million in 2030. As the chronic, degenerative diseases of arthritis, cardiovascular disorders, cancer, diabetes, and psychological disruption also increase with exponential rapidity, the necessity of finding ways to limit these preventable conditions becomes more and more evident. Before this trend reaches a plateau in approximately 2030 to 2050 A.D., medicine will evolve from a pathology management industry to a true health care system out of economic imperatives and humanitarian concerns. To do this, we need to move from individual to collective approaches and to create optimum health and productivity for all of humankind. Marking the cutting edge of this transformation is an unusual aggregate of groups: intentional communities, small towns, some multinational corporations, and many organizations operating on the principle that the same factors which determine health and longevity for the individual body and mind are the same for the larger or incorporated body and mind.

Writing this book required venturing into areas of economics, politics, and organizational development which seemed far removed from clinical practice and health research. Actually, this manuscript represents part of an ongoing study of the means of attaining optimum health, productivity, and performance for individuals and organizations. Exploring this rapidly evolving area has been made possible by grants from the California NEXUS Foundation, The Minneapolis Foundation, the Ruth Mott Fund, and The San Francisco Foundation. Several key individuals and organizations gave generously of their time and expertise. I would like to extend heartfelt thanks to Willis Goldbeck and Anne K. Kiefhaber of the Washington Business Group on Health; Cole Mandelblit of IBM

Corporation; George Pfeiffer of Xerox Corporation; and Norman
Cousins of the UCLA School of Medicine.

Additionally, many other individuals and their companies provided
data, materials, discussions, letters of support, and invaluable assistance
in translating the world of health care for the world of personnel and corporate development, and vice versa. For their generous assistance, I am
most grateful to Roy R. Anderson of Allstate Insurance; John J. Bagshaw,
M.D., of Physis; Robert N. Beck of Bank of America; Rinaldo S. Brutoco
of Dorason Corporation; Dennis Calacino of PepsiCo; Rick J. Carlson,
J.D., of the California Governor's Council on Wellness and Physical Fit-
ness; Fi-yin Chua of Wells Fargo Bank; Wallace Fulton of the Equitable
Life Assurance Company; F. Richard Cunningham of Parcourse; Clyde
C. Green, M.D., of Pacific Telephone; T. George Harris of *American
Health;* Joyce Hengesbach of PMI Mortgage Insurance Company; Rudi
Hurwich, management counselor; Frank Koch of Syntex Corporation;
James S. J. Manuso, Ph.D., of James S. Manuso and Associates; Marc
Michaelson of General Dynamics; Mark Rocchio of the Lawrence Li-
vermore Laboratory; Gordon Sherman, former president of Midas
muffler; and Frederick Crocker Whitman of Crocker National Bank.

Finally, there are my friends and colleagues who have always provided
sage counsel, constructive critiques, and most of all, their support and encouragement to continue! For their help I am most thankful to Anthony
Athos, Ph.D.; C. West Churchman, Ph.D.; Carol Cone; Dahlia Ducker,
Ph.D.; Leonard J. Duhl, M.D.; Ken Dychtwald, Ph.D.; Jonathan Fielding, M.D., M.P.H.; Albert R. Martin, M.D.; Rollo May, Ph.D.; Don W.
Miller; Don Michael, Ph.D.; and as always, Frances Wilcox. Each of
these individuals personifies the gift of standing on the earth and reaching toward the heavens.

Contents

Healthy People
in Unhealthy Places

CHAPTER I

INTRODUCTION:
Making the Workplace Healthier

An asbestos factory worker cannot breathe. In Salem County, New Jersey, bladder cancer is epidemic among men working in chemical plants. Workers in Palo Alto's "Silicon Valley" report severe headaches and vomiting due to allergic reactions to chemicals used in electronics manufacturing. In courtrooms on the East and West coasts distraught wives of prominent business executives press lawsuits contending that excessive stress induced their husbands' suicides. This dire litany could be extended indefinitely.

In seeming contrast, millions of men and women have given up smoking, are exercising and jogging, are eating healthier diets, have lost weight, are managing stress more effectively, and are moving toward optimum health and longevity. A 1961 Gallup poll indicated that approximately 24 percent of adults in the United States exercised regularly; that figure increased to 47 percent by 1977, and recent trends indicate an even greater rise in the future. No simple explanation can account for this trend, which involves nearly 100 million people and was characterized by George Gallup as "one of the most dramatic changes in lifestyle" he has ever measured in his public polls. Individual motivation ranges from a personal health crisis to a conscious decision to live a more fulfilling life. Then what? No matter what individuals do to assume a greater responsibility for their lives and their health, they soon recognize one evident fact. All of these efforts take place on the periphery of a forty- to fifty-hour block of time—work.

Work consumes most of an individual's life for the most important years, and is usually second only to sleep in the sheer number of occupied hours. This has been true down through the ages. Recently, however, attitudes toward work have been changing. Writing in *Quest/81*, author and philosopher Sam Keen noted a radical shift in personal, workplace, and cultural values: "Our changing valuation of work is a symptom of our changing view of all reality. The new iconoclasm is directed against the idolatry of economics, the myth of money, the assumptions that more is better, work makes free (the motto that was emblazoned on the gate over Auschwitz), technology can make us all healthy, wealthy, and wise. Many . . . have reached the top of the success ladder but are beginning to suspect it may be leaning against the wrong wall" (1981). Recent studies have indicated that approximately 5 percent of employed individuals in the United States have changed the nature of their livelihood in keeping with a break from these traditional values. The same decade has been marked by an unprecedented increase in employee dissatisfaction with virtually every aspect of work. For these reasons, as well as because of its inordinate influence upon every aspect of a person's life, the workplace is the most obvious focus when individuals move from a personal to a collective concern with the determinants of health and longevity.

According to the Italian physician Bernardino Ramazzini, who is considered the founder of occupational medicine: " 'Tis a sordid profit that's accompanied by the destruction of health. Many an artisan has looked at his craft as a means to support life and raise a family, but all he has got from it is some deadly disease." That was written in 1705. More recently, individual concern over personal health has grown into a significant cultural and economic influence. New health-related industries have arisen, as well as health-oriented social organizations and large-scale events. The concern for better diets has changed the shelves of supermarket chains; women's health collectives and the movement to humanize the birth process have had a substantial impact upon hospital economics and practices; other groups have influenced government programs such as nuclear energy plants, or insisted on the reduction of occupational hazards ranging from toxic chemicals to excessive stress. These aggregates of people have had a major influence upon every aspect of life as we evolve into the twenty-first century.

CAUTION: WORK MAY BE HAZARDOUS TO YOUR HEALTH

"My job is killing me" is more than a cliché; it is a tragic fact that has been evident since our prehistoric ancestors first recognized that hunters suffered the highest mortality. Modern hazards are often less visible, but just as deadly. According to conservative statistics, available in brochures and reports from the President's Council on Physical Fitness and Sports, there are over 14,000 job-related deaths and millions of disabling injuries every year. Low back pain is perhaps the most common disability for both blue-collar and office workers, with an estimated 75 million workers affected. In economic terms, this one malady costs $1 billion annually in lost productivity and $250 million in employee compensations. Other government studies have estimated 25 million unreported injuries per year, and over 390,000 bases of work-related disease, which result in more than 100,000 deaths annually. As shocking as these statistics are, they are limited to the effects of "visible" machine and chemical accidents in certain hazardous occupations. Among those affected are: industrial chemical workers, miners, plastic industry workers, insecticide makers, sprayers, painters, shoemakers, and medical technicians. Increased incidence of cancer of the liver and brain has been found among plastic industry workers exposed to vinyl chloride, respiratory diseases such as chronic bronchitis and emphysema among textile workers exposed to cotton dust, and leukemia and aplastic anemia among petrochemical and oil refinery workers. This list is expanding constantly as disease is shown to be linked to supposedly harmless electromagnetic radiation, or cancer-causing agents are demonstrated to affect workers' children, not the workers themselves.

At the same time it is becoming increasingly evident that there are also "invisible" hazards. Among these are noise and crowding in work areas, inadequate lighting and ventilation, psychological burnout, boredom, and aggressive or absent communications among workers and management, rush deadlines, job instability and fear of unemployment, erratic work schedules, and the presence of "stress carriers" and "workaholics" who actually disrupt more work than they accomplish. These invisible hazards are less well-recognized and yet are perhaps more amenable to immediate change. The Occupational Safety and Health Administration (OSHA) has recently listed the jobs highest in "occupational stress." Among those affected by these "invisible" hazards are: manual laborers, secretaries, inspectors, clinical lab technicians, office managers, foremen, and over fifty similar occupations. As a result of exposure to these invisible hazards, there has been an alarming increase in all minor and major stress-related disorders, alcoholism, prescription and nonprescription drug abuse, and suicide. Virtually every working individual is exposed to both visible and invisible workplace hazards. During 1981 the national health expenditures were more than $320 billion, more than twice as high as in 1976. This expenditure represents more than 9 percent of the Gross National Product (GNP) and that figure is increasing exponentially. Of that staggering $320 billion, estimates are that employers pay from a minimum of 25 percent to over 60 percent. Premature deaths cost business and industry $25 billion and 132 million lost workdays in 1981 alone. In the same year, it cost industry $700 million a year just to replace victims of heart attacks at all levels of employment. These costs are passed on to every consumer in the form of higher prices on all goods and services. Compared to these costs, the approximately $2 billion being spent annually on corporate health promotion programs seems like a bargain. Thus there is an enormous incentive to both corporations and individuals to lower or at least limit this vast drain on the economy.

Examples of the kind of costs which are forcing business and industry to confront issues of health maintenance and disease prevention abound on all sides:

1. A recent study indicated that smoking cost employers $27.5 billion with $8.2 billion in direct medical costs and $19.3 billion in indirect costs such as absenteeism. According to the National Interagency Council on Smoking and Health, the average one-pack-per-day smoker costs an employer more than $600 per year above and beyond the heart- and lung-disease risk to the individual. Lost wages due to cigarette-related illnesses have been estimated at over $3 billion (*Business Week*, 1976; Shimer, 1978).

2. For alcohol abuse alone, the total costs were $44.2 billion, with $11.9 billion in direct costs and $32.3 billion in indirect costs. Alcoholic employees experience twice the average rate of absenteeism as other employees (Du Pont, 1979; Erfurt and Foote, 1977; Follman, 1976; Schramm, 1977).

3. General Motors spent more money, $825 million per year, on health insurance and disabilities than on steel from U.S. Steel, one of its principal suppliers. Furthermore, these costs added more than $175 per automobile for its 1979 models. Disease treatment costs become a part of every service or product (Parkinson et al., 1982; Sapolsky et al., 1981; Stacey, 1980).

4. Similarly, Ford Motor Company estimates health care cost per employee at $3,350 per year and $290 per automobile during the year 1980. On a positive note, Ford saved $2 million annually from

the voluntary participation of 10,000 employees in a Health Maintenance Organization (HMO). That constitutes only 4 percent of its United States work force (Parkinson et al., 1982; *U.S. News & World Report,* 1980).

5. On any given day in 1982, the Metropolitan Life Foundation estimates, over one million workers will call in sick. In fact, more than 330 million workdays are lost each year due to illness and the resulting absenteeism (Metropolitan Life Association, 1982).

6. A survey by Pacific Mutual Life has estimated the cost of replacing a high-level executive between $250,000 and $500,000. Xerox Corporation estimates the cost of losing an executive at age 41 as $600,000 to over $1 million (*Behavior Today,* 1978).

7. Equitable Life Assurance has estimated the cost of one person with a chronic headache in 1979 at $3,394.50 per year.

a.	Visits to employee health center	$ 473.14
b.	Time away from work	56.61
c.	Work interference due to symptoms	2,206.95
	Work interference affecting superiors	72.80
	Work interference affecting co-workers	542.88
	Work interference affecting subordinates	42.12

(*Manuso,* 1978)

8. In 1980 the National Institute for Occupational Safety and Health estimated the cost of "executive stress" alone at $10 billion to $20 billion in the United States. That figure covers only the clearly measurable items as workdays lost, hospitalization, outpatient care, and mortality:

	Conservative Estimate	Ultraconservative Estimate
Cost of executive work loss days (salary)	$ 2,861,775,800	$1,430,887,850
Cost of executive hospitalization	248,316,864	124,158,432
Cost of executive outpatient care	131,058,235	65,529,117
Cost of executive mortality	16,470,977,439	8,235,488,720
	$19,712,128,338	$9,856,064,119

These statistics bring to mind Everett Dirksen's famous quip, "A billion here, a billion there—pretty soon you are talking about real money!" Their staggering proportions have thrust preventive health and holistic medicine concerns beyond the quarter of a million people directly involved in health care, upon the attention of the 200 million who are not.

SPHERES OF INFLUENCE

Given the enormity and complexity of hazards to health in the workplace, is there anything the individual can do? To clarify this critical question, it is helpful to picture an individual at the center of a series of concentric spheres surrounded by the vital health determinants which will be discussed throughout this book. We are not passive victims, but many of the adverse forces affecting our health can be corrected only by group action. Health in the workplace is one more area, along with stress management, auto safety, and nuclear weapons control, in which individuals are becoming empowered to take a more active role in determining their individual and collective destiny. At each level of the following diagram there are vital fulcrum points or "Spheres of Influence" where action can be effectively undertaken.

1. *SPHERE I—Individual Action:* At the center are personal health choices, such as stress management, "workaholic" behavior, "stress addiction," nutrition, physical activity, cigarette smoking, alcohol and drug abuse, under the control of the individual. Among steps an employee can take to maintain health at work are education in lifting techniques for prevention of back injuries, stretching exercises for secretaries and virtually all white-collar workers who spend long hours seated at a desk, stress management programs, and choosing healthier food from what is available in workplace cafeterias, or bringing nutritious food from home.

2. *SPHERE II—Group Action:* In the second ring are factors which can be influenced both by group action on the part of the employees and by management. Such hazards include toxic chemical exposure, noise pollution, poor air quality, poor lighting conditions, monotonous jobs. Reduction of unnecessary organizational stressors, improved employee-with-employer communications, introduction of modifications such as Japanese "quality circles," educational pro-

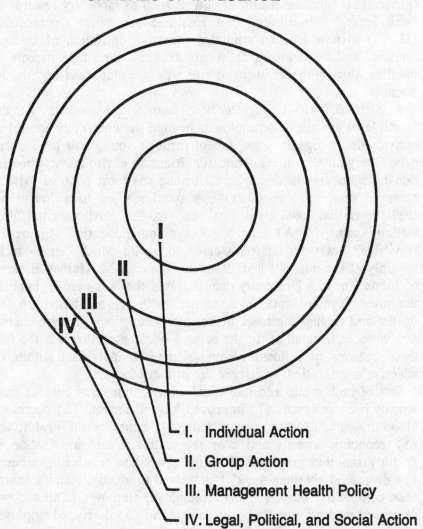

SPHERES OF INFLUENCE

I

II

III

IV

I. Individual Action

II. Group Action

III. Management Health Policy

IV. Legal, Political, and Social Action

grams in "medical self-care," are improvements which management and employees can undertake together.

3. *SPHERE III—Management Health Policy:* Health policies and incentives determined primarily by management belong in this sphere. These include health incentives such as monetary rewards or "well leave," subscription to a Health Maintenance Organization (HMO) plan which can minimize excessive utilization of medical services, and provision of child-care facilities for single parents or families when both the husband and wife are employed outside the home.

4. *SPHERE IV—Legal, Political, and Social Action:* At the fourth level are health determinants beyond the immediate control of individuals or organizations, except through voting and legal channels. Everything from economic conditions to environmental protection laws belongs in this sphere. Among the most obvious "visible areas of concern" are the OSHA standards, or hazardous-waste regulations that have been weakened by the Environmental Protection Agency (EPA) under the Reagan administration. Among the "invisible" but work-related hazards to health which can be tackled only at the national level is unemployment. M. Harvey Brenner of Johns Hopkins University demonstrated that a 1 percent jump in the unemployment rate is associated with an additional 36,887 deaths and related increases in hospital admissions, imprisonments, and violence in families. In the present book, however, it is the first three Spheres of Influence, emphasizing the individual within an adaptive organization, which are the primary focus.

Out of such group and individual efforts, numerous benefits have already been achieved: (1) improved job satisfaction; (2) decreased blood pressure; (3) improved morale; (4) better overall health; and (5) economic awards and peer recognition from participation in health promotion programs. For employers, the benefits have been: (1) decreased absenteeism; (2) improved productivity and a sharpened competitive edge; (3) better employer-employee relations; (4) decreased medical and disability claims; and (5) decreased employee turnover. All of these benefits are mutually enhancing and justify additional effort within each sphere.

THE ECONOMICS OF HEALTH PROMOTION

Health promotion programs in the workplace offer a structured environment in which to encourage health enhancement for the benefit of employee and employer. The challenge for health professionals is to recognize that many individuals and organizations are not at all interested in health per se since they are not in the health-care business but are concerned only about the delivery of their services and products and in turning a profit. Ultimately, health promotion programs in the workplace must meet and pass measures of cost-effectiveness or they will be discarded. However, there is absolutely no inherent reason why economic concerns are incompatible with effective health care. In fact, it is increasingly likely that economic concerns will have a salutory effect and help shift the emphasis in health care from crisis management to prevention and health promotion.

Companies have only begun to realize that their investment in health issues is not limited to benefit costs alone. Less than ten years ago virtually all medium to large employers used insurance companies and Blue Cross / Blue Shield for their employee health insurance. However, this has begun to change. Many companies run self-funded health plans, health maintenance programs, and a vast range of health promotion programs from jogging and smoking cessation to family counseling services. ". . . increased company involvement may well be a posture of active consumerism and resource management on the part of industry. Providers of health . . . are being challenged . . . by corporate America" (Levin and Wolfson, 1982). One of the most frequently cited means for regulating costs, used by companies rather than by outside insurance carriers, has been to structure health benefit packages so that employees are given more direct participation in the costs of care. Republic Steel uses a $100 deductible charge applicable each time an employee is admitted to the hospital, and Du Pont has initiated a trial benefits-package for its Texas employees that contains higher deductibles in return for higher catastrophic coverages. Many programs to date use these incentives to reduce excess utilization but do not use any direct positive rewards or incentives to employees for health promotion activities. At this point, the idea is that if employees share the costs of health care, they won't use medical care unless it is necessary.

This does not deny the value of or access to necessary medical care but does insist that such measures be utilized more conservatively in conjunction with a more general focus upon health maintenance. Among the proponents of humanitarian economics in health care is Bruce Stokes, of the Worldwatch Institute in Washington, D.C., who wrote an excellent editorial in *Science* under the title of "Self-Care: A Nation's Best Health Insurance." Clearly, Stokes recognizes that "in life-threatening situations, the ill should have the benefit of the best medical expertise, drugs, and medical technology that they and society can afford," but he also asserts that any national health care plan "should be tied to a program that would encourage people to take more responsibility for their own health. Self-care incentives should be built into any national health plan. If the first $500 or $1,000 that families spend on health care each year came out of their own pockets, there would be a built-in incentive to limit trips to the doctor and to practice more self-care" (1979). This is not indifference to ill health but the recognition of looming financial and social pressures. Such an approach is necessary to "create a public awareness that runaway health care costs are, in part, a social problem arising from overreliance on the medical system for treatment of even the simplest illnesses and that cost containment is a joint government and individual responsibility" (Stokes, 1979). It is possible to begin to work toward a health care system which restores individual involvement rather than relegating payments to a remote insurance carrier which fosters the illusion that medical care is free.

Another related illusion is that hospitalization plans, insurance, and intensive medical intervention can really compensate for the damage caused by a lifetime of unhealthy habits. If incentive programs are undertaken without adequate health education, without self-care groups and programs, or without individual people gaining economic and health benefits from reduced utilization, they will not be effective. Although such a system is yet to be created, it is possible and has been eloquently stated in *Strategies for Public Health* (1981) edited by physician Lorenz K. Y. Ng, as well as in *The Hidden Health Care System* (1981) by Lowell S. Levin of the Department of Public Health at Yale University. When individuals at home and in the workplace begin to assume a more active role in their personal and collective health, it may be possible to have a more cost-effective approach and these savings in dollars and sound health should be returned to the participating individuals.

When he was Secretary of the Department of Health and Human Services, Richard S. Schweiker stated: "We are going to stress . . . preventive health care. Another word for preventive health care is 'wellness.' For example, many companies are finding out that there is a big advantage to keeping their employees healthy. . . . We hope to encourage such programs by providing incentives for them . . . to give people incentives to stay well rather than get sick . . . to find out more about what people can do to live longer" (Cranton, 1981). Despite the prominence and consistency of these acknowledgments, health promotion programs have not advanced very rapidly. This is puzzling. A 1981 task force for the California Department of Health Services under chief physician Kathleen H. Acree pointed out that such programs are not necessarily very complex: "In one sense the planning of the health promotion program is very straightforward. Only a limited number of health behaviors have been shown to at all improve health. Even the methodologies for influencing the behaviors, while not totally satisfactory, are well-identified." If the need for individual and organizational health promotion has been unequivocally recognized and the means for implementation are readily available and such measures have proven out in limited but promising studies of cost-effectiveness, why are such programs not more evident?

A critical factor in this question, and one which has a direct bearing upon every aspect of health promotion in the workplace, is the need for *incentives*. To encourage involvement, there is a fundamental need to restore the economic benefits engendered by that participation, to any one person or group of people who voluntarily undertake health promotion efforts. Until such positive incentives are created at least to offset the innumerable negative incentives which already operate, any health promotion efforts will not have enough inherent or immediate reward to sustain them over time and they will fail. In an excellent article entitled, "The Health Promotion Organization," physician Lorenz K. Y. Ng and his colleagues of the National Institute on Drug Abuse show how the incentives tend to encourage sickness:

> . . . the health care system provides economic incentives for sickness rather than health, in that people receive financial re-

wards from most health care plans only when they are ill. Physicians are paid only for treating illnesses, and there is no incentive to focus on methods for promoting health. These negative incentives extend into other realms as well. . . . Such practices not only fail to reward those who are healthy or who make an effort to reward those who are healthy or who make an effort to stay healthy, but also implicitly penalize them. (*Ng, Davis, and Manderscheid, 1978*)

There is no other place, except the public school system, where sickness incentives are more prominent than in the workplace, where sick days can translate into time off, where disability claims can be tantamount to a paid vacation, and sickness care is seen as free or at least paid by a remote third party. None of this implies deliberate manipulation or deception on the part of the vast majority of working people.

The incentives of the system simply are conducive to certain behaviors. At present the scenario is one of infinitely escalating costs, diminishing returns, and negligible effects upon the health of the population, within a system where supply and demand are controlled by virtually the same organizations. Health promotion, in fact, may be inherently contradictory to the present system. An empty hospital earns no money; an empty organization or company earns no money; but for entirely different reasons both are vying for the time and occupancy of the same person.

By contrast, health promotion programs have used positive incentives such as courses in stress management, discounts on goods and services, memberships to recreational facilities and fitness clubs, salary increases, and even the creation of planned "well days" in place of unused sick leave. Health incentives are a controversial realm with potential for manipulation and abuse, and these issues are considered in later chapters in greater detail. There is a fine line between an appropriate incentive or encouragement and an undue inducement or coercion in matters related to employee health. Based upon his extensive work with over 200 companies of the Fortune 500, Willis Goldbeck, president of the Washington Business Group on Health, has clearly analyzed the need to be aware of multiple incentives and motivations in any health promotion program: "One should never approach a potential corporate supporter with exaggerated claims of future savings. Cost savings are a very legitimate reason for employers to be interested, but that reason alone is not sufficient. Community groups need to work with employers along the whole spectrum of logical, health, financial, environmental and ethical motivations for developing a wellness agenda in every community" (Goldbeck, 1982).

Any attempt to formulate a true health care system, i.e., one designed to elicit and sustain optimum health and longevity for the population as a whole, must keep the need for incentives in mind. In a memorandum to former California Governor Jerry Brown, attorney Rick J. Carlson, chairman of the California Governor's Council on Wellness and Physical Fitness, states three constraints which have held back the development of effective health promotion programs:

. . . first the lack of disincentives to deter people from using unnecessary and inappropriate curative medical services and as a result, contain stampeding medical care costs. Second, the lack of sufficiently powerful incentives to encourage people to assume more responsibility for their health and therefore utilize less medical care also resulting in cost containment. And third, the availability of money to develop realistic health promotion options to aid them in assuming that responsibility. (*Carlson and Goldbeck, 1979*)

These constraints have affected both individuals and organizations. Despite them, the movement to create the healthy workplace as an adjunct to and extension of individual lifestyle practices is becoming a reality in some innovative and prominent government agencies, school districts, major corporations, small businesses, several major universities, and numerous health promotion facilities.

BASIC PRINCIPLES OF WORKPLACE HEALTH PROMOTION

Turning to the question of what constitutes an effective health promotion program, there are certain consistent principles which need to guide both individual and organizational programs:

1. First and foremost is a vital principle which must be understood or all else fails: *The factors and conditions which promote individual health and longevity are precisely the same factors and conditions which promote the organizational health and longevity of*

the greater or "incorporated" body. Although this is a relatively recent concept in the United States, this principle is well-established
and applied internationally. In fact, the United States lags behind
most other industrial nations in this aspect of work life. For years the
Scandinavian countries, Germany, Japan, and Canada, among others,
have supported workplace health programs as a matter of policy. In
several countries both governmental and private organizations assist
employers to develop their programs. During 1982, Roy Shephard
and his colleagues at the University of Toronto reported on the results of a study of 1,125 employees of two large insurance companies
in Toronto. Benefits to both employees and employer were striking.
According to a report in the *Harvard Medical School Health Letter,*
the results indicated:

> . . . absentee rates went down in the company with the pro-
> gram 60 percent for the men, and 38 percent for the women.
> Monday and Friday absences alone went down 22 percent
> among the women. For a company of 1,400 employees, compa-
> rable in size to the ones studied, Shephard calculated there
> would be 3,500 fewer lost days—conservatively the equivalent
> of $175,000 in salaries and wages saved. . . . [E]mployees
> participating in the fitness program tended to stay with the com-
> pany. Their turnover rate was only 1.5 percent compared with
> 15 percent among nonparticipants at the same company and all
> employees at the other. Because the cost of hiring and training a
> new employee is high—about $6,300—this finding suggested an
> annual saving of more than half a million dollars for the com-
> pany with the fitness program. . . . [P]articipants reported
> feeling more alert, enjoying work more, and feeling that they
> had better relationships with fellow workers. Fully two-thirds
> felt more relaxed, more patient, and less fatigued during the
> workday. The Toronto study did not produce data to show
> whether actual sickness or payment for sick days was reduced,
> but other studies have suggested such a benefit. (*1982*)

Clearly the same factors were conducive to health both for the individual and the organization.

2. *Individual effort is necessary but not sufficient.* Anyone now
working in a corporation has probably seen a veritable barrage of
prepackaged stress management techniques and burnout remedies.

At best, these approaches are limited since the achievement of health in the workplace requires aggregates of individuals working together. Individual efforts which can be effectively introduced into the workplace are the primary focus of Chapter II and considered in Chapter III as well. Individuals can do a great deal to keep themselves healthy on the job. However, the most effective approaches to health promotion are intended to change the workplace, not just the worker. Effective programs require a commitment from employers and employees to a slow, deliberate developmental process built upon the careful evaluation of pilot projects. Such a process requires both time and financial commitments by the employers. A recent study by UCLA physicians Jonathan E. Fielding and Lester Breslow indicated which departments or groups are the most likely initiators and supporters of such efforts: "Personnel (35.1%), top management (20.5%), safety group (18.2%), medical department (14.3%), health benefits groups (7.4%), employees (1.3%), unions (.2%), and other groups (2.9%)" (Fielding and Breslow, 1982). These may indicate the most receptive resources for individual employees wishing to extend their individual health activities into the office environment.

3. *The employee and the employer, management and workers need the same information, objectives and incentives at the same time.* Suspicions on both sides inhibit positive steps toward health promotion. Two prominent companies in Illinois, Deere and Company and Caterpillar, have recognized this interdependence in their medical benefit programs. After lengthy negotiations with the United Auto Workers Union, which represents many employees in both companies, additional benefits were added including dental insurance. When costs skyrocketed, Duane H. Heintz, manager of Deere's health care services, recognized that the increased costs were not to put blame upon the union or management. According to Heintz, "We were all culprits. The hospitals were being operated inefficiently. The doctors were not sufficiently cost-conscious. As the people paying the bills, we were much too lax. The patients took advantage of what they felt were their contract rights. We were all guilty at some point for rising costs" (Higdon, 1981). Paying attention to this interdependence promises health and economic benefits for both individuals and organizations. In the realm of health promotion, everyone is an employee. According to a health plan advertisement, "Your company will be in better shape if you are." This

mutuality must be acknowledged. Bruce E. Buckbee, director of the Boston Fitness Group, states, "American businesses are just starting to recognize that you can't drain your employees for profit and not put anything back into the system" (Makower, 1982). Almost all of the articles and studies written about health promotion programs, including the excellent brochures *Building a Healthier Company* (1980) by Blue Cross / Blue Shield and *Fitness in the Workplace* (1981) by the President's Council on Physical Fitness and Sports, are addressed more to organizations than to individuals. This reflects the reality that individual efforts in isolation are limited. However, it is also evident that the most productive programs are those in which individuals and organizations work together for mutual benefit. Among the most outstanding examples are the programs at IBM, Xerox Corporation, Scherer Brothers, and Johnson & Johnson's Live for Life and Control Data Corporation's StayWell programs, which are discussed in Chapter V.

4. *Workers at all levels must participate.* "Workers may be wary or hostile to such management initiatives unless they participate in the planning and design of the programs from the beginning" (Carlson and Fullarton, 1981). In addition to providing invaluable input, such participation increases an individual employee's sense of control and self-esteem, which are essential prerequisites for any positive change in attitude and behavior. Because programs require the active support and participation of top management, employees at all levels need access to top decision-makers in planning and evaluation. Additionally, the support of middle management is critical since they will implement such programs. Top administration may approve such programs but at the same time demand increased productivity by middle management and the employees supervised by them. Among the most successful examples of such individual and organizational cooperation are the Johnson & Johnson Live for Life and the Scherer Brothers' programs where employees at all levels participated in a variety of planning committees and, through surveys, in the design and implementation of the program. This was accompanied by a significant increase in employee morale and job satisfaction *prior* to the implementation of the actual health promotion program.

5. *Limited health promotion programs are often more expensive and less effective than holistic programs which entail more subtle but permanent, positive change.* A one-dimensional, limited program such as weight control or one directed toward smokers or heavy

drinkers may not permit enough latitude for choice and success at small changes to lead to new motivation and other behavior changes leading to improved health. Not only are health risk factors interactive, but health promotion factors are mutually enhancing as well. Numerous studies have indicated that having a variety of linked programs increases the likelihood of a successful behavior change in one or more areas of an individual's life and workplace activity. In deciding which elements to include in an overall program, the following questions are useful: Does the program have a realistic timetable? When will employees participate and what levels of employees? Where will the program be held? Will employees be given time off to participate or will it be on their own time? Have labor and management issues been addressed? Who will support the program and who will pay for it? Most importantly, the outcomes of the program need to be measured and assessed to justify the continuity of that program. Through asking and answering these questions, the appropriate program elements can be selected, implemented, and evaluated in a systematic fashion. Asking these questions precludes a panacea approach and increases the likelihood of a program's success by raising the awareness of all participants.

6. *A program should offer the simplest and least costly components that can be expected to produce a positive result.* The highly successful IBM program, for instance, elected not to build elaborate and expensive facilities but to work in cooperation with the national YMCA and local YMCAs to provide health promotion programs and facilities. Free or nominal-cost community resources are growing and can be utilized. Smoking cessation programs are offered by the Lung Association and cardiopulmonary resuscitation (CPR) training is taught for free by the Red Cross or local fire departments. Smaller companies can benefit most through use of such programs. Among the more simple measures is to provide safe storage for bicycles or modest locker storage or changing rooms for employees who exercise on the way to work or during lunch hours. All of these steps have been demonstrated to be both inexpensive and effective.

7. *Any system of health promotion must respect individual needs and unique circumstances.* Regimented and prepackaged programs fail both the individual and the organization. Any program must acknowledge and respect an individual's right not to participate. Too often, little attention is given to appropriate activities for all employees who wish to participate in programs, including the disabled,

older employees, or individuals with chronic ailments which limit their participation. By contrast to the positive thrust of health promotion programs, there are fears that employees who are evaluated as less healthy or who do not participate in programs will suffer job discrimination or other work-related liabilities. By the same token, those who do participate should not have to support the higher incidence of disability and death among those who choose not to be involved. To take one example, running is a much advertised and excellent fitness activity which has been at the core of many limited "fitness programs." As beneficial as running might be, it is not suitable or desirable for everyone. Sedentary and / or older workers would not participate in such programs and are often intimidated by them, resulting in a situation of "perverse incentives" and negative peer pressure. For these individuals, activities involving stretching, breathing, and walking are a very positive step and need to be recognized as much as the jogging team competing for the corporate cup. Finally, confidentiality of both those who participate and those who do not participate needs to be ensured.

8. *A comprehensive or holistic health promotion program emphasizes the positive aspects of health rather than the negative risks.* "Any assessment or intervention program should capitalize on what people already do to maintain and promote health, and build on those strengths, as well as identify and develop new skills, beliefs, and behaviors to promote health" (Carlson and Fullarton, 1981). This emphasis marks an important distinction between programs of risk-factor identification, an extension of traditional pathology management, and health promotion programs to maintain the well-being of essentially healthy individuals.

9. *Changes in the overall workplace environment are necessary to elicit and sustain individual efforts.* Toxic substance exposure must first be reduced. Where this necessary first step has been completed, then questions of the health facilities are very important. W. Brent Arnold, of the Xerox program, has noted that if a "fitness program is located outside the business office, then employee participation will be cut at least one-half." Another example is the PepsiCo program, where employees may use the fitness facilities at any time during the day. Out of 14,000 employees in Purchase, New York, 11,000 registered for the program. In the Live for Life program of Johnson & Johnson there have been changes in the contents of vending ma-

chines and the cafeteria, designated nonsmoking areas, and accessible exercise facilities.

10. *Finally, health promotion programs need to be based upon some form of deductible or co-payment plan as part of every health insurance strategy.* This is a common practice in automobile insurance and needs to be extended into the realm of health insurance. According to physician Edward N. Brandt, Jr., Assistant Secretary for Health at the U.S. Department of Health and Human Services, "There is no question that the American health care system is over-utilized. . . . It's important to bring home to people—to everyone—what medical costs really are today. I'm not talking about large deductibles for devastating $25,000 or $100,000 hospital bills—I'm referring to going to the doctor for a minor headache" (Blanchard, 1982). In a more positive direction, participating employees should be given positive incentives such as "well leave," insurance premium reimbursements, or other incentives for maintaining good health. Such positive incentives are being utilized and have been effective in the preliminary studies. Individuals and organizations can do a great deal to achieve optimum health and longevity and should be rewarded for their efforts.

WHOSE RESPONSIBILITY?

Individual versus organizational responsibility for health promotion is a hotly debated question. Throughout the last decade there has been a widespread recognition of the role of an individual's lifestyle and behavior as a major determinant of his or her health. On the other hand, an individual's state of health, illness, and longevity is the result of a dynamic interaction between multiple determinants such as genetic endowment, family history, personal medical care, psychological attitudes, ability to manage stress, diet and nutrition, physical activity, as well as economic, political, and environmental determinants. While any one of these variables may override the others, all of these variables play a role in the person's subsequent health and longevity. If an employee is exposed to asbestos, it is highly likely that he or she will develop lung cancer whether or not he or she meditates, jogs, or eats a healthy diet. On the other hand, personal health choices are of great importance in swinging the balance between health and illness, life and death, in the vast majority of borderline cases. While holistic medicine has recognized all these dimensions, it has been used by some to justify "victim blaming." An exclusive focus upon personal lifestyles and behavior has tended to result in a neglect of the social, occupational, economic, political, and environmental causes of disease. Samuel Epstein of the University of Illinois, Department of Environmental and Occupational Health Sciences, has indicated that the lifestyle dimension of cancer has emerged as the basis of petrochemical industry objections to the regulation of its carcinogenic products and processes. An approach that places too much emphasis upon individual lifestyle ". . . trivializes past involuntary exposure to environmental and occupational carcinogens" (*American Medical News,* 1980). This is only one instance of the complex issues involved in any consideration of individual and organizational responsibility. Individuals are embedded in and influenced by major forces, such as familial, political, economic, and environmental determinants, which are not within their immediate influence. Each person affects and is affected by his or her environment like a fish in the ocean.

Within the last five years this general controversy has been brought into sharp focus. It has been within the area of "occupational health" that the often negative impact of environmental factors has been demonstrated most clearly. Among the more dramatic instances is the evidence that DBCP (dibromochloropropane) caused testicular cancer in some workers resulting in a "chemical vasectomy," or the groundbreaking study linking the effects of anesthesia on operating room personnel resulting in cancer, birth defects, and spontaneous abortions. Complicating the already complex area of individual and organizational responsibility for health particular to the workplace is the issue of cost. At the interface of issues of responsibility, money, cultural and organizational values, there is considerable friction and heated debate. James Fallows, in his highly provocative and influential article "American Industry: What Ails It, How to Save It" in *The Atlantic,* shows how blame for these conditions is spread about: "One view blames lazy workers and, to a lesser degree, indifferent management; a second blames government; and a third blames the very ethos of modern American life." To an extent, each of these groups bears a measure of responsibility.

In discussing responsibility, one must acknowledge that organizations and corporations are in the business not of health care but rather the delivery of service and products. Any health promotion program needs to be developed with this clearly in mind or it will fail.

Among the more articulate analysts of such complexities in organizational, particularly corporate, programs is Richard L. Pyle, an instructor in management at the University of Massachusetts. Writing in the *Training Development Journal,* Pyle points out that "Even strong proponents are recognizing the necessity of providing business with the logic and means of evaluation. . . . Fitness programs . . . must be viewed as functions concurrent with corporate objectives, and not simply as goodwill fringe operations" (1979). The challenge is to develop assessments which are sensitive and accurate enough to measure what people and programs are achieving. Over time, it is possible to formulate a series of reasonable, attainable objectives, but no program can meet all demands immediately or simultaneously.

Pyle has indicated that "Considerable anxiety has been felt about corporate fitness programs. The anxiety results from the inability to justify the investment for a program and facilities to corporate stockholders." Although this is a pervasive concern, it is possible to reconcile such issues by recognizing the demands of both the individual and the organization. Those opposed to corporate involvement in employee health often raise the criticism that the employer doesn't have a right to meddle in the personal lives of the employees (Pyle, 1979). Such an argument overlooks the fact that by virtue of relocation, time demands, weekend travel, job termination, and a host of other factors, employers are inevitably influencing every employee's personal life, all too often in a negative fashion.

There is a highly emotional controversy taking place in the courts as well as in many workplaces concerning the complexities of responsibility for the mental health of an employee. In six states, courts have extended workmen's compensation coverage to include cases of illness caused by "gradual or cumulative injury from work stress," and nine other states have permitted compensations for anxiety, depression, and other disabling psychological disorders. Alan McLean, eastern medical director for IBM, maintains that recent court decisions "have ignored preexisting emotional conditions as well as personality or family factors, all of which may underlie or contribute to an employee's mental illness" (Rice, 1981). Actually, IBM has long been noted for its humane employee policies but has drawn the line on psychological counseling and has encouraged the use of outside resources for its employees in this area. At one extreme is a misunderstood, but loudly extolled, model of the Japanese system of "lifetime security"; at the other are astoundingly arrogant pronouncements by a minority of organizations that health promotion programs are "coddling," or "knuckling under" to unrealistic and unfounded employee demands. Neither extreme is accurate. Closer to a middle ground is the observation of psychiatrist Sidney Lecker, who consults to several major corporations: "It is nonsense to say it's completely a matter of how the individual employee reacts to stress. The big factor is the overall quality of work life and the organizational climate" (Rice, 1981). Clearly, mutual responsibility is the only reasonable position. At the conclusion of an excellent *Psychology Today* article in 1981, senior editor Berkeley Rice concluded, "A more humane and, in the long run, perhaps more productive commitment might offer employees not only job security, but within reason, emotional security as well, particularly for those who have spent 20 years or more with the company . . . assuming responsibility for employee mental health may become a matter of legal obligation rather than an optional policy of management." If individuals and organizations each choose to accept a measure of responsibility, health promotion programs will be effective for individuals and organizations alike. When both the individual and the organization are sound, then it is an asset for all concerned.

LEADERSHIP FROM THE PRIVATE SECTOR

Virtually all health promotion programs are in private corporations. When this fact is pointed out, it is often greeted with reactions ranging from cynicism at best to hostility at worst. Critics point out that such programs are not altruistic, that they are created for an elite management group, and when they do extend to the majority of workers, are intended simply to squeeze more production out of the workers. To each of these accusations there is a grain of truth. There are no uniform motivations for the development of a given health promotion program. A few have been created from a careful analysis of employee medical benefit costs, while most have resulted from the interests of a key executive or even originated from the advertising department to promote a particular corporate image. While the health care industry itself and most government bureaucracies have been slow to react, private business has reacted swiftly and effectively. This is largely due to the spiraling costs of health benefits. "Employers picked up the tab for about $40 billion of the nation's $183 billion in health care expenses in 1978. In fact, employee medical benefit costs have risen so rapidly that they account for as much as 10% of total compensation in some companies. . . . All share a common goal: to contain the runaway cost of medical benefits. If nothing else, such efforts serve notice on the health care delivery system that the business establishment has abandoned its unquestioning role" (*Business Week,* 1979). These figures have grown considerably since 1978.

In 1981 a survey of chief executives in sixty-nine major companies by Harvey M. Sapolsky and his colleagues at the Massachusetts Institute of Technology concluded that measures such as "cost-sharing," "tightening claims control," "HMOs," and similar measures were not of great interest to corporations. Many of these measures were seen as coercive to employees and were unlikely to gain wide acceptance. However, on the subject of health promotion, Sapolsky stated, "There is no doubt of the popularity of preventive health measures as additional employee benefits. And if the claims made for these prevention programs by their advocates even partially materialize, then the future medical costs of many corporations may decline" (Sapolsky et al., 1981). At least in this study, management seemed more interested in genuine health promotion than in simply tightening up on disease and disability benefits.

Among the agencies which have fostered attention to health promotion in the workplace is the President's Council on Physical Fitness and Sports. During 1976, Richard O. Keelor, director of program development of the council, delivered a paper to the annual conference of Blue Shield. "Public expenditure alone," he pointed out, "has nearly doubled since 1970 [for health care], yet there has been no commensurate improvement in the health of Americans. . . . The death rate for heart disease, 355.5 per 100,000 in 1970, now stands at 353.1—25 years and untold billions of dollars later. . . . As costs mount, prevention is not only humane and practical, it is the only course we can afford." The issue now is not if prevention and health promotion are necessary but who will deliver these programs and what will be the components of such programs. Today, estimates by the President's Council indicate there may be as many as 50,000 health programs in the private sector ranging from diminutive substance-abuse programs to comprehensive physical and psychosocial facilities entailing corporate expenditures in the millions. Lists of corporations which have initiated employee health programs read like the Who's Who of the Fortune 500: IBM, Chase Manhattan, the National Aeronautics and Space Administration (NASA), Exxon, General Mills, Firestone, Johnson & Johnson, General Dynamics, PepsiCo, Goodyear, Phillips Petroleum, General Motors, Boeing, Xerox, Rockwell International, Kimberly-Clark, Control Data Corporation, and scores of others. More than 500 companies now employ full-time fitness directors, and hundreds of others have more modest programs. Details of these and other programs are discussed in Chapter V. Corporations are taking the lead in experiments with health promotion. Companies, which bear a major portion of health care bills, are beginning to look for ways to keep employees healthy and productively involved in their work. Even though the results of these programs will not be in for five or ten years, the burden of pathology management is so heavy, and its projects' costs so awesome, that many organizations and corporations are willing to invest right now in what seem to be probable solutions.

FOUR TYPES OF PROGRAM

While the actual programs vary, one factor remains constant. Voluntary health promotion practices by aggregates of informed individuals are at the very heart of any effective health promotion program. For this one essential requirement, there is no substitute. Before examining the type of programs, we might first ask, why should health promotion programs take place at the workplace, why not elsewhere? The advantages have been enumerated by physician Jonathan E. Fielding, co-director of the Center for Health Enhancement (CHEER) at the UCLA School of Medicine: "(1) access to people and time; (2) stability of the working population; (3) lower costs; (4) existence of management and organizational structure; (5) ability to conduct several interventions simultaneously; (6) strong social support networks; and (7) willingness of the working population to participate in occupationally sponsored programs" (Fielding, 1981). Governor Jerry Brown's mandate to the Governor's Council on Wellness and Physical Fitness for the State of California states, "More intensive, high cost treatment will do little to *prevent* chronic, debilitating and costly disease" and "the *health care setting and the workplace are the ideal places to initiate health programs* [author's italics]." Health promotion programs fall into four major categories:

1. toxic substance elimination and regulation;
2. health promotion policies initiated by the employer;
3. limited health promotion programs;
4. holistic health promotion programs.

Toxic substance regulation. Much of this has been in response to the data gathering, policy setting, and regulatory activities of the National Institute for Occupational Safety and Health (NIOSH). Whatever has been done amounts to little more than the proverbial drop in the bucket. ". . . most occupational diseases are not . . . easily linked and are notoriously difficult to trace. Safe exposure limits have been set for only about 500 of the approximately 70,000 chemicals in industrial use today . . . it has only recently become clear that in addition to such physical disorders as pneumoconioses, cancers and skin diseases, mental health problems can be caused by many chemicals, such as carbon monoxide, carbon disulfide and trichloroethylene" (Allport, 1981). The National Cancer Institute has conservatively estimated that 20 percent to 40 percent of all cancer is caused by occupational exposure. The difficulty in tracking down and regulating such exposure is compounded by the fact that 90 percent of American companies employ fewer than 25 people. It has been estimated that in these small companies, one out of every four workers has an occupational disease.

By contrast to this mounting evidence is the ironic dismantling of virtually all national and state regulatory agencies. Because the most effective means of curtailing such exposure is through surveillance and legislation, there are few courses of individual action. For physicians and workers there is a NIOSH publication entitled *A Guide to the Recognition of Occupational Diseases* (1981), which can be purchased from the U.S. Government Printing Office and helps an individual to become aware of toxic agents and indications of such exposure. Workers, managers, and physicians can also contact NIOSH's Health Hazard Evaluation Program in Cincinnati, which does conduct workplace evaluations if toxic exposures are suspected.

Although individual workers can do little, organized groups of workers can do a lot. The Public Citizen Health Research Group in Washington, D.C., has published a useful book called *A Worker's Guide to Winning at the Occupational Safety and Health Review*

Commission (Goldberg et al., 1981). The need for workers to organize to enforce their own rights is spelled out in detail. These issues are explicated in greater detail in Chapter III. One fact that remains constant in any consideration of toxic exposure is that virtually every resulting disease is preventable.

Health promotion policies initiated by employers. This second category is not a type of health promotion program per se but is a step in that direction. These policies, developed by management, usually bear upon issues of reducing medical utilization. While these are not inherently health promotion measures, they do indicate significant changes away from traditional acceptance of after-the-fact disease treatment. One of the most cogent analyses of this trend is contained in a book entitled *The Social Transformation of American Medicine* (1982) by Harvard sociologist Paul Starr. His historical analyses of the contemporary "medical-industrial complex" traces the movement of medical care away from the home into the marketplace, where it has become a lucrative commodity. According to his analysis, the physician's dominance of medical care has not been balanced by consumer representation, social accountability, or any rigorous attempt at cost control. Over the last forty years the rise of third-party health insurance, such as Blue Cross, employee health benefits, the politics of Medicare and Medicaid, and the expansion of hospitals and medical technologies has resulted in staggering costs. As the medical complex has grown, the federal government and big business inevitably have become increasingly involved since the government pays 42 percent of the nation's medical bill and corporations currently pay over $55 billion annually for employee benefits and medical costs. Although the movement is in its initial stages, both government and corporations are exerting their interest in cost control. As a result, Starr indicates, we are "witnessing and indeed taking part in the creation of corporate health care systems." Such systems are taking the form of corporate health programs as well as companies running for-profit hospitals, medical facilities such as dialysis units, and group medical practices. As one indication of the magnitude of this trend, he cites the development of the Washington Business Group on Health:

> In the early 1980s, spokesmen for business are calling for control over costs by the private sector. Though this approach has ideological affinities with the competitive model in health policy,

the two are not exactly the same. The chief instance of private-sector regulation is the business coalition. In 1974 the Business Roundtable, whose members consist of the chief executive officers (CEOs) of the largest corporations in the United States, created a new organization called the Washington Business Group on Health. The initial purpose was to defeat national health insurance, but the group increasingly became involved in other medical policy issues, particularly cost containment. Local business coalitions to encourage containment of medical costs have been the next step. By early 1982 about eighty such coalitions were in process of formation around the United States. Their agenda includes such issues as utilization review and review of capital spending by medical institutions. . . . It is not difficult to imagine a situation in which some corporations (i.e., employers) lean on other corporations (i.e., insurers, HMOs, hospital chains), which, in turn, lean on the professionals to control costs. (*1982*)

This transformation also engenders its own problems. Throughout the book, Starr maintains anticorporate sympathies since such approaches do not seek to serve the poor, or those indigent populations who are displaced from public services, or those with high rates of illness, or anyone from whom a profit cannot be derived. It is clear that he does not endorse the idea that corporate involvement will lead to reduced costs and greater efficiency, and eliminate excesses. However, his presentation is delicately balanced and clearly states that "History does not provide any answers about what should be done."

Although the book is an extensive analysis of the complex problems at hand, it is deficient in the suggestion of possible avenues of solution. Obviously, corporate involvement in health care, either through direct management or indirect health promotion programs, is not a panacea, but the health promotion programs which are evolving do indicate a range of substantial innovation and effectiveness. These programs may not provide the answers, but they do represent a significant evolutionary process toward the development of an effective health care system. If such programs enable individuals and organizations to accept more responsibility for preserving and enhancing their health, then the medical care system will be able to provide better services at less cost for those individuals who require such care.

From economic necessity, employers have moved out of a passive role in medical costs to one that is more active. Among measures they have pursued are: (1) reduction of hospital care since 40 percent of disease care is spent for excessive use of hospitalization; (2) insurance coverages extended to include second and third opinions on elective surgery—with large savings. This has raised the ire of many hospitals and physicians, although both the American Medical Association and the American Hospital Association have endorsed it. Second-opinion programs have proven to be one of the most effective of the cost containment measures; (3) more reimbursement for health services at home; (4) elimination of costly annual physicals which have little if any effect upon overall health; (5) greater use of preadmission testing and preauthorization for hospital admissions; and (6) the enrollment of more employees in Health Maintenance Organizations, which provide virtually all medical coverages but have a vested interest in minimizing the use of high-cost technologies. Greater use of HMO facilities is a growing trend. Some programs include active health promotion such as the "Total Health Care Project" currently under way at Kaiser Hospital in Oakland under the direction of the Kaiser system founder Sidney R. Garfield and his colleagues (Garfield, 1980). Each of these efforts have resulted in substantial savings with no loss of effectiveness. Former Secretary of Health, Education and Welfare Joseph A. Califano stated, "Corporations could have saved up to $150 million last year (1979) if just 5% of the employees of the Fortune 500 companies belonged to Health Maintenance Organizations [HMOs]." These are savings not only to corporations but potentially to individuals as well.

Perhaps the most significant and controversial innovations in the realm of corporate health policies involve "cost sharing" and "health incentives." Such cost containment strategies do save money for the organizations, but the savings are seldom if ever passed on to the workers, or even the middle management of the organizations involved. Cost sharing had been fought by labor unions, but unions too realized that medical costs were taking an increasingly larger share of funds that might be used for wage increases and other benefits. A range of alternatives are being utilized or considered under cost-sharing strategies and benefits: (1) assume all or part of the cost of worksite programs (IBM and Johnson & Johnson); (2) pay the costs of interventions for high-risk employees (Ford Motor Company); (3) pay only for interventions with clear evidence of effectiveness (New York Telephone); (4) train employees to perform in-house medical self-care such as monitoring blood pressure and cardiopulmonary resuscitation (CPR); (5) allow time off during work hours for health promotion activities (PepsiCo); (6) at the other extreme, completely drop all health benefits, raise workers' salaries, and let individuals create their own plans. While this last alternative may seem highly unlikely, there are indications that many individuals would welcome the opportunity to choose between one wage plus health coverages versus a higher wage without such coverages. Ironically, this idea is extolled by both the hard-liners who want to drop all health benefits in contempt of worker needs and health promotion advocates in the name of personal responsibility, participation, and cooperation!

Among the most innovative and promising programs utilizing cost sharing and health incentives is the Stay Well Health Insurance Plan undertaken by Blue Shield of California with Philip Nickerman, assistant superintendent of schools of the Mendocino County Unified School District in northern California. Working with Charles Parcell, vice-president of Blue Shield, the Mendocino County School System devised a plan whereby its 218 employees would earn money by staying healthy. Each employee was given the first $500 of a $500 deductible coverage for major medical insurance. That $500 per employee was placed in a credit union. When an employee has to seek medical attention, he or she has the bill sent to the Mendocino County School bookkeeper as a draw against his or her $500 allotment. At any point in the year, the employee can obtain information on the balance in the account. Employees can take the remaining money with them when they leave the Mendocino County School System. In this case the employees do not receive the unused money each year, but that remains an option for other trials. In testimony before the California legislature, Philip Nickerman stated, "In three years, we're going on our third year now, we've not had a raise in medical premiums. That's $80,000 cash savings to our office. . . . There were 60 employees that never even went to the doctor . . . we only had five employees that went over the $500" (Garamendi, 1980).

The Mendocino County program was distinguished from an earlier one initiated by the Teledyne Corporation by a "health education component." This may have been what made the Mendocino County program a success. Above and beyond the economic success, the Mendocino County program demonstrates the extraordinary impact on health when individuals are empowered to take responsibility for their own health care under the guidance of an effective health promotion program. Philip Nickerman noted, "I would like to mention that the effect it's had on our office has been phenomenal. We no longer deal with the employees against the management. We're all in this together. We have to be. People will come in and say, 'How are we doing? How much money are we saving?' Even our lowest employee is sitting there right along with the boss saying, 'We've got to make this thing go. It's really good. I'm getting 500 bucks I never got before'" (Garamendi, 1980). There are individuals who object to crass incentives such as these, but health incentives are a necessary reality of health promotion in the workplace and in general. During the Mendocino County program there was no evidence that employees avoided necessary medical care and there was abundant evidence of reduced smoking, reduced stress, and increased physical activity. This is an excellent example of a health promotion policy and program which benefits both the individual and the organization.

Limited health promotion programs. These are "limited" in the sense that it focuses upon one particular aspect of health care and tends not to utilize multiple approaches or organizational change per se to attain employee health. The problems with such an approach include unsuitability of prepackaged programs, high-cost health technologies which are identical to the high-cost sickness technologies, and facile solutions by instant experts to complex considerations. The actual materials to be used in any health promotion program must be well-developed, well-defined, effective, inexpensive, and readily available. The challenge is not to package and market these materials like competing brands of canned vegetables, but to have an individual or organization be aware of the options available and to put in the time and effort to create an effective program suited to requirements of both the company and the individuals involved. The personnel manager for a national bank's stress management program told me, "The only people deriving clear benefits from packaged stress management programs are the companies marketing these programs." There is a growing health promotion industry which promises, or, rather, threatens, to equal the pathology management industry in its technology and costs.

One type of limited health promotion program is the assessment of individual morbidity and mortality risk for chronic diseases, through screening and a health risk appraisal tool. Undoubtedly there is merit and benefit to such early screening and detection programs, but these are still within the disease model of medicine, which is distinct from health promotion. Medical assessments in these programs focus primarily upon the risk factors associated with heart disease, stroke, and cancer. This risk assessment is then followed by a risk reduction program comprising one or more of the following components depending upon the individual and organizational level of commitment:

1. Accident prevention and self-protective measures concerned with job safety and the visible, environmental hazards of the workplace; the traditional focus of occupational medicine.

2. Medical self-care programs including CPR training, basic first-aid blood pressure monitoring, and other aspects of lay medical care.

3. Smoking cessation, a very effective area since well-motivated participants can achieve initial abstinence rates of between 70 and 100 percent and long-term quit rates of up to 50 percent.

4. Alcohol and substance abuse programs, among the most long-standing and effective programs with success rates reported between 65 percent and 80 percent for long-term reduction in excessive drinking.

5. Hypertension control, including early screening, detection, and follow-up.

6. Weight reduction, an area where business can assist employees by providing meeting times and places as well as provision of low-calorie, low-fat foods and educational materials in the cafeteria.

7. Exercise and physical fitness programs, the most currently popular health promotion programs, usually limited to certain employee levels and among the most expensive to implement.

8. Stress management programs, often based upon "how to," prepackaged programs of limited effectiveness but better than nothing at all. Currently, the area of stress management is a prominent area of concern.

9. Nutrition and education in healthy dietary practices, relatively uncommon but growing rapidly, more far-reaching than single weight-control programs.

10. General health education approaches focused upon informa-

tion dissemination, without programs or incentives to actually encourage implementation.

It should be evident from this list that virtually every one of these practices is one where an individual can assume responsibility. In effective organizational health promotion the workplace also needs to change in order not to counteract these efforts, and in order to serve as an inducement for these practices to generalize throughout a person's life.

Just as with individual health practices, some organizations limit their health promotion activities to one or a few of these areas. As a result, such programs tend to be less effective and more expensive than a comprehensive, holistic approach. Early screening and detection programs will generally remain under the auspices of organizational medical departments, and those helped by them will be only 10 percent to 15 percent of the total number of employees in a given worksite. Even with such a limited number, the human and economic savings are large. Using the data from the Framingham Heart Study, Marvin Kristein has projected the impact of an early screening program for the coronary risk factors including hypertension, obesity, smoking, and high cholesterol levels. His estimates are that for every 1,000 employees screened in a company, a minimum of 100 would be found to have two or more coronary risk factors. High-risk employees, at 10 percent of the corporate personnel, can account for "40 to 60% of annual medical care spending on all company employees." These figures are consistent with estimates of the proportion of the population who use health service in hospitals, Health Maintenance Organizations, and private practices. For hospitals and physicians these figures translate into occupancy and profits, but for business, industry, and Health Maintenance Organizations they translate into absenteeism, decreased productivity, and losses.

An early screening program for coronary risk factors can translate directly into savings. For instance (1) smoking reduction could save $200 per person per year; (2) control of hypertension would save $260 per person annually; and (3) a 20 percent reduction in cholesterol could save at least $160 per person per year. Overall, if only 25 out of the 100 high-risk individuals could reduce their risk factors, the corporation's medical expenses could be reduced by as much as 10 percent to 15 percent per year. These are conservative estimates of the benefits from an early detection program. But what of the remaining 975 employees? These are the majority and larger population who would benefit by learning to sustain and enhance the health they already enjoy. It is for these individuals that comprehensive, holistic health promotion would be significant and cost-effective.

Holistic health promotion programs. These address the remaining 85 percent to 90 percent of all employees who have no early indications of disease and are relatively healthy. These consist of individual practice, organizational programs, changes in workplace environment, and policies which elicit and sustain health in the population as a whole. While the actual components are drawn from the limited programs described above, the unique characteristic of a holistic program is that it is not isolated and compartmentalized, while business continues as usual. One example of a limited program would be a stress management seminar in contrast to an overall effort to seek the roots of the apparent stress, in poor communications, disruptive noise levels, lack of health incentives, combined with instruction in stress management. While this is an extremely new area of research, there are indications that limited programs are often more expensive and less effective than comprehensive programs which create more permanent changes. The characteristics of model holistic programs will be discussed in Chapters IV and V.

COMMON SHORTCOMINGS
OF CORPORATE HEALTH PROGRAMS

Some shortcomings in existing programs should be pointed out here. During 1980 and 1981, Joseph Romm of System Sciences Incorporated conducted a study of 65 "health promotion and disease prevention" (HPDP) programs in diverse workplaces and came up with several important general observations concerning the present status of health promotion programs:

1. The program sponsorship is generally by management. Unions surprisingly enough have not initiated or actively sponsored many of these programs.
2. Presently, all HPDP programs have been introduced in the work setting as voluntary programs, to be selected by the employee if he or she desires.
3. There is not a well-defined or standard set of components

which make up health promotion and disease prevention programs in the workplace.

4. The components which are found in health promotion are primarily those dealing with behavior modification of lifestyle.
5. HPDPs have generally been initiated and remained at the executive level or home office. It has not generally trickled down to the blue-collar workers.
6. There is . . . a dearth of adequate information when costs and benefits of these programs are considered. (*Romm, 1981*)

These are a few of the findings of this major study, which outlines the applications and limitations of the limited as well as the few holistic health promotion programs now in the workplace.

Clearly related to these findings are the observations from a 1980 publication of the Office of Health Information, Health Promotion, Physical Fitness and Sports Medicine of the U.S. Department of Health and Human Services. In *Toward a Healthy Community* (DHHS, 1980), the authors identified six common shortcomings of health promotion programs. For individuals and organizations alike, these warrant careful attention:

1. "Fragmentation of effort." Programs are often implemented in a piecemeal fashion and this minimizes their impact.
2. "Overemphasis on initial motivation." Concerted advertising can induce momentary changes, but programs fail to provide support and maintenance over extended periods of time.
3. "Appeal to individual heroics." Group-based programs among aggregates of workers are more likely to be effective than victim-blaming approaches which insist that individuals "pull themselves up by their own bootstraps."
4. "Overemphasis on activities as opposed to results." Sporadic programs such as periodic screening have minimal value if the subsequently recommended work-style or health promotion practices are in fact not supported by the workplace environment or value system.
5. "Overemphasis on knowledge and information." This is the greatest potential pitfall. The plethora of information is usually well-known and disseminated but not applied. In applying what is already known lies the greatest challenge in health promotion.
6. "A 'We will do it for you', rather than 'Together we can do it

ourselves.'" Individual workers need to feel a sense of participation and ownership of the program from the very beginning as well as ongoing responsibility for its continuation over time.

These potential problem areas can be and have been remedied within a few model programs, which can serve as useful guidelines to ensure effective individual and organizational programs in the future. When all factors are considered, the one essential element remains the individual worker. In 1981, *Business Week* issued a cover story special report on "The New Industrial Relations," which pointed out that "workers have an unerring ability to spot exploitive schemes. . . . If a work improvement aims only at improving productivity, it quickly loses worker support. But a program that has only a vague plan of making workers feel better about themselves is likely to collapse for lack of business perspective." Both goals are clearly necessary. Describing Digital Equipment, the article notes, "Improved job satisfaction and improved productivity go hand in hand, and both are as important to workers as they are to managers." The same dual purpose applies directly to the effective design and successful implementation of health promotion programs.

HEALTH PROMOTION IN THE TWENTY-FIRST CENTURY

The move toward health promotion in the workplace is embedded in a major change of attitude toward work itself. A survey by psychologist Daniel Yankelovich reported that only 40 percent of all adults believed that "hard work always pays off" and that is the lowest response yet indicated. Related surveys of worker values among 250,000 employees in 400 companies by the Opinion Research Corporation of Princeton, New Jersey, have indicated, "American workers are more dissatisfied in their jobs than at any time in the past twenty-eight years. . . . Middle managers are more unhappy and feel less secure in their jobs than ever before. . . . Clerical workers, blue-collar employees, and managers in particular are becoming increasingly critical of the abilities of top managements" (*Behavior Today*, 1981). In a survey conducted by the University of Pennsylvania, at least 25 percent of the entire work force are overtly extremely discontented. That amounts to a minimum of

24 million people! According to author and philosopher Sam Keen, "the great God work is dead." It is increasingly evident that a profound shift has taken place in the values of most working adults. Concluding his report, Daniel Yankelovich noted that "A new breed of Americans, born out of the social movement of the 60s and grown into a majority in the 70s, holds a set of values and beliefs so markedly different from the traditional outlook that they promise to transform the character of work in America in the 80s" (1981). These changes can be seen throughout the world in the emergence of a planetary culture represented by limited but growing numbers stretching from Topeka to Moscow.

This movement has already been acknowledged as a powerful social and workplace force in William G. Ouchi's "Theory Z" and even more strikingly in the "7-S" model proposed in *The Art of Japanese Management* (1981) by Richard Tanner Pascale and Anthony G. Athos of the Business School of Harvard University. Japanese culture has traditionally operated within a holistic world view where parts are understood by looking at the whole, paradox is accommodated and accepted, and people are viewed as complexes of body, mind, spirit, and environment. There is an unusual nonadversary partnership between government, business, and employees resulting in careful attention to both productivity and well-being in the workplace. Japanese programs are not exportable to other cultures without extensive modification, but it is evident that the cultural values of East and West are moving toward greater accord. There is a widespread acknowledgment throughout the world and in particular to the United States that individual workers "want something more from their jobs . . . than wages, benefits, and job security" and that the workplace, "so long arrested at primitive levels of development, can now evolve into a . . . participative stage" (*Business Week,* 1981). Work and its monetary rewards are no longer the central values in the lives of a growing number of people. There is a certainty that an unprecedented number of men and women will live much healthier and much longer lives well beyond the age of 65 and beyond the period of life where work and its rewards provide meaning to an individual's life and family. Quantity of money and material goods has yielded to quality of life, self-fulfillment, a personal sense of purpose. These are not idle abstractions. Shifts in values have already resulted in innovations such as the personalizing of office environments, flex time, job sharing, quality of work-life programs, and the variety of health promotion efforts. Both management and labor in Japan, Sweden, the Soviet Union, and other countries have long recognized that healthy employees spare industry much absenteeism and lost productivity. In Sweden "the government devotes the largest single part of its budget to health and education, and if physical fitness programs can keep people well and fit, this is not only good in itself, but it is good economy" (Arnold, 1981). Actually, some of the most extensive programs and research have been carried out in the Soviet Union, where there is a long-standing interest in exercise physiology and sports medicine. A University of Leningrad study found that workers in fitness programs were less prone to industrial accidents and that absenteeism was reduced from "3 to 5 days per year per person." These few instances are not intended to create a Sputnik model of competitive health promotion but simply to indicate that efforts in these areas of health promotion are becoming worldwide.

Since the Industrial Revolution, workers have been viewed as interchangeable and disposable parts of a great machine. Such mechanistic concepts are outmoded and destructive. Our ultimate task is the restoration of human values to the workplace. Just as the Industrial Revolution engendered great social change, the current transition is equally significant and portends even greater changes. We are moving away from the environmentally destructive, highly centralized, disposable worker type of workplace toward one that is environmentally regenerative, necessarily decentralized, and based upon the life-affirming values of cooperation, interdependence, and dignity.

This change in values concerning work is symptomatic of an even more profound change in our view of all reality. There is an undeniable shift away from material saturation toward intangible values of meaning and purpose. While some critics view the paradoxical fusion of human values with hard economics with alarm and cynicism, it can be seen with optimism. For too long, arguments to acknowledge the human side of organizations have fallen on deaf ears. Perhaps it is because these dimensions have been translated into economic terms, that they will finally be acknowledged. Again, Daniel Yankelovich maintains that the "human side of the enterprise can no longer be relegated to low-level personnel departments" and has concluded that, "In the 1980's, knowledge of how the changed American value system affects incentives and motivations to work hard may well become a key requirement for entering the ranks of top management in both the private and public sectors. If this occurs, we shall see a New Breed of managers to correspond to the New Breed of employees" (1978). These changes in the workplace reflect a profound period of cultural transformation. Jonas Salk and his son Jonathan Salk have described this transition, primarily with reference to population growth and regulation, as a movement from "Epoch A" values of individualism, power, competition, independence, extremes, parts, and either / or to the "Epoch B" values of individual and group consensus collaboration, interdependence, balance, wholes, and both / and. This is not to imply that the previous values, scientific methods, and social systems were "wrong"; they have simply become anachronistic and inadequate. It is in this renaissance that we can fulfill the imperative of healthy people in healthy places.

CHAPTER II

Work and Stress

Although the stereotype of the harried business executive is the most common image which comes to mind in discussing workplace stress, every worker grapples with it. According to a national survey published by Blue Cross, five out of six workers at all levels of employment indicated stress as a major factor in their occupations resulting in "dissatisfaction, low self-esteem, angina, persistent coughs, neurotic behavior" and a host of stress-related conditions (Blue Cross, 1978). To address these problems, it is necessary to move beyond the Band-Aid approaches of burnout programs, meditation breaks, and employee compensation.

THE PERFORMANCE ZONE

There are many misconceptions concerning stress and its relationship to work. Perhaps the single most widespread misconception is that productivity and job performance are inevitably linked to stress. For purposes of this discussion, the classic definition of stress by the eminent researcher Hans Selye (1956) is still adequate: "Stress is the nonspecific response of the body to any demand made upon it." There have been innumerable elaborations upon this basic definition, when more precision has been required for research purposes, but this basic concept remains applicable to workplace stress. It is now a certainty that improved job performance is linked to increased stress up to a certain point but that a point of diminishing returns is soon reached where excess stress causes performance to deteriorate, whether the task is balancing a checkbook or determining a corporate fiscal policy. Although this is a very old and well-established observation, its implications are still not fully appreciated. As early as 1908, Robert M. Yerkes and John D. Dodson of the Physiologic Laboratory at Harvard University described this relationship between stress and performance. Today this relationship is recognized as the "Yerkes-Dodson Law." At the center of the curve is the "performance zone" where manageable stress results in high efficiency and productivity. Too little stress, at the bottom of the curve, or too much stress, at the top, cause performance and efficiency to decrease. Among the many implications of this simple principle is that each person will have a unique "performance zone" which will further vary from day to day. When individuals are within their optimum performance zone, stress results in feelings of energy, excitement, and stimulation, and decisions are readily made. Under conditions of stress underload or overload, the indicators are quite similar and stress results in irritability, a sense of time pressure, diminished motivation, as well as poor judgment and accidents.

Fortunately it is possible to become aware of the Yerkes-Dodson pattern and for each person to develop his or her own unique manner of achieving and remaining within the performance zone. An excellent and straightforward bit of advice is offered in the *Time / Life* Video Program series workbook *Stress Management: A Positive Strategy:*

> Whenever you feel that you may be functioning outside your comfort zone, examine the situation. Consider whether you have too little or too much stress. Then take whatever action you can to either increase or reduce the amount of stress you are experiencing, so that you can return to your comfort zone and function to the best of your ability. (*1982*)

It is possible to identify conditions of excessive stress, which is more frequently the case, and to implement a brief stress-management technique as a break in the cycle. This allows a person to remain within the productive zone. This process of breaking up a cumulative and potentially destructive "Type II" stress pattern into periods of transient and potentially productive "Type I" stress has been detailed in both *Mind as Healer, Mind as Slayer* (Pelletier, 1977) and *Holistic Medicine* (Pelletier, 1979). However, the first step requires recognition of those hazards of the workplace which create Type II stress reactions. Excessive stress is not an inherent part of optimum performance, and yet the image of the harried, aggressive workaholic remains a pervasive model. There is a wisdom in the cliché "work to live, not live to work" which, to our peril, has faded from our minds and hearts. Both the visible and invisible threats to healthy life are identifiable and resolvable. What remains in question is whether or not we have the individual and collective will to identify and correct these conditions.

SOURCES OF STRESS

Various attempts have been made to categorize the myriad possible sources of stress into a comprehensive model. One could apply the Spheres of Influence noted in the previous chapter to distinguish between those sources of stress over which an individual worker can exert a great deal of influence, through those which groups of workers can influence, to policies and practices which are under the control of management, all the way to the fourth sphere to stress factors changeable only by legislation or economic fluctuations. Another way of looking at sources of stress was developed by Alan A. McLean, eastern area medical director for IBM, who conceived of the variables and interactions as three intersecting circles. One circle termed "context" contains elements such as morale, organizational climate, economy, and family. A second circle encompassed "vulnerability" due to age, education, occupation, personality, and developmental influences. Finally, the third circle of "stressors" distinguished between change, uncertainty, conflict, and pressure which was "on the job" or "off the job" (McLean, 1976). This provides a way of understanding the wide range of individual variability to the same or different stress. When confronted with a deadline, one manager may drive herself or himself harder, a second might delegate work, while a third may feel overwhelmed and become ill. The interactions between context, vulnerability, and stressors determined the nature of the response. Yet another system differentiates four types of sources of stress, including recent events on the job, recent events away from the job, ongoing conditions on the job, and ongoing conditions away from the job (Adams, 1978). Each of these systems points up the complexity of the subject as well as the necessity of making some necessary but relatively arbitrary distinctions in considering how the invisible hazards of stress in the workplace interact with an individual's personal life at home.

In contrast to any neat diagram which can be drawn, all of these factors are in constant and inextricable interaction. They are more like layers of temperature difference in weather patterns than two-dimensional rings of a target. However, these distinctions can be useful, because a grasp of which source of stress can be altered, and by whom, is the first step toward individual and corporate action.

From the point of view of the vast majority of employees, the most immediate source of stress is the "little hassles" which disturb the working day. Most workers can more than adequately fulfill their job description. Competence is seldom the issue. Studies and self-reports from working people indicate that it is the minor hassles with other workers, time pressures, or difficult colleagues which constitute the major source of stress in the workplace, especially for office workers.

Prior even to these office or worksite hassles, it is the small troubles at home which carry over and create stress at work. According to extensive studies by noted stress researcher Richard S. Lazarus, it is evident that these "little hassles" which plague people every day may be more injurious to mental and physical health than major, traumatic life events. Lazarus and his colleagues at the University of California at Berkeley asked 100 white, middle-class, middle-aged men and women to keep track of their "hassles" and "uplifts" over a one-year period. Their results were a list of the top ten hassles and uplifts in order of frequency:

Hassles	*Uplifts*
1. Concern about weight	1. Relating well with your spouse
2. Health of a family member	or lover
3. Rising prices of common	2. Relating well with friends
goods	3. Completing a task
4. Home maintenance	4. Feeling healthy
5. Too many things to do	5. Getting enough sleep
6. Misplacing or losing things	6. Eating out
7. Yard work or outside home	7. Meeting responsibilities
maintenance	8. Visiting, phoning, or writing
8. Property, investment, or taxes	someone
9. Crime	9. Spending time with family
10. Physical appearance	10. Home pleasing to you

    (*Lazarus, 1981*)

When the researchers asked a group of college students and a group of Canadian health professionals, they received different answers. Only three hassle items, and not a single uplift, were common to all three groups: "Misplacing or losing things, physical appearance, and too many things to do" (Lazarus, 1981). Clearly, both individuals and cultural groups differ on the actual content of these lists, but the effect of such factors on daily life and well-being is universal.

Carry-over into the workplace is demonstrated in a pilot study by David W. Sheehan and his colleagues at Massachusetts General Hospital which indicated that both minor hassles and major events affect an individual's performance in the workplace. This study of 31 student nurses indicated that clusters of stressful events clearly predicted which nurses were most likely to suffer from a rash of physical accidents and job-related errors in the following weeks. Nurses evidencing a high number of stressful events were more susceptible to "accidents and errors," "muscle strains," "dropping or spilling things," "automobile mishaps," and "major errors in judgement" (Sheehan, 1981). In turn, each of these mishaps compounded the previous susceptibility in a negative stress cycle.

Recently, psychologists Perry London and Charles Spielberger have made explicit links between the little hassles, noted by Lazarus and other researchers, and stress in the workplace. From their research and others, they have noted "that the little problems do add up, taking more of a toll on health and well being than the rare major crises" (1983). Studies of groups of employees including air traffic controllers, high school teachers, physicians, and police officers appear to indicate that the impact of minor but persistent difficulties have more of an impact than dramatic occurrences. For business executives, men and women may have done very well in their previous jobs but were troubled when they were promoted to higher positions. They were almost uniformly capable of performing their jobs but the "petty details of their new position—not the burden of added responsibility—were the chief causes of their troubles" (London and Spielberger, 1983). Although it may seem obvious, it is being clearly demonstrated that the daily difficulties of domestic life do interact with the daily hassles of the workplace. Few would argue that personal events do not spill over and interact with workplace pressures in a positive as well as a negative manner.

Sources of stress within an occupational setting can be seen as a continuum, with many shades of gray between the two extremes. Below, in the left-hand column, are sources of stresses more common to management, while the right-hand column indicates the sources of stress more common to secretarial, computer terminal, and blue-collar occupations:

Management	Blue Collar
I. Work overload and excessive time demands and "rush" deadlines	Work stagnation and helplessness
II. Erratic work schedules and take-home work	Erratic work schedules and frequently changing shifts
III. Ambiguity regarding work tasks, territory, and role	Rigidity regarding work tasks
IV. Constant change and daily variability	Monotony; deadening, routinized stability
V. Role conflict (e.g., with immediate supervisor)	Too little contact or conflict
VI. Job instability and fear of unemployment	Job instability and fear of unemployment
VII. Responsibility, especially for people	Little responsibility or influence
VIII. Negative competition (e.g., "cutthroat," "one-upmanship," "zero-sum game," and "hidden aggression")	No competition or stimulation
IX. Type of vigilance required in work assignments and "team building" toward goals	Type of vigilance required in inherently stressful work (e.g., police, fire fighters, pilots, and air traffic controllers)
X. Ongoing contact with "stress carriers" (e.g., workaholics, passive-aggressive subordinates, anxious and indecisive individuals)	Social isolation and lack of support
XI. Sexual harassment	Sexual harassment
XII. Accelerated recognition for achievement (e.g., Peter Principle)	Inadequate recognition for achievement

Management	*Blue Collar*
XIII. Detrimental environmental conditions of lighting, ventilation, noise, and personal privacy	Detrimental environmental conditions of lighting, ventilation, noise, and personal privacy

In some cases, both management and blue-collar workers share the same stressors. There are different stress sources at different levels of the organization for different people. This can lead to awkward or difficult communications between managers and workers who do not appreciate the different kinds of pressures on the other persons.

In many instances, a recognition of such differences can help to improve individual and collective communication and serve to enhance the overall health of the workplace. Given the fact that "little hassles" may be equally important as major, traumatic life events in an individual's health, this opens new avenues of prevention at all levels of an organization. One approach to smoothing out these sources of stress is that of Willis Goldbeck, who has emphasized the use of "peer counseling." Goldbeck cautions against sophisticated psychiatric services at the highest level of professional sophistication since they are very costly and often unnecessary in coping with the little hassles. Actually, he has emphasized peer counseling to help resolve relatively "simple problems such as financial difficulties or problems on the job which can be taken care of more quickly and more efficiently than we are presently doing and in this manner we may avert more serious problems which require more expensive treatment" (1982).

With virtually all sources of occupational stress, the first step is the simple recognition and clear definition of the source and type of stressors. This is the essential step since each individual and organization has unique stressors which interact in a unique fashion. For this reason there is no single intervention or solution. Once the sources of stress are identified, a committed individual or organization can unquestionably rectify many of them in an appropriate manner.

HIGH-STRESS SITUATIONS

What occupations are most susceptible to occupational stress? One study undertaken in 1978 analyzed the health records of over 20,000 workers in a variety of occupations in Tennessee. The results were based upon death rates and admittance rates to Tennessee hospitals and mental health facilities and reflect the most extreme forms of occupational hazard. There was a surprisingly high incidence overall of stress-related disorders among these occupations (McLean, 1979). Based upon this and related studies, the National Institute for Occupational Safety and Health (NIOSH) has ranked 130 occupations and determined 12 occupations to have the highest occupational stress:

1. Laborer
2. Secretary
3. Inspector
4. Clinical lab technician
5. Office manager
6. Foreman
7. Manager / administrator
8. Waitress / waiter
9. Machine operator
10. Farm worker
11. Miner
12. Painter   (U.S. News & World Report, *1978*)

Among other high stress occupations, in alphabetical order, are: bank teller, clergyman, computer programmer, dental assistant, electrician, fireman, guard / watchman, hairdresser, health aide, health technician, machinist, meatcutter, musician, nurse's aide, plumber, policeman, practical nurse, public relations person, railroad switchman, registered nurse, sales manager, sales representative, social worker, structural metal worker, teacher's aide, telephone operator, and warehouse worker. These occupations span the range from management to blue collar and underscore the fact that no one approach to occupational stress is suitable for everyone.

Within each of these occupations the largest single group which is most affected in sheer numbers is Caucasian males, "age 20s or 30s, married, five or more years of experience, and working in presupervisory and premanagerial jobs . . . the 'take off phase' for both family and career lives." Although this group of males comprises the largest numbers affected by occupational stress due to their majority position in the overall work force, two groups who tend to be disproportionately and more adversely affected are minorities and women. There is increasing evidence that minorities are affected most adversely due to factors such as "the 'old boy' network of middle-aged, white middle management [where] minorities must face de facto segregation, hierarchically, within the power structure" and "the absence of minority mentors or senior role models for minority employees to emulate." Furthermore, "stemming from their previous contacts with large, white dominated institutions imbued with the 'plantation syndrome' ('we' must fix 'them'), minorities have learned to be distrustful and disbelieving of large institutions" (Manuso, 1979d). Although such stressors are not unique to minority groups, they are more exaggerated and can have more tragic consequences.

Occupational stressors are also compounded even when the minority is that of women in the workplace. Beginning with the popular and accurate bumper sticker that "every mother is a working mother," and judging by the recently emerging studies of women executives, it is evident that women are under equal if not greater occupational stress than their male counterparts. Whether in the boardroom or in the "cottage industry" household, women appear to be at excessive risk in their occupations. Household work is usually ignored in discussion of work and health, but a unique fifteen-year study of Oregon housewives indicated that they faced "a significant excess of cancer deaths" of the breast, ovaries, colon, lungs, uterus, and stomach (Morton and Ungs, 1979). In fact, housewives had the highest job-related cancer death rate of any occupation in the study. Aside from toxic chemicals and low-level radiation from microwave ovens, the sources of stress include boredom, isolation, and lack of self-esteem.

Many of the pressures associated with minorities in general appear to hold true for women in the workplace. Nancy Milio of the University of North Carolina's School of Public Health points out that "The relative health of women will decline by the turn of the century, as more women enter the workforce . . . women's death rates from heart and respiratory diseases are expected to rise while men's are expected to decline . . . in the future women will die of cirrhosis of the liver at a rate almost equal to men, and their rate of death from circulatory and digestive diseases will not improve as rapidly as that for men . . . given the opportunity for comparable jobs, women face the same work environmental risks as men: asbestos, toxic chemicals, coal, noise, heavy workloads, and rotating workshifts" (*American Medical News,* 1981). While the environmental risk may be the same for women as for men, the psychological stress factors may be higher. A study from Stanford University showed that "four times as many young women with MBA degrees seek psychological counseling as do men with the MBA . . . women showed significantly more psychological and physical signs of stress . . . stomach upsets and a variety of non-specific physical ailments" (*San Francisco Examiner,* 1981). Researchers noted that women were more apt to be "living out the myth of the 'superwoman' trying to be model homemakers as well as successful in business." One cardiologist, Robert S. Elliot, stated his conclusions that today's woman is more stressed than men in noting, "A woman is expected to act like a lady, think like a man, and work like a dog!" While a cynical interpretation of such results may conclude that women cannot manage occupational stress, it is far more likely that women in the workplace are demonstrating a greater sensitivity to and willingness to point out sources of occupational stress rather than ignore the relatively minor and correctable early indicators until they proceed to the point of an "unexpected" coronary or psychological "burnout." Given the decades of data indicating that women have tended to be healthier and evidence greater longevity than men and that these differences are largely lifestyle related, the best outcome from women's presence in the workplace would be to "feminize" it. The psychological workplace could well stand to be shifted away from "macho" competition toward a model based upon cooperation and interdependence, and thus improve the quality and quantity of life for both the female and male worker.

RESPONSE TO OCCUPATIONAL STRESS

The majority of health impairments which result from stress are not dramatic instances such as heart attack. According to recent data, the most common symptoms in order of decreasing frequency are: (1) anxiety and / or neurosis (25 percent); (2) depression (20 percent); (3) stress-related, psychosomatic disorders (headache, low back pain, hypertension, gastrointestinal tract) (15 percent); (4) alcohol and other drug abuse (15 percent); (5) situational adjustment problems (e.g., divorce, finances, death in the family) (10 percent); and (6) other disorders (e.g., severe mental and / or physical morbidity or mortality) (15 percent). From the organization point of view symptoms result in the statistics of absenteeism, reduced productivity, and disruption in the workplace.

Before discussing the three most common individual responses to a stressful working environment, we might mention a rare but curious mass response. "Assembly-line hysteria" was described by researchers for the National Institute for Occupational Safety and Health. As early as the mid-1970s, researchers had noted the phenomenon of the rapid onset of physical disorders among masses of assembly-line workers. According to NIOSH clinical psychologist Michael J. Colligan, "All of a sudden, people become so weak that they have to be helped from the floor; there's a lot of rapid breathing, and if there is a lot of hyperventilation there may be spasms—it's general pandemonium" (Peterson, 1979). These reactions are in the absence of environmental toxins. The reactions verge on panic. Outbreaks of "assembly-line hysteria" or what is termed "mass psychogenic illness" in the psychological literature, occur most frequently: (1) on assembly lines where each worker performs the same repetitious tasks over and over; (2) among workers where opportunity for advancement is low or nonexistent; (3) under high noise conditions; (4) where workers are less educated; (5) where workers are dependent upon their jobs for their families' survival and yet are more dissatisfied with their bosses and their work in general than unaffected workers; and (6) among women workers. Often one person's complaint of headaches, nausea, chest pains, or fatigue appears to be the catalyst; this appears to create extreme psychological stress among other workers and the outbreak expands in a geometric fashion. For the catalyst person, the original symptoms may have been due to an environmental toxin or stress, but the ensuing epidemic has no such specific cause.

There are indications that the nature of the symptoms are determined by culture. During the 1970s a case was reported in Malaysia among women working in electronics plants. They were using microscopes to work on semiconductors and began seeing demons! Among the most famous cases of mass hysteria is the report of Duke University psychologists Alan C. Kerchoff and Kurt W. Back in *The June*

Bug (Herbert, 1982). Women in a North Carolina textile mill claimed they were bitten by bugs, but no unusual insects were discovered. Upon closer examination, Kerchoff and Back concluded that the apparent epidemic was due to the pressures of unwanted overtime during the month of June, which was the peak of production. Most recently, psychiatrists from Harvard and UCLA investigated an outbreak of fainting, abdominal pain, and nausea among 41 elementary school students in a chorus meeting of over 400 students in Massachusetts. This study is of particular interest since physical exams of the stricken students did indicate a trace of a toxic chemical, n-butylbenzene-sulfonamide. Further testing, however, found the same level of this chemical among the healthy students and the chemical appeared to be a surface contaminant of the plastic urine-containers. The incident was ruled to be mass hysteria. According to investigators Gary W. Small and Jonathan F. Borus, "Whenever mass illness occurs the likelihood of obtaining positive results from toxicology screening will increase as environmental pollution becomes more widespread . . . no single finding is [adequate] . . . chemical tests, psychological variables, and other epidemiologic characteristics must all be assessed" (1983).

Such panic episodes are often accompanied by hyperventilation, breathing in a rapid pace from the upper point of the lungs, a reaction which in turn signals a full "fight or flight" episode to the body and mind. While such episodes appear most often in assembly-line areas, outbreaks have occurred in schools, secretarial pools, computer terminal areas, or in work areas characterized by a high density of organized and structured activities and where tension is likely to mount. Such phenomena suggest that the corporate body itself may suffer from stress. Individual stress reactions are not simply cumulative; they may compound one another in an exponential fashion.

THE WORKAHOLIC RESPONSE

Individual response to occupational stress can fall into three basic styles: (1) workaholic behavior; (2) Type A behavior; and (3) burnout. "Workaholic" is a loosely defined term which connotes an individual who is addicted to work per se even more than the results of that work. Although the term has acquired a pejorative sense, workaholics are not inherently detrimental to themselves or others. A more realistic and relatively neutral definition has been proposed by Marilyn Machlowitz in *Workaholics: Living with Them, Working with Them* (1980) as "people whose desire to work long and hard is intrinsic and whose work habits almost always exceed the prescriptions of the job and the expectations of those with whom or for whom they work." One of the surprising conclusions reached by Machlowitz was that the workaholics she interviewed were "remarkably satisfied with their lives." In fact, she concluded from her interviews that "satisfaction with work and with life are more apt to be intertwined than mutually exclusive." This finding is consistent with research in longevity in which "job satisfaction" has been determined to be a significant predictor of both health and longevity. At the negative extreme there are the impaired workaholics who are inflexibly addicted to work to the detriment of all other dimensions of their lives. According to New York psychiatrist Lawrence Susser, who specializes in treating workaholics (presumably those who are dissatisfied with their way of life), "workaholics are lauded as some type of contemporary hero . . . they're among the brightest and most successful people within a community or company. But what's the price they pay? . . . Workaholism will make you sick, ruin your marriage and your relationships. It can actually kill you" (Staver, 1981). Although workaholic behavior can occur at any level of an organization, it is a particular hazard for those in management positions.

During 1980, *The Wall Street Journal* sponsored a Gallup organization study of 306 chief executives of the country's 1,300 largest corporations. Respondents in that study clearly exhibited strong workaholic tendencies and consistently reported working sixty to seventy hours a week, traveling six to ten days per month, and, frequently, putting work and career before family and their own personal health. Virtually all of the chief executives reported more personal pressure in their present positions than in middle management, where the occupational pressures seemed greater. As a result "over 60% believe that personal and family sacrifices are needed to succeed . . . and almost one-quarter of the executives state that physical and mental health suffers" (*Behavioral Medicine,* 1980). Regional and job specific variations were also of significance, and chief executives of western companies reported more job-related ailments than those of eastern companies. Also, executives of smaller businesses reported a greater percent of physical health ailments than those in larger companies. On a more positive note, the executives found that health promotion programs were a means to alleviate the excessive occupational stress.

Research by Waino Suojanen of Georgia State University and Donald Hudson of the University of Miami raises the interesting possibility that workaholics might actually be incurring a form of addiction to adrenaline, a hormone produced by the body in stressful situations and closely resembling amphetamines. Also suggesting an addiction is an abundance of norepinephrine, another stress-induced secretion, which is characteristic as well of certain Type A behavior discussed in the next section. According to the researchers, a workaholic requires larger and larger dosages of these hormones and creates a managerial style where he or she "tries to build fires in order to put them out, or manufacture crises he can stand up under" (Harrigan, 1981). Such a manager is termed an "ACORN," which is an acronym for "addictive, compulsive, obsessive, real nutty," as opposed to an "OAK" executive, who is "open, adaptive, and knowledgeable." In contrast to Machlowitz's work, they point out that impaired workaholics not only adversely affect themselves but also have a very negative effect upon peers and subordinates. They are stress carriers. Their behavior, which has tended to be highly prized by American organizations, is increasingly coming into question. Usually such behavior continues until the person "gets transferred or dies of a heart attack" (Harrigan, 1981). While such a toll is preventable, it occurs all too frequently.

Estimates indicate that approximately 5 percent of the working population are workaholics. A relatively high percentage of these individuals are on the positive end of the continuum and are characterized as contented or functional workaholics. Marilyn Machlowitz identified four factors correlated with a workaholic's degree of happiness: "(1) acceptance of their work habits by their families; (2) autonomy and variety in their work; (3) a good match between their personal skills and styles and those required by their jobs; and (4) their general state of health" (Ferguson, 1981). Those workaholics who had all four factors going for them generally felt positive about themselves. Those who lacked one or more tended toward the impaired workaholic side of the range and were prime candidates for "occupational burnout," which is discussed in a later section. A key characteristic of contented workaholics appears to be that they genuinely enjoy their work. Dick Vermeil, head coach of the Philadelphia

Eagles, said in an interview with Machlowitz: "I do what I do because I enjoy it very much; I don't really consider it hard work." There are no definitive conclusions which can be drawn from this initial data being collected on impaired and functional workaholics, but at least a distinction is being made.

It is an important first step to recognize that contented workaholics genuinely enjoy their work, rather than being driven by a neurotic concern for control and manipulation, and that they are flexible and can disengage from work addiction to enjoy the many other dimensions of life and relationships. Most often, the biggest problem is not the work itself but the inability to do or enjoy anything else. These individuals cannot take pleasure in their leisure and are uncomfortable in social situations. They often feel distressed, anxious, and dissatisfied when they are not working, which leads them to work harder and longer in an increasingly anxious and isolated lifestyle. A workaholic's family may be crumbling or he or she cannot sustain good personal relationships. When a crisis does occur, then they do not have the human resources to rely upon for help and support. The scale noted below is a way of measuring workaholic tendencies. Since, as we have seen, a workaholic is neither a positive nor a negative designation, the score should not be taken too literally. The best use of this scale is simply to raise one's awareness of these tendencies.

Work to Live
Live to Work

Circle the number of statements with which you agree and add the number of circles to get your score (maximum is 10).

1. My work is one of the most rewarding and fulfilling parts of my life.
2. I would probably work just as much as I do now even if I had no need to work to support myself.
3. One of my main goals in life is to find and do the "work that is play."
4. I use a daily list of "things to do" to help me make the best use of my time.
5. Most of my friends would probably agree that I usually have a great deal of energy—and I get much of this energy from my work.
6. I frequently work on weekends and holidays.

7. I am so involved in my work that it is difficult for me to take vacations.
8. I frequently break dates and cancel appointments so that I can get more work done.
9. My work is so much a part of my life that distinctions between "work time" and "time off" get blurred.
10. My involvement in my work sometimes causes problems for my family and friends.

SCORE _____ (*Ferguson, 1981*)

Extreme workaholic tendencies (8 or more) need to be balanced. Among the measures suggested by physician Tom Ferguson (1981), founder and editor of *Medical Self-Care* magazine, are: (1) focus on the aspects of work that are most enjoyable and delegate or minimize those that you dislike; (2) ask yourself: "What work would I do for free?" and try to evolve your work in that direction; (3) decide how much time you want to spend working and limit your work accordingly; (4) schedule open time into your work life, since breaks can actually enhance your performance when you return to work; (5) learn to say "no" to new demands on your time; (6) try to remain oriented toward the positive aspects of your work such as the freedom and opportunity to be of help to others; (7) place a value on time away from work, since this offers the opportunity to reassess life values and make decisions concerning life changes and directions; and most of all (8) remember to appreciate your family and friends, since they often feel overlooked and unimportant in the busy blur of a workaholic's productive but isolated lifestyle. Overall, says Ferguson, "workaholics are lucky people. Not only do they tend to love their work . . . but also the cure for their characteristic problem is quite pleasant: learn to relax . . . do more of what they like and less of what they dislike, and spend more quality time with their family and friends" (Ferguson, 1981). From these observations it is clear that high productivity and performance are possible without the disintegration of a personal life, possible heart disease, or psychological burnout but that this requires insight and a willingness to initiate small but vital changes in work performance and lifestyle.

TYPE A BEHAVIOR

Closely related to the workaholic orientation is Type A, or inflexible, time-pressured behavior. This has become recognized as a risk factor in heart disease. Work addiction is only one aspect of the complex Type A syndrome, although the closest correlation of a true Type A individual is with the impaired workaholic. There are also Type B, or functional, workaholics who are able to work long hours at high levels of performance and not exhibit excessive, hostile competitiveness or an excessive time pressure and urgency. There is a whole spectrum in between the extremes, and anyone can move along that continuum in either direction. Type A behavior is actually a constellation or cluster of behaviors that are primarily learned and therefore can be changed. *Today* program commentator Jane Pauley described Tom Brokaw with "You've heard of the Type-A personality. Well, Tom is an A-plus. He can't stop." For purposes of several major studies concerning work-styles, the designation of Type A has referred to individuals who constantly put in many extra discretionary hours of work per week versus the designation of Type B, discussed later, for those who were more easygoing and relaxed about their work schedule. Another characteristic of Type A is a strong "need for power." Such individuals are generally "more argumentative and aggressive; they engage more often in competitive sports; they are sexually more active; they accumulate prestige supplies; like fancy clothes and cars; and they tend to join organizations and ally themselves with those who have affluence" (Pines, 1980). When a person with these qualities finds his drives inhibited, he reacts adversely to that stress and becomes susceptible to illness and heart disease.

There is no need to detail Type A further since complete descriptions can be found in the classic book *Type A Behavior and Your Heart* by cardiologists Meyer Friedman and Raymond Rosenman (1974), in *Holistic Medicine* (Pelletier, 1979), as well as in numerous other books and magazine articles. In brief, Friedman and Rosenman spell out the clearest characteristics of Type A behavior as (1) excessive competitive drive; (2) ambitiousness and achievement oriented; (3) chronic sense of urgency; (4) inclination to take on multiple commitments; (5) concern for meeting deadlines; (6)

impatience; (7) inability to relax without feeling guilty; (8) drive to accomplish tasks quickly; (9) preoccupation with quantity rather than quality; and (10) behavior unrelated to anxiety, fear or worry (adapted from Friedman and Rosenman, 1974).

For purposes of this discussion the traits of a Type B personality are: (1) Lack of sense of urgency; (2) no need to display achievements; (3) lack of free-floating hostility; (4) the ability to play for fun and relaxation rather than competition; (5) ability to relax without guilt; and (6) ability to work without agitation (adapted from Friedman and Rosenman, 1974).

These two poles represent the range of behavior which is possible, and the most important characteristic appears to be the ability to move flexibly along this continuum in an appropriate response to internal or external demands. When executives achieve this full range, they often become more productive than they were. It is a myth that the less Type A you are, the less you will achieve.

Despite the widespread acceptance of such behavior as a coronary-risk factor, there are refinements in current research which may lead to further insights and greater usefulness for this valuable concept. Cardiologist Robert Elliot of the University of Nebraska has found that Type A behavior did not consistently correlate with measures of cardiac output and other hemodynamic indicators. In his studies, thirty top executives were given math quizzes, challenged in a video game, and monitored during other stressful situations. Under these conditions some Type A executives remained physiologically very calm, while others who did not test out as Type A actually were found to be "silent hyperreactors" who showed great physiological strain. These latter had "decreased stroke volume, decreased cardiac output, increased total peripheral resistance and marked blood pressure rise" (Kornfeld, 1981). These "hot Type A's," or overreactors, exhibit hostility, impatience, and aggressive competitiveness and generally react much too strongly and disproportionately to situations. According to Elliot, the physically calm Type A's may explain the "throngs of crabby Type A's whom we all notice at the funerals of their Type B contemporaries!"

A related series of studies has refined and clarified the psychophysiology of Type A behavior even further. At Duke University Medical Center, Redford B. Williams and his colleagues studied blood pressure and blood flow to muscles as well as the levels of five hormones (norepinephrine, epinephrine, cortisol, testosterone, and prolactin) in Type A and Type B individuals. Measures were taken for each group before and after two different tasks of mental arithmetic work and reaction time. They found clear differences between Type A and Type B responses. The Type A individuals produced excessive physiological responses beyond what was required simply to achieve the task. On the arithmetic task, Type A's produced excessive blood flow to muscle and excessive levels of norepinephrine, epinephrine, and cortisol. On the reaction-time task, Type A's produced excessive levels of testosterone and, in those who had a history of high blood pressure, also excessive cortisol levels. These findings are very significant since both cortisol and testosterone are known to encourage hardening of the arteries, a major risk factor for heart attacks. Also, epinephrine and norepinephrine are known to increase blood clotting, and if a clot lodges in a coronary artery clogged with cholesterol, it could deprive the heart of oxygen and lead to a heart attack. All of these findings make explicit and clear links between the psychological responses of Type A versus Type B behavior and the physical changes which result. According to Williams and his colleagues, these studies "have potentially far-reaching implications for understanding mechanisms underlying the increased coronary disease risk observed among Type A persons" (Williams et al., 1982). Beyond the value of such findings for basic research is their demonstration that the Type A response is excessive and not conducive to improved performance. In fact, such excessive reactivity may actually be counterproductive, as we saw in the earlier illustration of the maximum "performance zone."

Findings such as these are preliminary but are extremely important in order to offset a tendency in work situations to stereotype one form of behavior versus another as good or bad, based on superficial judgments. There is no one right way to work or achieve optimum performance: there are a virtually infinite number of effective workstyles which need to be individually adapted for a particular person in each work environment.

The most complete overview to date of this complex area was prepared by the National Heart, Lung and Blood Institute of the National Institute of Health under the title "Coronary-prone Behavior and Coronary Heart Disease: A Critical Review" (Weiss et al., 1981). There are many surprises emerging in recent studies. Top executives apparently suffer less cardiovascular disease and somewhat fewer stress-related complaints than middle-management employees and clerks. For one example, the presidents and vice-presidents of the 500 largest industrial companies had 40 percent fewer fatal heart attacks than middle managers of those same companies. In the often quoted words of one top executive, "I don't get ulcers; I give them!" Another study, by NIOSH, showed that top executives had fewer heart and circulatory problems and indicated a greater risk for the secretarial to middle-management range. Among these workers the NIOSH study also found a higher incidence of boredom, frustrated ambition, and job malaise. One example was cited of clerical workers who used video display terminals and reported very high levels of workload, lack of control over their job activities, boredom, and feelings of stagnation in their career development.

Studies of executive versus middle-management stress suggest that there may be a different physiological response to stress between these two groups. In any response to problem-solving stress, there is an increase in norepinephrine, which stimulates a person's performance and creates an upswing in coping ability. However, at a certain point this increase actually begins to impair work performance. Some individuals are able to keep norepinephrine levels within this narrow frame of high performance by an intuitive sense or learned process, which needs to be explored further. Unfortunately, many more individuals go beyond this threshold and continue to produce excessive norepinephrine which contributes to further inefficiency. Robert S. Elliot has demonstrated that such a pattern of destructive norepinephrine overload is less likely to occur among top executives because of differences in work-style. Among top executives, "Those . . . in upper management tend to set their own schedules and are rarely forced to do more than they can do, not only because they are in charge but also because their ability to schedule themselves properly is part of the reason they have made it to the top. The real issue from my perspective boils down to how much decision and latitude you have over your life and job" (*Medical Tribune,* 1981).

As one result of this internal difference in their approach to work, the top executives exhibit less epinephrine overload. Possibly these differences in work-style and in the different nature of job demands between top and middle management result in quite different psychophysiological states. Long-term secretion of excessive norepinephrine eventually leads to arterial and heart problems, but its more controlled secretion may account for the lesser mortality among upper management. As was mentioned earlier, norepinephrine overload is closely related to and quite similar to the adrenaline addiction characteristic of the impaired workaholic and, like any addiction, can lead to physical and psychological deterioration. Finally, it is possible that this epinephrine addiction is compounded by the fact that the same individuals turn to excessive consumption of coffee, alcohol, and cigarettes, which further stimulate norepinephrine production! Future research may find that moderate levels of norepinephrine may be a mediator of healthy competitiveness while excessive levels may be characteristic of nonproductive, hostile competitiveness. Findings such as these are fascinating since they indicate a concrete means of understanding and working with the preventable toll of self-destructive work-styles.

Turning from the psychophysiological basis of Type A behavior to its manifestations in the workplace, one of the most outstanding studies was conducted in 1979 by psychiatrist Ari Kiev and his associate Vera Kohn. For their study, Kiev and Kohn mailed 6,000 questionnaires to members of the American Management Association with a focus upon the two groups of top management and middle management, those with the title of manager. There were 1,422 replies from top management and 1,237 from middle management for a high response rate of 44 percent, indicating a high interest in the subject. Generally, "the results do not support the popular image of the harried executive for whom stress is the norm as he or she faces a daily barrage of crises, pressures, and frustration" (Kiev and Kohn, 1979). Also, the executives appeared to handle stress very well without excessive physical or psychological difficulties and did not feel that their health had been adversely affected by their work. Results such as these appear to contradict the findings of the *Wall Street Journal* study discussed earlier. Some of this variance is accounted for in the differences in the populations studied, as well as in details of the findings. However, the variance indicates the need for more systematic study.

Both the top and middle managers did agree on the four leading causes of stress at the workplace:

— "Heavy workload / time pressures / unrealistic deadlines."
— "Disparity between what I have to do on the job and what I would like to accomplish."
— "The general 'political' climate of the organization."
— "Lack of feedback on job performance."

As for the major stressors away from the workplace, among the two groups there was also considerable agreement about the top three: (1) "financial worries"; (2) "problems with children"; and (3) "physical injury, illness, and discomforts." Overall incidence of major, traumatic life events such as death of a spouse, divorce, or marital separation was low for both groups and tends to support the importance of the "little hassles" rather than major life events as suggested earlier. Both groups also agreed upon their four leading indications of psychological distress:

"I am irritable and angry if things don't go my way."
"I am restless and can't seem to relax."
"I worry about things that worrying won't help."
"I have difficulty concentrating."

Again, extreme maladjustment through insomnia, habitual smoking, or heavy drinking were quite low in occurrence. Data such as these show that individual and organizational stress is identifiable and potentially resolvable.

At this point, the one critical difference which cuts across both top and middle management was how these stressors were handled. Surprisingly, there appeared to be as many Type A individuals as Type B individuals in both top and middle management. In the Kiev and Kohn study, managers were divided into Type A or Type B based upon their response to one specific workaholic tendency, "I work excessively (for example, take work home / work on the commuter train / go into the office weekends)." This study disproves the common stereotype and misconception that has erroneously linked achievement, effectiveness, and optimum performance with either Type A or workaholic behavior. It is possible to be Type B or a functional workaholic and achieve success in the workplace, with considerably less physical or psychological disability. "Type A managers reported a noticeably higher level of stress than Type B managers did, particularly with respect to symptoms like restlessness and inability to relax, loss of interest in leisure activities, and imbalance between work and home life." Furthermore, Type A's were found to be more stressed than Type B's on every stress indicator. These findings confirm other studies in the psychological, medical, and workplace literature that "Stress is rooted in personality. People with one kind of personality create stress for themselves; those with another kind of personality do not, or they do so to a lesser extent"

(Kiev and Kohn, 1979). Recently, researcher Craig E. Daniels reported a study of the correlates of Type A versus Type B behavior in a group of middle- and upper-management male executives. According to his study, the Type A executive had more "indigestion . . . migraine or tension headaches and motion sickness. They used more aspirin, were more likely to use Valium, drank more coffee, engaged in more aerobic exercise, and were more optimistic." By contrast, the Type B executive at the same level of stress and responsibility evidenced a different response to the same environmental conditions. Type B executives had "lower incidence of pain in the arms, shoulders or wrist, . . . were more likely to jog, play tennis, walk distances greater than one mile for recreation, engage in yoga . . . and were less likely to use valium" (1982). Studies such as these clearly indicate marked differences in coping-style and stress management given comparable internal and external challenges. It appears increasingly likely that the "fault . . . is not in our stars, but in ourselves." Given the same set and level workplace and personal life changes, demands, or stressors, certain individuals will barely survive while others thrive. Furthermore, as we will discuss later, it is possible to identify and learn the characteristics of those individuals who thrive under stress.

Changing Type A behavior is not an easy task. In fact, ongoing studies appear to indicate that such behavioral changes are difficult to both induce and sustain even under the motivating threat of the possibility of a fatal heart attack. At the present time a five-year program is under way in the San Francisco Bay Area under the title of the Recurrent Coronary Prevention Program. Under the RCPP an attempt is being made to alter the Type A pattern in more than 1,000 postcoronary men and women. One group is receiving usual medical care from their own doctors. The second group is meeting periodically with a cardiologist to discuss nutrition and exercise, while the third group is split into smaller groups focused upon altering Type A behavior. Patients in the third group practiced physical and mental relaxation techniques as well as phrases to ponder and apply to their lives, such as William James's statement that "The art of being wise is the art of knowing what to overlook." After the first year, the study indicated, the patients receiving instructions in a healthier lifestyle, diet, exercise, and relaxation demonstrated a rate of recurrent heart attacks "significantly below the national average of 6 to 9% annually." Preliminary results such as these are very encouraging and it appears that changing Type A behavior is easier than changing eating habits. There appears to be a very positive effect from just the group meetings themselves. According to Stanford University psychologist Carl Thoresen, "A lot of these people never had any emotional support in their lives. . . . Many were so individualistic that they had cut themselves off from other people almost totally" (Smith and Sherman, 1982). Many of the approaches used in the study have been very straightforward and applicable in everyday life. Among the techniques noted by Thoresen are: "At the heart of it is becoming more trusting, more caring, more loving, less suspicious. . . . Simple behavior changes you can practice are: talking more slowly and less emphatically, interrupting others less and focusing your full attention on what they have to say. It is also good to gesture less abruptly with your head and hands and cut down on fidgeting and juggling. . . . Try to find humor in the situation. . . . Type B behavior comes more easily in a peaceful environment. So cut back on violence and highly competitive events on TV, including the 11 o'clock news and Sunday football. Forget prime time altogether" (Smith and Sherman, 1982). These suggestions may seem simple, but the real difficulty is in practicing these guidelines, not just hurriedly acknowledging them in typical Type A fashion.

The need to build such intervention programs into the workday and at the workplace was brought out by the researchers in this program: "intervention programs built into the working day would not only be well received by participants but would have a significant influence on Type A behavior" (Thoresen, Telch, and Eagleston, 1981). Motivating positive change is perhaps the most formidable obstacle in an individual or organizational approach to health promotion. Rather than bemoaning the difficulties in motivating large numbers of individuals, it is possible to specify certain strategies which do appear to be effective and can be adopted and adapted by some individuals even though they may constitute a minority.

Drawing upon the Kiev and Kohn study, three techniques of stress management were favored by a substantial majority of both top and middle management. Type B managers appeared to be substantially more effective in actually implementing these stress management strategies. Below is a list of the top three strategies with the percent of top versus middle managers who used that technique indicated after each strategy:

1. "Delegate responsibility instead of carrying entire load my-self" (used by 90 percent of top management and 86 percent of middle management).
2. "Analyze stress-producing situation and decide what is worth worrying about and what isn't" (used by 85 percent of both groups).
3. "Establish daily goals and set priorities to accomplish the most important objectives" (used by 81 percent of top management and 83 percent of middle management). (*Kiev and Kohn, 1979*)

Although the conclusions are tentative, there are clear indications that stressful situations at work occurred more often and with more impact for Type A's than B's at both management levels. By large margins, the Type A's tended to speed up themselves and co-workers in response to stress, while Type B's changed gears, broke the work routine, and provided themselves and others with periods of rest and relaxation each day. Type B's also apparently utilized the above stress management strategies with greater effectiveness. Success and performance are not synonymous with the hard-driving, inflexibly competitive, and hostile stereotype of management. Recent studies appear to indicate quite the opposite, and that is good news for individuals and organizations.

BURNOUT

Before turning to a more detailed consideration of individuals who thrive rather than suffer under stress, there is one other major type of response to stress to be considered, and that is "burnout." In many work settings, especially human services, burnout has been a growing concern in recent years. The plethora of "anti-burnout" programs, however, is almost uniformly oriented toward crisis intervention rather than health promotion. Clearly the consequences of burnout are very high, but after the fact interventions are likely to remain more costly and less effective than overall health promotion.

One of the best inquiries into this area is *Burnout: The High Cost of Achievement* by Herbert J. Freudenberger (1980), who reports his own recovery from burnout after working eighteen hours a day in his private practice and running a storefront free clinic in the East

Village of Manhattan. Among the indications of burnout are chronic fatigue, low energy, irritability, and a negative attitude toward oneself and one's job. In listening to individuals suffering from burnout, certain themes consistently emerge, such as "trapped or attacked," "need to get away or escape," "feeling weighted down," "exhaustion or depletion," "sensations of emptiness and loneliness," "being blocked by obstacles or circumstances which are insurmountable," and finally, "giving up or drowning." At the workplace these personal feelings translate into difficulty concentrating on or making decisions, failure of short-term memory, and overall impatience, cynicism, irritability, and rigidity or resistance to new input and ideas. According to research by Christina Maslach of the Department of Psychology at the University of California at Berkeley, burnout appears to have three phases. First, there is an emotional exhaustion, a feeling of being drained, used up, and of having nothing more to give. Second, there is a cynicism, a callous, insensitive regard for people, a "don't-knock-yourself-out-for-anyone" attitude. Finally, the burnout victim comes to believe that he or she has been unsuccessful and all job effort has been fruitless.

Burnout affects both men and women at every level of employment. Although burnout is a potential in every profession, there is a growing literature which addresses the specific hazards of burnout for specific types of professionals such as physicians (Halenar, 1981; Roeske, 1981; Gardner and Hall, 1981), judges (Behavior Today, 1980), public administrators (Morrison, 1977), accountants (Sapp and Seiler, 1980) and CPAs (Gaertner and Ruhe, 1981), credit managers (Hunt, 1981), bond dealers (Euromoney, 1980), and air traffic controllers (Lefton, 1981). For individuals in these stressful occupations or related areas, these articles can provide invaluable insights and some techniques for managing occupational stress before it results in the burnout phenomenon. Those individuals in any profession who appear most susceptible are employees who measure their success or failure largely by standards other than the usual external standards of income or corporate position. Ironically, it appears that the most susceptible individuals are those who enter their work or profession with unrealistically high expectations of making the world a better place or those who had the most sparkle and are literally crushed with disillusionment.

Burnout appears to be more common among the helping professions such as teaching, social work, nursing, clergy, and police

(Golin, 1981), although the greatest concern appears to be among corporate managers. Writing in *The Wall Street Journal,* Robert S. Greenberger described the dilemma of executives who "don't really want to be in the job any longer, but they won't blow the whistle on themselves" quoted sources who said that "10% of the overall executive population exhibits the cynicism that could be a harbinger of burnout" (1981). Quite often there is a distinct developmental profile where the individual makes a significant early impact in his or her career and is identified as having high potential and being "up and coming." This leads to early and rapid promotion. Unfortunately, these management-quality people soon find themselves managing other people and the details of their career rather than having time and latitude for more creative input. One person who reported such an experience was a creative man in a large New York advertising agency who moved rapidly up the corporate ladder to just such a plateau and discovered that the more managerial responsibility he got, "the less I could do the things I liked and could do well. I had become a supervisor" (Greenberger, 1981). At this point, managers tend to become cynical and disillusioned. The result can be an impaired workaholic who becomes addicted to work per se rather than the results, a prime candidate for burnout.

Burnout is not inevitable, and its treatment or prevention can be as simple as one executive's decision to "make sure that every day I sat down with a real person and talked about a real problem, instead of pushing paper around" (Greenberger, 1981). There are also highly effective workshop programs by such individuals as Diane Ryerson and Nancy Marks of Ryerson Marks Associates of Teaneck, New Jersey (*Behavior Today,* 1980). Members of one profession which suffers from an inordinately high incidence of burnout are teachers. The occurrence has reached crisis proportions. Many excellent teachers are leaving education for business; new teachers are not entering the profession, and those who remain do so at great risk to their personal health. In order to address this crisis for teachers, Christopher F. Wilson and Deborah L. Hall, of the San Diego Department of Education, have written *Preventing Burnout in Education* (1981), which is an excellent step-by-step guide for educators and other professionals to evaluate the stress in their lives and to develop effective stress management skills. Having teachers learn such skills is valuable to them per se and of even greater value because of their influence upon primary- and secondary-grade children. Children can learn these life-affirming skills also, often more readily than adults. Perhaps there will be programs developed for children and young adults to foster these skills at an early age and prevent many of the chronic diseases of adulthood which have their psychological and physical roots in the early years.

Just as "stress" and "workaholic" are not pejorative terms, neither is "burnout." As with workaholic or Type A behavior, it is possible to give an impressionistic assessment of burnout tendencies. Below is a self-administered scale which can indicate such tendencies. Respond to this questionnaire by thinking back over the last six months of your life. Read each question and then give yourself a score for each one, ranging from "1" indicating "little or no change" in the last six months in the item, to "5" indicating a "good deal of change" in the item. Allow yourself about 30 seconds for a response and add up the total number of points to the 15 items as your final score for a maximum of 75. This scale is a "Brownout / Burnout Inventory":

1. Do you tire more easily? Feel fatigued rather than energetic?
2. Are people annoying you by telling you, "You don't look too good lately?"
3. Are you working harder and harder and accomplishing less and less?
4. Are you increasingly cynical and disenchanted?
5. Are you often invaded by a sadness you can't explain?
6. Are you forgetting? (appointments, deadlines, personal possessions)
7. Are you increasingly irritable? More short-tempered? More disappointed in the people around you?
8. Are you seeing close friends and family members less frequently?
9. Are you too busy to do even routine things like make phone calls, read reports, or send out Christmas cards?
10. Are you suffering from physical complaints? (aches, pains, headaches, a lingering cold)
11. Do you feel disoriented when the activity of the day comes to a halt?
12. Is joy elusive?
13. Are you unable to laugh at a joke about yourself?
14. Does sex seem like more trouble than it's worth?
15. Do you have very little to say to people?

SCORE _____

As with the previous workaholic scale and Type A checklist, do not be alarmed if your score is high (51–75). These self-administered scales are not definitive by any means. Actually, the greatest value of such self-administered scales is to take the first step toward correcting burnout tendencies by recognizing them. Once the recognition occurs, it is then possible to consider alternative choices of action. The following chart contrasts professionals who thrive on long work hours on the left versus those who do not on the right:

Professionals who thrive on long work hours:	Professionals who experience the overwork syndrome:
Ability to postpone thinking about problems.	Rumination about work problems.
Ability to respond promptly to evidence of fatigue.	Lengthening workday to compensate for diminished productivity.
Avoidance of drug and alcohol abuse.	Use of alcohol or drugs as an escape from stress.
Enjoyment of scheduled vacations.	Tendency to postpone vacations.
Stable domestic situation.	Chaotic family life.
Ability to maintain friendships.	Loners.
Engagement in regular exercise.	Sedentary lifestyle.
Varied interests outside work.	Narrowed interests.
Sense of humor.	Inability to laugh at self.

(*Adapted from Rhoads, 1978*)

Factors on the left are inherent characteristics of some individuals or have been learned by them. It is this element of learning and adaptation which makes burnout prevention possible.

WHO THRIVES?

Much is currently known about the adverse effects of stress. At this point it may be more valuable to learn not who gets sick but who stays healthy and why. Our focus should shift from the diagnosis and treatment of disease to discovering the means of eliciting and sustaining optimum levels of health and performance. It is evident that certain individuals and organizations can actually use stress to achieve personal growth and development, to raise productivity, stimulate creative thinking, introduce innovative ideas and procedures, enhance their job performance as well as that of their peers and subordinates, and foster teamwork and cooperation. According to *The Art of Japanese Management* by Pascale and Athos, an effective corporation is based upon the "seven S's" of strategy, structure, systems, staff, skills, style, and superordinate goals. Western organizations have emphasized the first three while Japanese firms have given equal emphasis to the last four, which "act as a lubricant in the organizational machine to keep the hard S's from grinding one another away." In these four elements may be found the means by which stress is transformed into productivity and performance. One quotation from Takeo Fujisawa, co-founder of Honda Motor Company, was very striking: "Japanese and American management is 95 percent the same and differs in all important respects." Just a few subtle but critical distinctions can make the difference between successful performance and workaholic, Type A, and burnout experience; the qualities of highly functional individuals and organizations appear to constitute this vital 5 percent difference.

What distinguishes the people who exhibit optimum performance? Recently, Suzanne C. Kobasa of the University of Chicago defined certain qualities in stress resistant people. Her research began with a retrospective study of 670 middle and upper-middle managers of Illinois Bell Telephone. All of the men were white, Protestant, college graduates, between 40 and 49, and married with two children. In comparing two groups of these men using the Schedule of Recent Experience, she found that 126 men had high stress scores but below-average illness as compared to 200 men with comparably high scores and exhibiting the predicted level of illness (Kobasa, 1979). However, these scores were obtained retrospectively. Of greater significance was Kobasa's later study of 259 executives, collecting information about them at three different times over two years. At the end of two years it was evident that the executives who remained healthy under stress had certain characteristics in common which Kobasa termed "hardiness." There were three characteristics of these executives: (1) "a sense of commitment to rather than alienation from the various aspects of their lives"; (2) a belief that "they have control over their lives rather than feeling externally controlled" and

(3) a search for "novelty and challenge rather than familiarity and security" (Kobasa, Hilker, and Maddi, 1979). Those executives who remained healthy had an attitude toward life and their work which was high on commitment, challenge, and control, and felt supported in that orientation.

Actually the healthy executives' attitudes toward change and challenge appeared to be the most important factor determining their state of health. These executives were not so much cowed by adverse circumstances as challenged by them. To rate this dimension of challenge, Kobasa asked the executives to what extent they agreed with such statements as "Boredom is fatal" or "I would be willing to give up some financial security to be able to change from one job to another if something interesting came along." Those executives who strongly agreed with statements such as these were rated high on the "challenge" scale. One further refinement was to distinguish a willingness to accept challenge without being reckless. Toward this end Kobasa interjected statements such as "If a job is dangerous, that makes it all the better." Those who scored high in agreement with such statements were termed "adventurous," which was defined as excessive risk-taking. Overall, the healthiest executives exhibited a high orientation to challenge and a willingness to take some, but not excessive, risks. It appears that the hardy executive "aims not only at survival, but at the enrichment of life" and actually experiences better health in the face of minor and major difficulties than those who have tried to avoid stress or remain uninvolved in their work as well as their personal lives. Kobasa's findings indicated that such attitudes toward work stress can decrease an executive's chance of being ill by as much as 50 percent.

Individuals can encounter occupational stress and thrive rather than retreat or merely survive. Furthermore, there is every indication that it is possible for employees to learn those personality dispositions and perceptions of stress associated with healthy and functional workers. Just this knowledge alone can help individuals to recognize that they are not passive victims of stress and can practice and adopt a more viable approach to the unavoidable stress inherent in work. These observations are highly consistent with those of Hans Selye regarding "eustress" (1978a), which is an essential amount of positive stress which varies from person to person. Richard S. Lazarus in *Psychological Stress and the Coping Process* (1966) pointed out that stress does not reside solely in the person or the situation but depends largely upon how the person appraises and reacts to the particular situation. These theories were borne out by another study conducted by Kobasa (1981) among 157 lawyers and 75 army captains who were similar in many characteristics to the executives. Surprisingly, the lawyers did not exhibit any relationship between stress scores and physical illness. Kobasa interpreted this as an indication that lawyers tend to believe that they perform best under pressure and that their roles as advocates, adversaries, and cross-examiners actually prepare them to confront and manage stress. By contrast, the 75 army captains showed higher physical illness than expected. This may be due to the fact that they may have joined the military seeking novelty and challenge and find themselves in an environment in which security and rigid role-definition stifles such needs.

Kobasa applied the same approach to a group of 100 gynecology outpatients who were mostly white, 25 to 35, middle-class, employed, and married. Those 40 women who were classified as high in stress but low in psychological symptoms of stress, such as depression or anxiety, exhibited "hardiness." They reported significantly more commitment to work, family, and self, more personal control, and more vigor in the face of challenge than 60 comparable women who were high in both stressful life events and psychological symptoms. This study is now being extended to follow up on 2,000 women in the same life situations.

Studies are beginning to emerge focusing on individuals who have learned to optimize their response to unavoidable stressors. A recent study compared physician and lawyer lifestyles in Massachusetts and indicated that physicians found their work less stressful and more satisfying than lawyers even though physicians reported longer work hours. Two hundred and eighty-nine doctors and 316 lawyers were matched to obtain comparable groups. Interestingly, over half in each group found gardening to be a major relaxation. Physicians reported less smoking, used seat belts more, and jogged more. Actually, about 75 percent of respondents in both groups indicated at least one ongoing physical activity, alcohol consumption was reported by 80 percent of each group at least once per month, and 25 percent reported meditating. Overall, the "happiness" reported by both groups by age 55 was comparable (Carpenter, 1980). The dimension of "work satisfaction" appears to be important in determining both the quality and quantity of life for all levels of employment. In fact, "work satisfaction" is the single most accurate predictor of longevity, followed by "overall happiness." According to noted researcher Erdman Palmore, these two psychological measures predicted an individual's longevity better than standard physical indicators, risk factors such as tobacco use, and even genetic inheritance. In a classic study, in *Mental Health of the Industrial Worker* (1965), Arthur Kornhauser reported that 40 percent of his sample of 407 auto workers had overt symptoms of mental health problems. The key element distinguishing psychologically healthy workers was work satisfaction. For executive personnel, there is a very striking correlation between work satisfaction and longevity. In a study of 1,078 executives of the Fortune 500 companies, Metropolitan Life Insurance Company has found that, "for all ages combined these corporate executives recorded mortality only 63 percent of that among their contemporaries in the general population. . . . This favorable longevity is believed to reflect in large measure the physical and emotional fitness of business executives for positions of responsibility. . . . It may well be that work satisfaction together with public recognition of accomplishments, is an important determinant of health and longevity" (*Statistical Bulletin,* 1974). Other studies which bear this out are described in *Longevity: Fulfilling Our Biological Potential* (Pelletier, 1981), since these are vitally important considerations for every working person.

Data such as these are beginning to give a clearer picture of those lifestyle factors which foster high performance and significant personal life satisfaction amid high stress occupations. Related to this line of inquiry is the excellent work of Israeli researcher Aaron Antonovsky, an American-born professor of medical sociology at Ben Gurion University of the Negev, who has studied the survivors of Nazi concentration camps. Although he found that most concentration camp survivors were predictably poorly off by the usual standards of psychological and physical health, he did find a small subset of women survivors who were functioning very well. From these and other basic insights Antonovsky formulated a theory of "generalized resistance resources" which are protective against excessive stress. A key component elaborated in his pioneering book *Health, Stress and Coping* (1979) is that education and information regarding stress and its management creates options for people. It permits them to choose an effective means of utilizing, rather than being victimized by, stress. Also of particular interest to Antonovsky is a stable and continuing social network and social support system. Among many examples he cites the often quoted study of 6,928 persons in Alameda County in the San Francisco Bay Area. This study has clearly indicated that individuals with many personal and workplace social ties such as marriage, close friends, dear relatives, church memberships, and supportive work groups have a greater life expectancy than comparable people who do not. Added to the characteristics of "hardiness" defined earlier—commitment, control, and challenge—the strong social support system rounds out the profile of the person who thrives on stress.

"Social support" has been defined by Sidney Cobb in his presidential address to the American Psychosomatic Society as "information leading the subject to believe that he is cared for and loved, esteemed, and a member of a network of mutual obligations" (1976). Social support can be in the form of family, friends, work colleagues, an animal, or even a plant. A large body of research is accumulating to document that social support from one or another of the above sources helps protect people from becoming ill in a wide variety of situations. These include exposure to toxic chemicals, depression, alcoholism. Social support also seems to protect against arthritis and tuberculosis, and low birth weight in infants, and postpones death in the aged. Accelerated recoveries or spontaneous remissions such as reported by Norman Cousins also appear to be correlated with solid social support.

Clearly the oldest and most well-founded influence upon a person is the family of birth or nuclear family, and later the extended or chosen family, including peers in the workplace. The nine-year ongoing study of 6,928 adults in Alameda County in California, using the 1965 survey of the Human Population Laboratory of S. Leonard Syme of the School of Public Health at Berkeley and Lisa F. Berkman of Yale University, showed that "people who lacked social and community ties were more likely to die in the follow-up period than those with more extensive contacts" (Berkman and Syme, 1979). Socially isolated women were at a 2.8 times greater risk and men were at a 2.3 greater risk. After the researchers controlled for the influences of other factors such as socioeconomic status, obesity, smoking, alcohol consumption, physical activity, as well as utilization of preventive health services, social support was demonstrated to be a major determinant of health. Such findings are clearly consistent with Aaron Antonovsky's (1979) findings. In *The Seven Laws of Money* (1974), former vice-president of the Bank of California and economist Michael Phillips makes the point that people use money to bring them security, respect, freedom, and good health but that the "real sources of these desired goals are your family and friends." Social support brings benefits that money cannot buy. In the vast research literature, we also learn that people who are married live longer than those who are single, widowed, or divorced (Ortmeyer, 1974; Pelletier, 1981); that widows, especially in the first year following bereavement, have many more psychological and physical symptoms as well as a higher risk of dying themselves (Taylor, 1981). Overall, the implications are clear that social support plays a vital role in swinging the balance between health and disease, life and death.

In thinking about promoting health in the workplace, it must be kept in mind that social support is just one of many influences, all interacting. The role it plays in health or disease is dependent upon its strength relative to other contributing factors. If an employee is heavily exposed to cancer-causing agents, clearly the effects of social support can only be minimal. However, when exposure to visible or invisible hazards is milder, then social support systems appear to play a very significant role. The single most frequently reported stressor in the workplace is "interpersonal and inter-unit relationships": do a person's colleagues and work units get along? do they communicate well? do they help and support one another? and when inevitable conflict and disagreement arise, how are they managed? Here, social support can clearly affect the outcome. Alan A. McLean of Cornell University Medical College has stated, "Work stress is most apt to produce symptoms when an individual is particularly vulnerable and his environment is unsupportive. . . . On the job, the work environment and the presence or absence of union support are important factors, but so are wide-ranging aspects of the worker's life including his family, his community, and the national economy" (*Clinical Psychiatry News,* 1980). Through the medium of peer support, personal health and performance practices can be extended into the workplace, where the dimensions of "support, cohesion, and affiliation" (Kiritz and Moos, 1974) become vitally important in coping with the pressures of the work environment.

A supportive family and work environment is one of the greatest assets in positive adaptation to organizational stressors. A variety of factors have been identified as indigenous organizational stressors. Although the determination of specific organizational stressors is unique to each individual workplace, common stressors have been identified and very significant preventive programs have been initiated by innovative companies. At this time, the extension of individual stress management techniques into the organizational setting is one of the most significant approaches. This fact is underscored by an extensive report on a wide range of workplace health promotion efforts by Harvey M. Sapolsky and his colleagues at the Massachusetts Institute of Technology. Drawing upon interviews with key executives in sixty-nine companies, the research team found "little impetus to seek changes in health benefits" and that "top management rarely expressed a deep interest in health care costs preferring instead to wonder only whether or not benefits were up to date with those of major rivals" (Sapolsky et al., 1981). Surprisingly this attitude held true toward a wide variety of measures including cost sharing by employees, tightening of claims control, promoting HMO membership, and limiting access to expensive medical services. Most significantly, the one area which was viewed as most favorable was health promotion programs, where Sapolsky and his researchers found: "Nevertheless, there is no doubt of the popularity of preventive health programs as additional employee benefits. And if the claims made for these prevention programs by their advocates even partially materialize, then the future medical costs of many corporations may decline" (1981). Many companies including Equitable Life Assurance, New York Telephone, IBM, Johnson & Johnson, and Control Data Corporation have created stress management programs to enhance employee skills in this area.

Much research in the area of social support in the workplace assumes a rather passive model of the individual, without the capacity to cope with stress on his or her own or to create a supportive environment. Recently psychologists Dana Bramel and Ronald Friend of the State University of New York at Stony Brook challenged the classic Hawthorn Effect findings of the 1920s because they supported a view of workers as "nonexploitive and free of class conflict" (1981). Beyond the specific issues raised in this challenging article, is the implication that employee attitudes and attitudes toward employees are undergoing substantial changes. Individual workers are exhibiting more "hardiness," exercising personal control and direction, a personal sense of commitment, seeking challenge, or reaching out for needed support. And just as individuals can grow in this way, it is possible for aggregates of workers to create a positive work environment, and their own networks of support. David Harris, commissioner of New York's Suffolk County Department of Health Services, has noted that organizations can create a supportive environment by taking "the human factor" into account. According to his experience, "Stress management is just another name for good management" (*Clinical Psychiatry News*, 1981a). He includes measures such as: matching the employee to an appropriately challenging job, setting appropriate performance standards, improving communications, and allowing workers to work at their own pace. Outside sources of support must also be recognized. Workers with social support of the family suffered fewer health complications at the time when a factory closed and, according to a spokesman at Eastman Kodak, when executives remained in a health program, their wives had a lot to do with it. The wives were apparently sensitive to the health issue through women's magazines. Ways of enhancing such support within health promotion programs are discussed in Chapter IV.

THE MIND / BODY LINK IN STRESS RESEARCH

During the last decade the subtle internal processes by which stressful events can affect health have been mapped with increasing precision. There are extraordinary breakthroughs taking place in understanding how stress affects individual health. This fascinating field has been called *psychoneuroendocrine influences* by Vernon Riley of the Pacific Northwest Research Foundation in Seattle and *psychoneuroimmunology* by Robert Ader of the University of Rochester School of Medicine. It is not the purpose of this chapter to explore this research except to note that it is providing clear links between mind (psycho), the brain and nervous system (neuro), and the body's ability to defend against infection and tumors (immunology).

These studies clearly indicate that minor stress, major life events, disruptions in social support systems, and difficulties at work can dramatically affect the body's system of defenses so that a person becomes more susceptible to a number of conditions. The particular disorder is influenced by many other factors including genetics, smoking, viruses, and environmental pollution, but unrelenting, inescapable Type II stress appears to be the most frequent precipitating cause. Among the discoveries to date is research by psychiatrist

George Solomon at the University of California School of Medicine in San Francisco, which found that "baby rats handled during the first three weeks of life had a more vigorous immunological response [that is, they made more antibodies] as adults than their uncuddled cohorts." Throughout life, social supports, as scientists refer to friends and family, provide strong preventive and therapeutic aids. A recent Johns Hopkins study found that widowed men who remarried lived longer than those who did not. In a study of pregnant women undergoing numerous life stresses, 90 percent of those who faced these changes alone developed complications before or during delivery, as compared with 33 percent of those who had "good social support" (Hales, 1981). Other studies have noted links between "sudden death" and events which were overwhelmingly negative or positive. On a positive note, it is becoming increasingly clear that laughter and humor may indeed be the best medicines. From the writings of Norman Cousins to the research of Harvard psychiatrist George Vaillant, it is evident that healthier individuals rely upon humor and stable, enduring relationships at home and in their work to maintain and enhance health. All this research underscores the importance of the psychological climate in the workplace.

Central to the study of psychological health in the workplace is a worker's relative sense of empowerment versus helplessness. In contrast to conditions left over from the Industrial Revolution, a new work ethic is developing which seeks a sense of power, efficacy, freedom, and responsibility. The effects of this upon an individual's health are beginning to be understood. In his excellent book *Helplessness* (1975), psychologist Martin E. Seligman at the University of Pennsylvania documented the extraordinarily debilitating effects of helplessness and the equally potent, positive effects of choice and responsibility. Although most of this research has been based upon animal studies, the physical effects of "inescapable stress" have been clearly demonstrated to include: "Severe deficits learning to escape from other aversive stimuli, become submissive in competition for food, fail to escape from frustrating situations, and show less aggression when subjected to additional shock. Physiologically, inescapable shock leads to catecholamine depletion in the central nervous system, activation of the hypothalamic-pituitary-adrenal axis, weight loss, and gastric ulceration. Finally, uncontrollable aversive events increase psychological distress in humans" (Visintainer, Volpicelli, and

Seligman, 1982). Most recently, Seligman and his colleagues have demonstrated explicit links in the immune system, between inescapable stress and whether or not laboratory animals reject or succumb to cancer. Their research, and that of many others, indicates that uncontrollable stress does suppress or diminish the normal activity of the immune system and increases susceptibility to cancer. Summarizing their experiments, the researchers concluded, "inescapable shock decreased tumor rejection [i.e., tumor rejection decreased by experience of inescapable shock] was not a function of shock per se but resulted from the animals' lack of control over shock. The psychological experience somehow interfered with the ability of the organism to resist tumor development. . . . This demonstrates that a psychological variable can decrease an animal's ability to reject a tumor" (Visintainer, Volpicelli, and Seligman, 1982). There is a growing body of evidence beginning to link these findings from animal research with human stress and feelings of helplessness, including research conducted by Stephen E. Locke (1982) of Harvard Medical School. Many of the links are not yet clear; it is certain that helplessness on the negative side versus a sense of individual efficacy or empowerment on the positive side is a major determinant in swinging the balance between health and illness, life and death. Psychoneuroimmunology constitutes a major breakthrough area in the research of the 1980s. Results of these studies will be of particular pertinence to work environment health promotion programs since the workplace tends to foster powerlessness and helplessness. In fact, there already appears to be enough evidence to advocate that an essential, underlying goal of any health promotion program should be to enhance an individual's sense of efficacy, involvement, and influence.

STRESS MANAGEMENT

Two extreme points of view characterize the field of stress management. At one extreme is the advocacy among certain professional groups and in the media of stress avoidance. This is neither possible nor desirable. Business executives are told that stress can disable or even kill them when that is not necessarily the case. Unfortunately, "many business corporations in their eagerness to set up stress-management programs, gyms on their top floors, and cardiac units in the medical department, seem to be buying into this negative, narrow view of stress. The executive is told that excess is harmful and that attempts will be made to reduce it; but in the meantime, use biofeedback or the exercise machine to ready your body for the assault" (Pines, 1980). An individual executive or worker is not helped to realize that stress not only is controllable but can be positive. Many well-intentioned but frequently ineffective packaged programs have sprung up to remedy this false workplace emergency. This point was underscored by a *Wall Street Journal* headline which noted, "Stress-Management Plans Abound, But Not All Programs are Run Well" (Guenther, 1982), and that is precisely the case. Quoting psychologist James S. J. Manuso, the article stated, "Unfortunately many companies are buying what is really a stress lecture. Often they're sold a stress management program and they end up getting a stress lecture." Actually, this occurrence is not entirely the fault of the individual or company selling the program, since all too often a company prefers to deal with the superficial symptoms of stress rather than the real causes. According to clinical psychologist Marilyn Ruman, "If an organization is not willing to make changes, they're just offering employees a Band-Aid" (Guenther, 1982). When a seller offers and a company purchases a panacea program, both are deluded.

Early stress research fostered such a view by emphasizing the contribution of stress to illness and assuming that a person is essentially a passive victim of external life events. As research and applications have evolved and become more sophisticated, these concepts have been refined, but the general misconception that a person should avoid stress in order to remain healthy and functional has tended to persist. This misconception has had a direct impact upon stress management programs in the workplace. It has resulted in a situation characterized by Suzanne C. Kobasa, "Mounting economic, political and consumer pressures place ever-increasing amounts of stress upon employees at all levels in the organization. As a culture, we are increasingly unwilling to believe that stress at work is necessary. The business or industry with much stress is regarded as failing in its responsibility to employees. Furthermore, the cultural trend toward rest and relaxation as an ideal of life is supported by the communications media. . . . Labor unions and employers are under pressure to increase job protection and curb changes that might affect workers . . . more and more . . . angry and frightened employees attempt to enlist . . . aid in the avoidance of stress" (Kobasa,

Hilker, and Maddi, 1979). While there is widespread agreement that this is an accurate rendering of the current situation, there is equally widespread disagreement concerning a course of action. Any action plan must be built upon two assumptions: excessive and unnecessary exposure to visible and invisible hazards is preventable, and when individuals and organizations work together, they both derive substantial benefits. Unfortunately, attempts at stress avoidance have become so unrealistically extreme that a national magazine featured an article which advocated staying off the Los Angeles freeway following the occurrence of stressful life events for fear of being involved in an accident. There may be many reasons for avoiding freeways, but this reasoning is unduly alarmist.

At the other extreme is a macho misinterpretation of the positive aspects of stress which condemns any attempt at stress management as escapism or views stress management or meditation breaks as a weakness, similar to tranquilizer abuse. A great deal of such sentiment appears to be a backlash phenomenon, in response to stress management or health promotion programs which assert that stress is to be avoided. Other objections have sometimes borne a seed of truth. *Business Week* quotes statements by Gerald E. Fisher, president of the Center for Organizational Development in Rochester, to the effect that longer vacations and exercise rooms are a "great cover-up" because they help executives to dissipate the symptoms of too much stress without eliminating the source. The same article mixes sense and diatribe in quoting Charles E. Thompson, of the Thompson Medical Center in Chicago, who considers the stress management techniques of meditation and biofeedback to be "a lot of garbage," and Reginald P. Cherry, director of the Houstonian Preventive Medicine Center in Houston, who declares, "Executives are often bored with these stress programs because they already know how to deal with stress" (*Business Week,* 1979). This latter observation is a reasonable response to stress management programs when they are prepackaged, one-dimensional, and based upon inaccurate assumptions.

Since there is evidence that too little stress actually leads to the same consequences as too much stress, in the form of accidents, lack of attention, fatigue, and irritability, mere stress reduction is clearly not the goal. Stress management is. The same *Business Week* article quotes John H. Zimmerman, a vice-president of Firestone Tire and Rubber Company: "Stress is what you make of it, and that can be the difference between coping and collapsing." Reducing executive job-related stress may not be in the best interests of an organization. Stress is a neutral term which has taken on a negative connotation. Any approach to stress management and health promotion needs to acknowledge that well-managed stress can motivate, stimulate, and provide the needed challenge for creativity and heightened performance.

At the center of the stress management controversy is one simple question: Is it worth dying for? While that may seem unlikely, the phenomenon of sudden death from excessive stress has been well-documented. A series of notable studies showed that aerospace workers at Cape Kennedy who were as young as 29 to 31 actually dropped dead of stress-induced heart attacks without warning when they learned their jobs were being phased out. Autopsies indicated that their heart muscles had ruptured in seconds by a stress-induced outpouring of catecholamines. An individual needs to ask if a given challenge is literally worth risking everything. The answer to that question is a question of personal values. Cardiologist Robert S. Elliot put it this way: "Clarify your values and live according to what is important to you, not your mother's bridge club. Take stock of your life. If your body is giving you signals—pain in the chest, chronic fatigue, depression—don't deny them. Get things right in your life. Insight will save you . . . to ignore the strain of stress through liquor, Valium, and aspirin, is simply to hasten the steps toward disorder, disregulation, disease, even death" (Breo, 1981). These are strong words. In his work with patients, Elliot advocates a "six-months-to-live" exercise, where each person is told to live as if he or she had only six months to live. From such a point of view life priorities do fall into place. Work satisfaction might continue to rank high in a list or be balanced with personal and familial values. The key element is insight and a willingness to be bluntly honest. Solutions to stress management may involve dramatic changes such as divorcing a spouse or quitting a job but more often involve relatively small adaptations, or giving up a futile quest. In fact, as I have worked with many individuals and organizations, I have come to see the sudden occurrence of rapid, external change such as a divorce, an affair, or buying a sports car as an indication of danger, like the potentially suicidal person who suddenly appears calm since he has finally decided to end his life. Under conditions of great uncertainty, a decision can be calming. But growth can take place more quietly. Upon the completion of a stress management program, many individuals have stated, "When I entered this program I expected a great change to happen and I was disappointed when that did not occur. Instead, I realized that many small changes did happen which made the big one unnecessary." A concerted, systematic effort leads gradually to significant lifestyle change. There is no magic, but there are steps which can be taken toward informed awareness, acknowledging stress as unavoidable yet also realizing that stress responses can be improved and optimized.

Certain basic steps are common to all successful stress management programs:

1. *Recognition*—learn to recognize and anticipate both internal and external sources and situations of stress.

2. *Hardiness*—develop an attitude of "hardiness" consisting of commitment, acceptance of challenge, and a sense that the sources of stress can be controlled.

3. *Practice*—engage in the systematic practice of any stress management technique which works for you: clinical biofeedback, Autogenic Training, Herbert Benson's "relaxation response," meditation, Edmund Jacobson's Progressive Relaxation, yoga, Charles Stroebel's "quieting response." The essence of these is a pause which allows an individual briefly to disengage from stressful circumstances and to renew physical and psychological abilities. Every individual has a unique, idiosyncratic response to stress, and each of the above methods will have a different effect upon different individuals. For example, Jacobson's Progressive Relaxation, detailed in his own book and in *Holistic Medicine* (Pelletier, 1979), is probably best for a person who exhibits muscle tension, while Wolfgang Luthe's Autogenic Training, described in his own book and in *Mind as Healer, Mind as Slayer* (Pelletier, 1977), is better for a person who is responsive in the cardiovascular system. The more a relaxation procedure is consistent with an individual's own predisposition, the more effective and long lasting it will be.

4. *Generalize*—become engaged in or continue a lifestyle involving moderate aerobic physical activity, a diet consistent with the U.S. Government Dietary Guidelines of the McGovern Committee and available from your local chapter of the American Heart Association, a serious involvement in career, and an equally involved and fulfilled personal and family life. Frequently a stress management program is the first place an executive or employee learns about per-

sonal health care, and this often grows into concerns for diet and nutrition, physical activity, and healthy environments. Any one of these approaches requires systematic practice, like any skill from riding a bicycle to playing a musical instrument. It is possible to learn to play the infinitely complex instrument of the human mind and body to their optimum health and productivity.

5. *Action plan and audit*—develop a realistic plan of action and a self-audit based upon your desired end point. For some individuals the goal may be to lose a specified amount of weight in a given time, to counteract a workaholic addiction, or even finish a work project by a self-imposed deadline. Chapter IV spells out the nature of such plans in greater detail. Whatever the action plan and self-audit contains, it should be adhered to and taken seriously.

6. *Extension*—develop the means to create relationships and environments which are supportive of these practices. Help others at work or in the community recognize their value, i.e., move from the inner sphere of influence described in Chapter II to the wider spheres.

In response to the widespread recognition of organizational stressors, a veritable barrage of literature (Behling and Holcombe, 1981; Organ, 1979; Quick and Quick, 1979; Beehr and Newman, 1978) and programs has resulted. Among the most responsible and effective clearinghouses for such information are the Washington Business Group on Health in Washington, D.C., and the National Center for Health Education in San Francisco. They can provide assistance about the relative merits of program components and the qualifications of those offering the materials. Each individual and organization is both unique and dynamic. Any effective health promotion program must be adapted to the particular circumstances through consultation and then systematically followed through over time. That is a challenge which simply cannot be met by a program described in an article or a prepackaged program.

There are several books which provide basic program information, such as *Executive Health* by Phillip Goldberg (1978), *Managing Stress* by physician Leon J. Warshaw (1979), who is vice-president and corporate medical director of Equitable Environmental Health, Incorporated, and an excellent seven-part series of booklets focusing upon stress management by psychiatrist E. Joseph Neidhardt (1981) and his colleagues at the Western Center for Preventive and

Behavioral Medicine in Vancouver, Canada. Recently there have been two effective attempts to use video facilities and interactive learning systems such as the StayWell program of the Life Extension Institute of Control Data Corporation (1982) and the *Time / Life* Video Program series of five interactive video cassettes entitled *Stress Management: A Positive Strategy* (1982). The Control Data program is centered around slide presentations in major health areas under the supervision of a trained counselor, in order to adapt the program content for a particular work group or organization. In the *Time / Life* program there is a series of five half-hour-long video tapes which are keyed to a workbook. At designated points in the videotape, the viewer is asked to turn to a specific section of the workbook for a more intensive discussion of a particular area, such as sections on "Self-Assessment: Personal Signs of Stress" or "How to Manage for High Performance and Low Stress." After completing the section, the individual or work group can return to the videotape. One large national bank has found that using the *Time / Life* series in conjunction with an employee assistant counselor from within the bank itself has resulted in an effective program which is well-adapted to the unique workplace of that particular bank. The adaptation of general program content so as to extend personal health practices into the workplace is also a key element.

Carrying out any stress management program requires ongoing flexibility and adaptation. Such qualities underlie most successful careers. Harvard University psychiatrist George Vaillant, in *Adaptation to Life* (1977), describes a longitudinal study of 268 Harvard men from the classes of 1939 to 1944. One consistent finding was that the health and happiness of these adults were greatly influenced by their "capacity for working and loving." This was not a genetic endowment or a lifestyle set in childhood or adolescence but the direct consequence of gradually learned coping styles. In stress management such capacities must be learned, practiced, and applied like any other skill. Vaillant's study clearly indicated that "Isolated traumatic events rarely mold individual lives. . . . Unexpected events do affect our lives . . . but the quality of the whole journey is seldom changed by a single turning. What makes or breaks our luck seems to be the continued interaction between our choice of adaptive mechanisms and our sustained relationships with other people." Life is a great deal more than a dire series of predictable adult life crises. Each developmental stage also holds the opportunity to engage in the situation and develop the skills necessary for the inevitable challenges ahead.

This point is echoed in the work of Suzanne C. Kobasa, quoted earlier. She describes a process that "assumes that life best led is a strenuous process, and that fulfillment of human capabilities is ultimately more satisfying than is rest, leisure, and easy security. We call it existential psychotherapy, and regard it as good preparation for modern times" (Kobasa, Hilker, and Maddi, 1977). It is possible for individuals to become more aware of and involved in internal thoughts and reactions, to be willing to influence life events and experience through active participation, decision, and choice, and to view change and its attendant stress as an inevitable opportunity for growth and transformation.

VISIBLE AND INVISIBLE HAZARDS

Individuals can do a great deal to keep themselves healthy at work, but many occupational health hazards can be remedied only by fixing the workplace, not just the worker. Not all organizational stressors can be eliminated and not all hazards can be solved by changes in behavior and attitude. In Sphere II of our diagram in Chapter I (p. 7) are the health factors which require group or company action. These factors fall in two categories: the physical, environmental hazards such as chemical exposure, noise, radiation and microwave emissions, and the psychosocial hazards of peer support, crowding, patterns of communication or lack of performance feedback. Although the former are most common among blue-collar workers, there is a growing body of evidence from "clinical ecology" pioneered by physician Theron G. Randolph (1978), and other sources, that white-collar and secretarial workers are exposed to risks from computer terminals, copying-machine chemicals, and radiation. There is mounting evidence that all workers are exposed to both physical and psychological hazards and the only difference is a matter of degree.

CHAPTER III

Toxic Hazards of the Workplace

Environmental health hazards are becoming one of the major political, economic, and human issues of the decade. To the list of known carcinogenic agents to which everyone is exposed, new chemicals and substances are literally added daily. There is growing acceptance of the fact that "80% of human cancers are caused by environmental influences" (Thomas, 1980), but the actions resulting from this longstanding view are highly fragmented and often contradictory. When the inquiry is extended to other environmental hazards unrelated to cancer, the results are staggering. This ominous situation is described by many organizations and in a number of books, including the Environmental Defense Fund; Robert Boyle, *Malignant Neglect* (1979); Nicholas Ashford, *Crisis in the Workplace* (1976); Paul Brodeur, *Expendable Americans* (1974); D. Berman, *Death on the Job* (1979); and Barry Commoner, *The Politics of Energy* (1979). This literature is growing and it is not my intention to duplicate it here. However, no discussion of health in the workplace would be complete without an acknowledgment and overview of this escalating problem. The stress described in Chapter II is of course compounded by the anxiety caused by exposure to toxic substances.

Furthermore, toxic hazards of the workplace are only part of a much larger problem. In agriculture, there are dangers in the use of pesticides, herbicides, soil enhancers and fertilizers; in the home environment, where energy conservation trends have created highly insulated environments, inadequate ventilation and toxic gases combine to create new threats; in consumer products, hazardous agents have been found in over-the-counter as well as prescription drugs, ceramic glazes, cosmetics, food additives, aerosols, adhesives, and hobby materials. In the workplace, exposure to chemicals, radiation, noise, and dust is compounded by pollutant by-products of virtually every product that is manufactured.

While there is virtually uniform agreement that many of these substances are hazardous, regulation and protection measures are plagued by political and scientific problems at every turn. Scientists do not agree on measurement procedures, do not agree on "safe" dosage or toxicity levels, are uncertain how to estimate human exposure, and cannot provide explicit links between exposure and subsequent health problems. All such inquiries are increasingly conducted in an atmosphere unduly influenced by large manufacturing donations through political action committees (PACS) which have distorted objective inquiry even further. At present the situation is one where there is little consensus on what is to be measured, how measurement is conducted and by whom, how to interpret the resulting data, and how to relate any of these factors to subsequent human health problems. Obviously this is a concern of overwhelming magnitude which is not about to be resolved in this or any other discussion. With this important reservation in mind, it is possible to selectively address representative hazards in the workplace since that is among the most common sites of exposure and is also the source of most of the hazardous agents released into the environment.

Researchers such as Devra Lee Davis of the Environmental Law Institute in Washington and Marvin Schneiderman, former statistician at the National Cancer Institute and now with Clement Associates in Washington, have predicted that industrial chemicals may cause an upsurge in cancer deaths between ten and twenty years from now. This is a well-documented and widely held position. In fact, there is an indication that such an upsurge has already begun. "Deaths from some types of cancer associated with occupational exposures such as brain cancer and multiple myeloma, appear to be increasing already in men between the ages of 45 and 84" (Boffey, 1982). By contrast, some writers maintain that the workplace and general environment have actually been growing less hazardous in recent years. Recently, Sir Richard Doll and Richard Peto, two internationally prominent epidemiologists at Oxford University, have written a 115-page overview of cancer trends and causes in the United States. Overall, the two researchers conclude that 75 percent to 80 percent of all cancer deaths could, in principle, be prevented if enough were known of the causes. Somewhat surprisingly, their estimates of cancers caused by the products and carcinogenic chemicals of industry is relatively small. They have concluded that "occupational exposures" account for only 4 percent of American cancer deaths and pollution in the air, water, food and earth accounts for even less. The effect of air pollution must be relatively small, they say, because populations with comparable smoking habits but living in areas with markedly different air pollution have roughly the same rate of lung cancer mortality. (*Boffey, 1982*)

By contrast, they have estimated that "tobacco use" accounts for as much as 30 percent of current cancer deaths. This is identical to the independent estimate of the 1982 Surgeon General's report on smoking. Furthermore, the Oxford researchers suggest that "nutritional factors—such as calories, fat, fiber, vitamins, trace elements, and other substances that may affect the formation and transport of carcinogens in the body—may ultimately be found of comparable importance" (Boffey, 1982). Based upon findings such as these, some cancer epidemiologists "have published estimates that occupational exposures and environmental pollution are relatively minor causes of cancer compared with such personal 'lifestyle' factors as smoking, diet, alcohol, and even sexual and reproductive behavior" (Boffey, 1982).

Conflicting data such as these appear to place involuntary exposure to carcinogens at the opposite extreme of voluntary, hazardous lifestyle practices such as smoking. That is not the case, since any given incidence of cancer derives from multiple influences. Their interaction, such as between smoking and asbestos exposure, may constitute the greatest hazard of all. This position has been addressed by the *Harvard Medical School Health Letter:* "Occupational cancers seem to be a small fraction of the total, but that is no consolation to the affected individuals, and there is no justification for exposing workers to hazardous conditions. . . . On the basis of current knowledge, the most important steps an individual can take to protect himself or herself from cancer would be these: *not smoking,* drinking only in moderation; and, probably, consuming a low-fat, high-fiber diet. People handling chemicals in the workplace should take personal precautions to avoid contact and should work to see that safety and health standards are enforced. Due caution should be exercised around all forms of radiation—including sunlight, X-ray machines, and other sources of radiation" (1982). Workplace exposure to hazards needs to be minimized or preferably eliminated. There should be no easing of efforts to clean up the workplace and the total environment. Even if occupational exposures account for the conservative 5 percent incidence, that translates into more than 20,000 unnecessary cancer deaths every year and that statistic cannot be ignored. When compounded by invisible hazards such as stress and hazardous behaviors, these factors may ultimately constitute the greatest threat to human health and life in the workplace.

Two major obstacles to identifying and correcting workplace exposure to toxic chemicals and radiation are: (1) employees are often unaware of such exposure or the consequences related to such exposure; and (2) the effects of exposure may not be evident for decades and sometimes not in the employees themselves but in their children. At the present time, the National Cancer Institute has estimated that "20% to 40% of all cancer is caused by occupational exposure. Up to 40% of all skin problems in adult males are caused by workplace exposure" (Allport, 1981). Obviously, statistics such as these are alarming. An atmosphere of great emotion surrounds the regulation of such exposure. Before considering this issue, it must be acknowledged that it is extremely difficult for an individual or even a group of workplace peers to evaluate exposure.

One of the most effective means of regulating such exposure is based upon the activities of the federal government's National Toxicology Program (NTP), which comprises representatives of several agencies such as the Food and Drug Administration, NIOSH, and the National Cancer Institute. Legislative action must occur at a national or at the very least a state level (Sphere IV in our diagram). Depending upon the political climate, debate waxes and wanes. On the one hand is Ralph Nader stating, ". . . there must be a broad sensitivity among the citizenry to this massive, continuing destruction of workers' bodies. As a form of violence, job casualties are statistically at least three times more serious than street crime" (Donway, 1980). On the other are cavalier dismissals by spokesmen from large petrochemical companies, claiming that lifestyle factors rather than exposure to carcinogens are responsible for cancer incidence. The unfortunate reality is that there are over 70,000 chemicals in industrial use today and safe exposure limits have been established for only about 500 of these agents. The issue of "safe exposure" is at the crux of the problem, since even the most ardent lobbyists against petrochemical manufacturers make extensive use of the products of these manufacturing processes in their homes, automobiles, and offices. Lewis Thomas, president of the Memorial Sloan-Kettering

Cancer Center in New York City, makes this central question clear: "Is there such a thing as a threshold dose of a carcinogenic chemical below which there is no carcinogenic effect at all, or is there no such thing as a totally safe, totally non-carcinogenic dose? . . . Until we find this out, the dilemma that faces our regulatory agencies and almost all our major industries, most notably the chemical industry, is almost unsolvable" (Thomas, 1980). As difficult as that stance is to maintain, it is the most likely to yield effective legislation out of the tension between the extremes of anti-industrialism versus environmental destruction.

While the process of identifying toxic agents in the workplace must proceed in a methodical manner, that cannot serve as an excuse for delaying immediate action in those areas of workplace exposure where there is already clear evidence of hazardous effects. In those instances the hesitancy is more likely in the name of politics and vested economic interests than in the name of scientific objectivity. *U.S. News & World Report* prepared a chart of several clearly "suspected" hazards which provides a dramatic microcosm of the extent of the problem and numbers of workers involved (see p. 90).

Actually, this list is a small fragment of a much longer table which listed toxic exposures in over 100 occupations ranging from athletes to migrant workers, due to over 500 biological hazards. This more complete listing by occupation is contained in the February 28, 1979, issue of *Patient Care*. This is an essential reference for anyone engaged in the jobs which are noted here, since toxic exposure is extremely likely.

The toll of carcinogenic exposure in industry can be clearly seen in the link between asbestos and lung cancer. This link, first pointed out in the 1960s by physician Irving J. Selikoff of New York's Mount Sinai Medical Center, is a vivid example of the issues surrounding any one of the tens of thousands of hazardous agents. During World War II, more than four million workers were exposed to asbestos, which was used in navy yards to fireproof ships. To date, thousands of lawsuits involving subsequent lung cancer have been lodged against Johns-Manville Corporation, which was the largest asbestos supplier during that period. Asbestos is one of the few agents clearly recognized as carcinogenic. Given this widespread evidence of asbestos as a carcinogen, the litigation should be straightforward, but that is not the case. Settlements have been complicated by the agreement of experts on both sides that an asbestos worker who also smokes

10 SUSPECTED HAZARDS IN THE WORKPLACE

As cited by federal agencies, here are some of the major agents linked to on-the-job diseases—

POTENTIAL DANGERS	DISEASES THAT MAY RESULT	WORKERS EXPOSED
Arsenic	Lung cancer, lymphona	Smelter, chemical, oil-refinery workers; insecticide makers and sprayers—estimated 660,000 exposed
Asbestos	White-lung disease (asbestosis); cancer of lungs and lining of lungs; cancer of other organs	Miners; millers; textile, insulation and shipyard workers—estimated 1.6 million exposed
Benzene	Leukemia; aplastic anemia	Petrochemical and oil-refinery workers; dye users; distillers; painters; shoemakers—estimated 600,000 exposed
Bischloromethylether (BCME)	Lung cancer	Industrial chemical workers
Coal dust	Black-lung disease	Coal miners—estimated 208,000 exposed
Coke-oven emissions	Cancer of lungs, kidneys	Coke-oven workers—estimated 30,000 exposed
Cotton dust	Brown-lung disease (byssinosis); chronic bronchitis; emphysema	Textile workers—estimated 600,000 exposed
Lead	Kidney disease; anemia; central-nervous-system damage; sterility; birth defects	Metal grinders; lead-smelter workers; lead storage-battery workers—estimated 835,000 exposed
Radiation	Cancer of thyroid, lungs and bone; leukemia; reproductive effects (spontaneous abortion, genetic damage)	Medical technicians; uranium miners; nuclear-power and atomic workers
Vinyl chloride	Cancer of liver, brain	Plastic-industry workers—estimated 10,000 directly exposed

has a much greater risk. It appears that smoking cigarettes in combination with inhalation of asbestos produces a potentiating effect and greatly increases the cancer risk. Sometimes this variable is used to obscure the fact that asbestos exposure alone was and is a major cause of cancer.

The long, grinding process of evaluating hazardous agents with scientific rigor is of little solace to the individual with terminal lung cancer. This obstructed and overly laborious process also held true for the regulation of PCB, polychlorinated biphenyls, which were identified as hazards in 1933 but not regulated until more than thirty years later! Asbestos, PCBs, benzene, and formaldehyde are clear instances where immediate action needs to be undertaken to protect the health of workers, even while further research is going on.

Beginning in 1950, William J. Blot and a team of researchers of the National Cancer Institute conducted a survey of cancer mortality in those United States counties where the petroleum industry is most heavily concentrated. That study was concluded in 1969. The results published in 1977 found "Male residents of these counties experienced significantly higher rates for cancers of the lung, the nasal cavity and sinuses, and the skin (including malignant melanoma) compared to male residents of other counties with similar demographic characteristics" (Blot et al., 1977). Overall, thirty-nine counties were found, including Contra Costa County in California, Galveston County in Texas, and Gloucester County in New Jersey. Obviously, petroleum industry officials contested these findings. The National Cancer Institute emphasized the "preliminary" nature of their study, and little if any action has resulted. More recent studies by the National Cancer Institute and NIOSH have confirmed these findings: (1) "a higher than normal incidence of brain cancer among workers at two oil refineries and three petrochemical plants" (*American Medical News,* 1980a); (2) oat-cell lung cancer is much higher among "transportation equipment operatives" such as cabdrivers, truck drivers, and auto repair mechanics, with clear indications that "components of gasoline and diesel engine exhaust" are the carcinogenic agents (Wegman and Peters, 1978); (3) a study presently under way by NIOSH at the Augusta Chemical Corporation in Augusta, Georgia, is looking over the medical records of 1,100 past and present workers in that factory who have been exposed to tanaphthylamine, one of the older and more potent known carcinogens.

Particularly tragic findings also implicating industrial exposure to petrochemicals resulted from a study by John M. Peters and his colleagues at the University of Southern California School of Medicine. These researchers compared the medical and familial records of 92 children under age 10 who had brain tumors with 92 matched controls. The mothers of children with brain tumors reported skin exposure to chemicals at three times greater frequency than the controls and there was a strong link between "paternal occupations involving solvents, and employment of father in the aircraft industry" (Peters et al., 1981). Occupational exposure to chemical solvents by one or both parents was linked to brain tumors in their children, although the parents exhibited no obvious negative effects. While the report could not specify the precise carcinogenic agent, it cited strong supporting evidence from other studies which would urge extreme caution.

In instances such as these there is a clear imperative to legislators and employers to eliminate hazardous exposures. For individual workers, it is important to be aware of hazardous exposures, report this to the medical department and also notify NIOSH's Health Hazard Evaluation Program in Cincinnati, which can undertake workplace evaluation on request by workers or management. Under the present administration these agencies are being weakened, but worker initiative is still possible. While the impact of one employee upon hazardous chemical exposure is limited, aggregates of workers bringing such exposure to light is the first and necessary step to instituting effective safety precautions. A useful manual in this regard is published by the Public Citizen Health Research Group, 2000 P Street, N.W., Washington, D.C.: *A Worker's Guide to Winning at the Occupational Safety and Health Review Commission* (Goldberg, 1981).

There is an inevitable lag between the discovery of a cancer-causing agent or one that results in birth defects and the translation of that discovery into coherent action. That time lag is partially the result of the need for more scientific evaluation, but more often it is due to procrastination and cover-ups on the part of the industries involved. According to former California Governor Jerry Brown, "Thousands of workers are now dying from cancer and asbestosis because asbestos manufacturers covered up the hazards of asbestos. Workers who were exposed to the pesticide DBCP without warning of its hazards are now sterilized, and have a substantial risk of cancer" (Brown, 1980). After the scientific data are in, political action groups, vested interests, and economic influences slow down the process of cleaning up the hazards. In his excellent book *The Closing Circle* (1971), Barry Commoner speaks for the need of "closing the circle" of ecological reality so that the final cost of industrial growth must include the economic and health cost to every individual as well as the cost of repairing the damage or recycling the waste materials of the products consumed. At the same time that synthetic chemicals have been correlated with increases in cancer rates, production has grown from one billion pounds per year in 1935 to over 300 billion in 1975 and is growing geometrically. Closing the circle will come only via the demands of aggregates of workers and the public as a whole insisting upon prevention in the workplace and political action based upon informed ecological principles. Research into toxic hazards in the workplace must continue while we implement preventive measures, rather than sit passively for conclusive findings while exposed workers die by the tens of thousands.

In California, under the title of *Preventing a Toxic Tomorrow,* former Governor Jerry Brown established the Toxic Substances Coordinating Council by executive order with the task of creating a "uniform state policy on carcinogen regulations and coordinating intra-agencies strategies to deal with our problem hazardous waste sites" (1980). The first of the nine areas of bills and budgeted programs was Occupational Safety and Health (Worker Right to Know). Here the program would "require manufacturers to inform employers and for employers to train workers in the acute and chronic health risks posed by chemicals to which they may be exposed during normal work operations or reasonably foreseeable emergencies" (1980). Ironically a new solar-powered state office building dedicated to the late anthropologist Gregory Bateson, across from the capitol in Sacramento, is the subject of occupational health concerns. Large numbers of workers have reported nausea, headaches, and fainting since the offices were occupied in 1982. Positive intentions and environmental concerns are necessary but not sufficient to ensure the healthy workplace.

Clearly, action on toxic exposure in the workplace requires action in Sphere IV in national policy and legislation. However, perhaps the single greatest failure of health promotion programs in the workplace or for the public as a whole is the failure to educate individuals on the hazards of toxic substance exposure. Individual initiative becomes doubly important when one recognizes that borderline exposure to an environmental toxic agent will be enhanced or reduced depending upon the lifestyle factors of stress, nutrition, physical activity, and peer support. Addressing these two spheres of influence and their interaction is an essential aspect of any comprehensive approach to health promotion. In concluding his report on *Preventing a Toxic Tomorrow,* former Governor Brown emphasized: "The spectre of a toxic tomorrow is indeed before us. We are investing now in a future 20 to 30 more years away. Since repercussions often do not appear until 30 years after exposure, we must either wait until the 21st century to assess the deadly costs of our industrial processes or take action now." For both the hazards of stress and a toxic environment, that challenge represents a clear and present choice.

CHAPTER IV

Health Promotion Programs

If we examine the factors in an organization which affect employee health and performance, we see that these same factors can be responsible for the overall health and performance of the organization. When an organization works with employees to create positive conditions, those same conditions will make the organization healthier, more productive, and ultimately more profitable. Although this principle is deceptively simple, it should not be underestimated.

PRELIMINARY QUESTIONS

Certain critical questions need to be asked and answered before any program can begin. If they remain unanswered, then there is almost certain failure. Willis Goldbeck, president of the Washington Business Group on Health, has outlined the minimum information which must be known about an organization's climate toward health promotion:

— product line(s)—(do these involve occupational or environmental hazards)
— type of employees (assembly line, high technology, executive, clerical)
— the relationship and relative authority of the medical director, benefits manager, president, and chairman (where does health promotion fit in)
— mix of health benefits the company offers (and therefore, an idea of their costs and the impact their plan design has upon the utilization of and demand for medical facilities and services)
— the extent to which the company is unionized . . . what union(s) . . . what is their position on health issues . . .

when is their contract up for renegotiation (or what was just agreed to)

— officers and others who may serve on hospital or school boards or hold local political office (often part time). (*Adapted from Weinberg, Kiefhaber, and Goldbeck, 1980*)

Assessing each of these factors is essential to the initiation of any health promotion program.

To begin to organize an effective program, several steps need to be taken:

1. It is necessary to identify the organizational stressors characteristic of the company. If they are not easily pinpointed, various "symptoms" will serve as clues. For instance, misdirected activity, little initiative or creativity, complaints of being left out of decisions, or suspiciousness might point to lack of clarity of responsibilities. When there is lack of performance feedback, the symptoms are often excessive need for approval, complaints of nonrecognition, mistakes being repeated, and a sense of overall frustration and being on a treadmill since workers do not know when a goal or objective has been reached. Chronic conflict sometimes surfaces in a "blame game," in excessive competition, superficial cooperation accompanied by sabotage, or withholding of information. When the organizational structure or management style is wanting, then the symptoms might be excessive agreement in order to play it safe, indecision or decisions taking too long to implement, and projects that go unfinished due to busy activity with low output. Finally, excessive deadlines can manifest as misunderstandings in priorities, work imbalance with some workers doing too much and others too little, missed deadlines, and frequent unplanned overtime or excessive meetings which result in complaints and stress.

2. The next step is to decide which of these sources of organizational stress can be dealt with at the individual level and which require group or company-wide action (Spheres I, II, or III). A person, for instance, who sets unrealistic deadlines needs to be brought into the work group in order to see the problem. Or perhaps the work group itself sets its own unrealistic deadlines (Sphere II). If a number of Type A–oriented individuals need stress management skills, that might be taken care of at their own private initiative, or by a company-sponsored program (Sphere III).

3. These same two steps can be applied to identifying and assign-

ing responsibility for the positive aspects of the work environment, such as opportunity for advancement, substantial peer support and teamwork, or a comfortable physical environment in which to work. These are the assets of the work environment, the resources to build upon. In one program that I established in a national bank, the district managers decided to use their "asset" of peer support. They met once a month to brief each other on the "debit," which was a series of conflicting directives from a top manager, who was later incorporated into the same group very effectively.

4. The next obvious but often neglected step is the assembly and evaluation of various resource materials and model programs. All too often these materials are not even gathered and evaluated according to the needs of the particular company. The result is that the work group or organization selects a program which aggravates rather than resolves the organizational stressors. In making this evaluation, there are several qualities which might be kept in mind. They have been identified by Leon J. Warshaw as necessary for a successful program. Among these qualities are that the program content should be "relevant," "flexible," "interactive," "not based on fear or prejudice," "take advantage of group dynamics and peer pressures," "provide opportunity for individuals to get personalized information," "involve employees' spouses and other family members," "information should be accurate and up-to-date," "employees should be involved in the design and modification of the program," and "mechanisms for evaluation of its effectiveness should be built into the program" (1979). These factors will be examined in more depth when we discuss the structure of health programs, but they should be kept in mind before any consultants or existing program models are chosen.

The Bibliography lists hundreds of different resources useful at the planning stage. One of the most useful, overall guides to such programs is the booklet *A Practical Guide for Employee Health Promotion Programs* (1979) by the Health Planning Council of Madison, Wisconsin. Under the direction of a multidisciplinary team of psychologists, nurses, physicians, and people from business, the council developed a list of "inevitable do's" for health promotion programs which are similar to the qualities suggested by Leon J. Warshaw. Of equal importance is their list of "inevitable don'ts," which include: expect overnight success or initial cost savings, overpromise results, give up, preach at or harass nonbelievers, stagnate—since programs must be revised and changed to remain fresh—and expect improved health behaviors from purely recreational programs. The Health Planning Council of Madison, Wisconsin, has adapted a helpful list, from the publication *Employee Fitness* by the Canadian Ministry of State for Culture and Recreation, fitness branch, of the twelve common features of successful programs "plus one": (1) strong leadership; (2) administrative support; (3) accessibility (on-site of nearby facilities); (4) availability (right programs at the right time); (5) assessment (continuing evaluation); (6) recording (techniques should be devised for monitoring the progress of participants); (7) group exercise and other activities; (8) challenging physical programs (participants come to be improved not humored); (9) continued motivation, stimulation, and incentive; (10) organization (careful attention to the mechanics and details of program operation); (11) visibility and variety; (12) continuity and extension (the program should work with, and not against related company and community organizations); and (13) (the plus one) "fun." Bulk copies of two handbooks listing and elaborating upon these thirteen points are entitled *Fitness in the Workplace* and *Building a Healthier Company*. Both can be obtained from the Washington, D.C., office of the President's Council on Physical Fitness and Sports or from Blue Cross / Blue Shield. Although there can be no rigid "checklists" for establishing an organizational fitness program, these thirteen guidelines are a sound approximation.

WHY DO COMPANIES START HEALTH PROMOTION PROGRAMS?

No employee health promotion program can be successful unless it has the full support and encouragement of the administration and the labor organizations to which the employees might belong. According to Willis Goldbeck, "support from top level executives will make or break a program . . . to date, health promotion programs are generally sponsored by management" (Weinberg, Kiefhaber, and Goldbeck, 1980). Virtually every health promotion program has been sponsored by management; unions have initiated or actively sponsored few if any such programs. A study by the Washington Business Group on Health pointed out that some unions actually oppose such programs because of the concern that money allocated to health promotion would reduce management's commitment to job safety. Even at present, "only 43% of the small companies, those which annually gross $100,000 to $200,000, provide any medical insurance at all. As a consequence, employers consider offering basic and major medical protection a higher priority than offering health promotion services. Employees often feel the same way" (Weinberg, Kiefhaber, and Goldbeck, 1980). In the words of one worker, "Money should be spent cleaning coke ovens before it is spent on 'frills' like smoking cessation." Without a doubt, basic safety measures and adequate employee health benefits should be given first priority. At the same time, it must be recognized that such benefits may be used excessively or inappropriately if a minimal level of health education and promotion is not introduced.

There are at least as many motivations for companies to start health promotion programs as there are programs. Interestingly, perhaps the least frequently cited reason is the cost of medical disabilities or even a concern over the ubiquitous "bottom line." Some employers enact programs out of a sense of social responsibility or union pressures. A program at a Chicago printing company began after an irate pressman hurled his lunch pail into a press, causing $30,000 in damages. More often, programs have been initiated by a key executive who has recovered from a heart attack, or after the death of a key person which could have been prevented. The remaining top executives respond in the form of a health promotion program. At least one major program was started to keep the corporate image consistent with their product; others have been established as a competitive perk in seeking key personnel. Kenneth A. Plummer, director of education at St. Catherine's Hospital in Chicago, noted, "Many companies are adding physical fitness programs because the firm gets a tax break and because it is a benefit that many of the top executives would otherwise buy for themselves. The notion that fitness programs can save money for the company is just a rationalization for something they wanted to do anyway" (Staver, 1979).

Many programs begin on a modest scale. The first program in an American company began in 1894 at the National Cash Register Company in Dayton, Ohio. That program began when John H. Patterson, the company president, authorized morning and afternoon exercise breaks for employees. Following that, Patterson installed a gymnasium and built a 325-acre park for his employees and their families, an impressive step even by today's standards. Pioneering programs began at NASA in 1968 at its Washington headquarters. In cooperation with the Heart Disease and Stroke Control Program of the Public Health Service, the space agency provided an exercise program, three times per week, for 259 male executives from ages 35 to 55. After one year the participants completed questionnaires and were given complete medical examinations. According to Richard O. Keelor, former Director of the President's Council on Physical Fitness and Sports, the findings were most impressive. In a 1976 address to the Blue Shield Annual Program Conference, Keelor noted that "Half of the regular participants reported improved on the job performance and better attitudes toward their work. . . . Nearly all the regular participants said they felt better. . . . More than 60 percent lost weight. . . . Many participants quit smoking or cut down, and nearly half said they were paying more attention to their diets." The outcome study of the NASA program was based on subjective measures; it indicated that 93 percent of those who strictly adhered to the program reported feelings of better health compared to only 21 percent of those who did not adhere to the program.

It is estimated that there are at least 500 corporations with such programs according to *The New York Times* (August 24, 1981). One company which was an early innovator is Metropolitan Life Insurance Company of New York, which maintains a Center for Health Help and programs in smoking cessation, hypertension, nutrition, physical fitness, weight control, stress management, and breast self-examination. In one of the longest-standing programs, at General Mills in Minneapolis, the medical department provides extensive health assessment and their employee assistance and substance abuse programs are linked with community resources. In the main office the physical fitness programs use in-house facilities, and a nutrition education program is carried out in the cafeteria, where there are displays of the calorie and fat content of various foods. A "reward smoking cessation program" is being conducted by a Texas division of Dow Chemical. Their program used a series of health incentives using $50 incentives and finally a boat and motor to get one-quarter of the 33 percent of their employees who smoked to join the "I am a quitter" club. Physical fitness programs constitute a key starting point in many programs including Kimberly-Clark, Xerox, PepsiCo, and Sentry Insurance Company of Stevens Point, Wisconsin, which provides medical screening, stress testing, classes in risk factor reduction, and extensive facilities including a gymnasium, swimming pool, racquet and handball courts, and various exercise equipment. For Campbell Soup in Camden, New Jersey, the medical department has a colon-rectal cancer detection program which has saved $245,000 and an extensive screening program for cardiovascular risk factors, which is their number one medical problem. Hypertension control programs have evaluated over 10,000 employees since 1968, and in-house programs have been initiated. An interesting question here is how much emphasis is given to salt reduction in soup as either an individual or corporate concern, since salt consumption is a major risk factor.

At Chase Manhattan Bank, former president David Rockefeller had a charismatic effect with his personal involvement in that program limited to vice-presidents and above. There has been a five-month wait to join the bank's cardiovascular fitness program. There is even a rule that if an executive's attendance falls below one and a half sessions per week, he or she may be dropped from the program. Yet another dynamic leader, Malcolm Forbes, has been known to fire off memos to department heads when their participation in the company's fitness program is good and to admonish them when it lags. One of the most ambitious programs is being offered by the Rockwell International Corporation of El Segundo, California. Starting in 1960, the Rockwell program has encouraged every employee and his or her family to participate in a daily exercise program following a battery of medical tests. Facilities for this program include an enormous recreation center with several clubhouses, a track, tennis, golf courses, basketball, volleyball courts, and even picnic areas. By sharp contrast the National Science Foundation in Washington, D.C., has no facilities at all. In a cooperative effort with a YMCA directly across the street, NSF created a special group rate in a program which included use of the gym, track, exercise classes, and swimming. At New York Telephone, Converse rubber company, and Union Carbide quiet rooms are provided for relaxation breaks.

Among the attempts to extend personal health practices into the workplace, some exemplary programs are the use of nutritious food choices in the cafeterias and vending machines at Johnson & Johnson, Kimberly-Clark, Boeing, and Levi Strauss; there are no-smoking work areas for employees or smoking areas provided if the company has adopted a no-smoking policy in Johnson & Johnson and Campbell Soup; and there is great support for physical fitness programs which is equal to or a close second to the emphasis upon stress management programs. Toward the end of physical fitness, some companies such as Xerox, Johnson & Johnson, Shaklee, and Kimberly-Clark have provided showers and lockers for employees as well as encouraged employees to use the facilities by providing time and access during working hours. Optimally, these programs are undertaken while simultaneously addressing the reduction of unnecessary organizational stressors. Without these concurrent efforts at individual plus organizational stress management, these programs could be viewed as "blaming the victim" or as an effort to reduce or mask legitimate employee grievances.

Since there are at least 400 such programs, these lists could be extended virtually indefinitely. Details of a few exemplary programs, such as those of Xerox, Kimberly-Clark, Johnson & Johnson, IBM, and Control Data Corporation, are considered in the next chapter. Amid this array, is there any common ground? These programs range from large to small, have extraordinary facilities to none at all, some cost millions and others barely reach $100. Each is a serious and laudable beginning which deserves support and objective evaluations. One clear message from these divergent programs is that if you are a key individual or employer who is interested in such programs, then select a program appropriate to your setting and employed population and get to work. A great deal of the groundwork and experimentation has been done and this is unquestionably to your advantage.

Although there is a widespread consensus that employees who are healthy are more creative and productive, there are very little, if any, data, to support this conclusion. On the one hand are ardent enthusiasts such as PepsiCo's John Sculley, who has stated he "can't remember the last time one of our managers had a heart attack," and on the other are dissenters such as Alan McLean, eastern medical director of IBM, who has termed psychological counseling programs "a deadly form of paternalism" (Hastings Center Report, 1982). Between these two positions serious efforts are currently under way to assess whether employer-initiated programs in the areas of stress management, physical fitness, smoking cessation, weight loss, hypertension, and employee assistance are actually effective. Another element in this complex equation is insurance carriers, who have been relatively slow in providing health incentives because they are locked into a system of simply passing on increased costs to their clients. At least one major insurer, Blue Cross / Blue Shield, has given considerable support to corporate health programs. As part of a $2.85 million campaign to advertise various companies' efforts, they ran a full-page advertisement in the December 4, 1978, issue of *Business Week,* describing Xerox's program. That ad stated: "It only stands to reason that if your company can institute a program to keep your employees healthy and well, your company's health care costs can possibly be lowered." However, insurance carriers, including the Blue Cross and Blue Shield, are still waiting for definitive proof. This is a bit of a "Catch-22" since the viability of such programs will depend upon flexibility and innovation by insurance carriers to provide incentives. Insurance carriers cannot be passive observers because their policies affect the outcome. Roy R. Anderson, vice-president in the corporate headquarters of Allstate Insurance in Northbrook, Illinois, wrote me at length on this subject: ". . . as long as the insurance companies can continue to get the needed premium increases, their business just gets bigger and bigger. But the rub is that the system is now too big and much too costly" (1981). If insurance carriers do not respond innovatively to these trends, it is likely that more companies will turn to self-insured programs and self-administered health plans which can be run more efficiently and at less cost. At the present time several evaluation programs are being conducted by the Washington Business Group on Health (Goldbeck, 1982), the California NEXUS Foundation (Pelletier, 1983), and the National Center for Health Education (DuVal, 1982). Until these studies are completed, hard questions remain about the value of health promotion programs in increasing productivity and arresting the spiraling costs of medical care.

EMPLOYEE ASSISTANCE PROGRAMS

Many limited approaches to corporate health promotion fall under the heading of "Employee Assistance Programs." These focus upon psychological counseling, smoking cessation, alcohol abuse, hypertension control, and, in some instances, cancer screening. These programs focus on the minority of employees whose health problems cause the greatest expense, in medical benefits and lost productivity. In any given organization it is possible to identify a small percentage, usually 10 percent to 15 percent, who utilize between 80 percent and 90 percent of all medical services. After examining the records of

2,238 patients, drawn from 42,880 cases, Christopher J. Zook and Frances D. Moore have linked "high-cost users of medical care" to "harmful personal habits." In particular, Zook and Moore noted that "high-cost users" showed "a pairing of diagnoses that are commonly associated, such as alcoholism and benign inflammatory disease (e.g., cirrhosis of the liver), alcoholism and neurologic deficits; smoking and benign pulmonary disease or peripheral vascular disease; and obesity and degenerative vascular disease of the heart (or diabetes)" (Zook and Moore, 1980). Findings such as these are increasingly striking. Rehabilitation and medical care for this small percentage of employees become very expensive. Employee assistance programs are designed to reduce these statistics through early detection and treatment, improved working conditions, and health education.

For most organizations the first step in any employee assistance program is an overall health risk assessment. Although this is a requisite step, it cannot be used as the only intervention, since information alone has been proven to be ineffective in actually achieving health promotion. Ironically, only providing assessments and information may result in greater concern and frustration, for they lead employees to recognize occupational health hazards but do not give them the influence or skills to correct the conditions. The steering committee of former Governor Jerry Brown's Wellness in the Workplace project formulated specific criteria for the use of risk assessments:

1. Risk assessment is an educational tool to be utilized only in conjunction with risk reduction / health promotion interventions, never independently;
2. Any risk assessment tool should have a current mortality / morbidity data base, and the capability of assessing mental as well as physical health-related characteristics and behavior;
3. Risk assessment should be used in periodic followup / evaluations to measure and reinforce change;
4. Risk assessment, like all health promotion programs, must respect confidentiality and the rights of the individual to privacy—about alcohol and drug use as well as other sensitive issues of health. (*Brown, 1981*)

When these assessments are applied to an employee population, two distinct groups are found. One group is "high-risk" individuals, the actual or potential "high-cost users" of medical services. The other group is "low-risk" individuals who are relatively healthy. Both groups will benefit from the same general health promotion programs, but the high-risk employees require more medical supervision, counseling, follow-up, and will benefit greatly from the creation of special support groups designed to address their special problems. These individuals have been referred to as "High-Risk / High Yield" by G. H. Collins of New York Telephone since any change in the health status of identified high-risk groups will have a noticeable personal and economic benefit (Jennings and Tager, 1981). Programs of employee assistance are of considerable benefit in these instances.

Among the organizations using health risk assessments are Mattel Inc., the San Francisco Department of Public Health, Kimberly-Clark (as one aspect of their larger program), and NASA, which utilizes the Health Hazard Appraisal (HHA) combined with other physical assessments and followed by special counseling, medical referrals, and other services. Health assessments such as the HHA have been detailed and discussed at length in Chapter IV of *Holistic Medicine* (Pelletier, 1979) and other publications. Among the programs which include more extensive health assessment and employee assistance is the Health Care Management program developed by the medical department of New York Telephone (*Business Insurance,* 1981). This program provides medical treatment and physical examinations but emphasizes health promotion and disease prevention. There are nine areas of prevention and health promotion in the program including: (1) smoking cessation; (2) cholesterol reduction; (3) hypertension control; (4) fitness training; (5) stress management; (6) alcohol abuse control; (7) colon-rectal cancer screening; (8) breast cancer screening; and (9) healthy back education for proper lifting. One of the primary motivations by New York Telephone was the cost of providing traditional coverages to its 80,000 employees in more than 1,000 locations. Projected costs of medical benefits for 1980 were $187 million, which was equal to 12 percent of the company's total wages. Of even greater significance was that the $18 million was 11 percent higher than in 1979 for the same benefits. When these programs were assessed, the company used conservative statistics and assumptions and found some striking results. Data were collected and analyzed by physician Charles A. Beery, former chief medical director for NASA, under a grant from the Health Insurance Association of America and details of these findings are available from their Washington, D.C., headquarters (1982). According to their data, the annual savings to the company was $4,540,000. The nine programs cost $2,840,000 to conduct and left a net annual gain of $2,700,000, which is impressive by any standards. Out of all nine programs, the greatest impact upon personal and corporate health as well as the greatest savings were evident in smoking cessation, alcohol abuse control, and hypertension control.

More recently, New York Telephone completed an eighteen-month study on stress management and elected to continue meditation as part of their overall program. Using three forms of relaxation, Patricia Carrington of the Department of Psychology at Princeton University assigned employees to one of three groups and asked each person to practice the meditation or relaxation twice daily for fifteen to twenty minutes each time. From this study she found that 70 percent to 80 percent of the employees continued the practice for the full study and that the two most effective methods were her own "Clinically Standardized Meditation" and the "Respiratory One Method" of Herbert Benson from the Howard Medical School. Overall, the employees reported much less depression and hostility, decreases in stress disorders and absenteeism, and an increased ability to think more clearly. Most importantly, the company devoted a lot of time and money to the successful project with the full support of its medical department. This is most significant since programs such as these require the commitment of the organization as a whole to effect such large-scale programs for large numbers of employees. Even with these impressive results, programs such as that at New York Telephone clearly require further development and more widespread implementation.

Employee assistance programs are generally inexpensive and are a highly visible employee benefit with considerable savings for the employer. Often these programs consist of not more than three counselors, usually clinical psychologists or social workers, who are able briefly to help employees or to refer them on a confidential basis. Employees must be assured of confidentiality or these programs simply do not work. One reason for the relatively low utilization of such programs is that employees often doubt confidentiality or are still concerned about the stigma of seeking psychological help. This issue of confidentiality cannot be overemphasized. Willis Goldbeck has noted that court decisions have made it increasingly difficult to use health records for placement, promotion, firing, or hiring. Nonetheless, "Even with certain statutory protections, worker confidence, and therefore, worker participation in any voluntary program, will be affected by their perception that restricted access to their medical records has been assured" (Weinberg, Kiefhaber, and Goldbeck, 1980). "Stress management" programs are often more popular than psychological counseling programs, precisely because learning to manage stress is less stigmatizing and even somewhat fashionable.

With employee assistance programs based primarily upon psychological counseling, alcohol abuse, and cardiovascular risk reduction, a number of companies have reported significant results. Annual cost savings were calculated by multiplying the number of workers rehabilitated in a program times a certain period of their average salary. Among the results are a $2,221,362 savings by the United States Postal Service, $2,000,000 by New York Transit, $448,400 by Kennecott Copper with a program involving both workers and dependents, and $67,996 by the University of Missouri, to cite only a few examples. There was also a 40 percent decrease in use of health benefits at the University of Missouri and a 53 percent decrease in absenteeism at Kennecott Copper. One of the largest employee assistance programs, instituted by General Motors at over 130 sites, has been of benefit to over 44,000 employees or 7 percent of their total North American employees. At the end of one year of the program, results indicated 40 percent less time lost, a 60 percent decrease in sickness and accident payments, a 50 percent decrease in accidents, and a decrease of 50 percent in overall grievances. General Motors estimated at least a 3-to-1 return on dollars invested. An Oldsmobile program involved 117 hourly workers at a cost of $11,114 and achieved a 49 percent decrease in lost time, a 29 percent decrease in disabilities, and a 56 percent decrease in leaves of absence. Comparable results were obtained in a Pontiac program. These programs, as we have said before, involve few staff members and clearly demonstrate themselves to be cost effective.

Finally there is the intangible human element, for both the individual and the organization, which is often overlooked in the fixation upon the eternally elusive "cost-effective" health promotion program. There are many benefits beyond the econometric measures being developed, of equal if not greater importance. Former director of the corporate fitness program at the General Foods Corporation, Peter J. Brown, has enumerated these benefits: "reducing overhead costs as a result of more productive employees (although this is difficult to objectively prove); gaining a reputation for caring about the human side of the workplace; and gaining a useful tool for recruiting managers and top graduates from the business schools" (Staver, 1979). Similar benefits may include reduced turnover of employees, improved public image of the organization, and other secondary gains which are not specific to health promotion in their impact and benefit. Observations such as these have evolved out of growing awareness by employees and organizations that values are changing. In May 1981 a special cover story report of *Business Week* was entitled "The New Industrial Relations": "With the adversarial approach outmoded, the trend is toward more worker involvement in decisions on the shop floor—and more job satisfaction, tied to productivity." Increasing demands for more skilled and better-educated workers at all levels of employment have placed a new emphasis upon an active, participating process in decision making. Both business and labor are realizing that "people problems" and solutions are as important as generating capital and new technology.

MEDICAL SELF-CARE

One dimension of an overall health promotion program which is frequently overlooked is the area of medical self-care. Medical self-care focuses upon certain aspects of personal health care which individuals can safely and routinely perform for themselves, such as breast and testicular self-examinations, throat cultures, as well as the burgeoning number of home diagnostic aids such as pregnancy tests. While critics of medical self-care berate this trend as turning the United States population into hypochondriacs consuming medical tests like aspirin, it is also having positive health benefits. An excellent journal, *Medical Self-Care,* edited by a physician, covers these developments (Ferguson, 1982). Because employees may avoid medical services in order to circumvent having damaging information being placed in their records or, on the other hand, use medical services inappropriately or excessively, it seems essential to include self-care education and information in an overall health promotion program. Several major organizations have included medical self-care as an important element in their programs. ARMCO steel company in Middletown, Ohio, utilizes a 167-page book on health practices for employees and their families. California Blue Shield in Mendocino County, California, with their Stay Well Health Insurance Plan, the Bank of America, Control Data Corporation, and Xerox are among the corporations using medical self-care as part of their health programs. These efforts utilize newsletters, pamphlets, lectures, medical care controls, as well as the popular and highly effective self-care manual *Take Care of Yourself* (1976) by physicians Donald M. Vickery and James F. Fries.

A common error is to equate medical self-care with the annual physical examination. There is widespread agreement that annual physicals are of benefit to clearly defined high-risk individuals, but that for reasonably healthy individuals a physical examination "perhaps every two or three years in adult life remains reasonable" (*Harvard Medical School Health Letter,* 1980). Although the yearly physical remains a pervasive myth, it has been referred to as "a costly indulgence" (Hackler, 1980). Franz Ingelfinger, the late eminent physician and editor of the *New England Journal of Medicine* stated his reservations in an article entitled, "Can You Survive a Medical Diagnosis?" (1980). Medical self-care approaches have been supported by innovative insurance companies such as Equitable Life Assurance. There needs to be a great deal more effort and cooperation between organizations and insurance carriers, particularly in this important area of medical self-care, and health education.

FINANCING HEALTH PROMOTION

Effective health promotion programs in the workplace do not have to be elaborate or expensive. Evaluation of such programs does not have to be expensive, either, in order to demonstrate even modest success. In reviewing the reported economic benefits of health promotion programs, Willis Goldbeck notes, "We have enough anecdotes about success all over the country, and occasionally someone suggests that the wild claims of 50% success or 75% success by a given employer may not be proven to be totally accurate, especially if there was a great academic rigor applied to the evaluation. Let me assure you in today's climate there is not an employer that I have ever met that wouldn't be tickled to get a 10% savings in anything!" (Goldbeck, 1983). Clearly, neither the facilities nor the evaluations need to be extensive to ensure an effective, cost-saving program. Only a few firms have large facilities or staffs and most utilize or share existing facilities such as health clubs and YMCAs. Some hospitals are even entering the competition by offering free or low-cost programs in order to help protect their share of "health" as well as the "disease" market. Actually, it appears that some of the more elaborate programs with extensive athletic facilities are often less effective than those which utilize less visible but more effective measures, ranging from smoking education to communications.

In the instance of limited programs, the most frequent form is that of a "fitness" program based upon physical exercise. Although these represent an admirable beginning, they are not adequate. Programs based exclusively on physical fitness often involve expensive facilities and may "place undue emphasis on a performance standard which may intimidate, and, thereby, prevent people from taking up an appropriate fitness activity from them . . . a balanced fitness program includes on-the-job activities related to the activities of work" (Brown, 1981). When a program begins with physical fitness, it needs to be extended into other areas. Excellent programs have been established where companies enroll workers in independent health clinics rather than build their own facilities, as with Cardio-Fitness in New York City and Fitness Systems Incorporated in Los Angeles. The spectre of large expenditures for elaborate facilities and staff is a frequent deterrent to organizations considering health promotion programs. In deciding whether there are to be off-site or on-site facilities, there is no single best solution. If the program does not involve physical exercise at the outset, there is no need for physical facilities at all. Kimberly-Clark has a program which was initiated by the construction of a $2 million gymnasium, while IBM has utilized the services of community YMCAs; both programs have been demonstrably effective.

To date, approximately 49 percent of the health promotion programs I have studied are financed by employers, 24 percent by employees, and 22 percent by a cooperative effort of employers and employees. Since the costs of starting and maintaining health promotion programs are of great concern to organizations, former Governor Brown's study for the Wellness in the Workplace program elaborated a number of different approaches: in some, employers "assume the entire cost" (IBM and Johnson & Johnson); "pay for the costs of interventions for high-risk employees" (Ford Motor Company); "pay for interventions with high levels of demonstrated effectiveness" (New York Telephone Company); or "allow time off during working hours for wellness program activities" (PepsiCo) (Brown, 1981). Unless employers contribute time, resources, and support to health promotion efforts, employees will not take the programs seriously. Former Governor Brown's report noted the importance of financial as well as nonmonetary "health incentives." These incentives are intended to help employees be more discriminating in their use of medical services and also to provide them with a share of the savings which the organization is gaining from employee participation in health programs. Such incentives encourage individuals to participate in decreasing their own medical costs by making informed decisions about when to use, and not to use, such services.

To encourage deskbound workers to become involved in health promotion, the Hospital Corporation of America in Nashville, Tennessee, initiated a program of paying employees 6 cents for each mile they bike, 24 cents for each mile they walk or run, and 16 cents for each mile they swim. One 42-year-old employee, Mary Greer, is a switchboard operator and now runs 25 miles per week. She has also eliminated most red meat and salty food from her diet. She reports less fatigue, no longer has sinus headaches, and has reduced her dress size from 13 to a 7. Recently she received a check for $97 for her voluntary efforts from the Hospital Corporation and quipped, "It pays for the running shoes."

Education and guidance in medical self-care also become important here: "There are certain non-behavioral factors such as genetic disposition, age, gender and existing disease which leave a person with little control over the need for or use of medical services. Some people will defer essential health services because of a financial incentive, thus exacerbating otherwise controllable illnesses" (Brown, 1981). On the other hand, the assessment of employee populations can result in greater utilization of medical services, when undetected conditions such as hypertension are discovered. However, such an increase in use of medical services may not necessarily result in increased costs, because the early, preventive use of medical services will prove less expensive than later treatment of established disease. With these cautions in mind, the *Wellness in the Workplace* report cited examples of various health incentives which have proven effective. Among these are rebates by some insurance companies or premium reductions for people who do not smoke and who drink moderately, maintain a balanced weight, and have safe driving records. There have been financial rebates to employees for more appropriate use of medical services in the Mendocino County Unified School District or in the San Francisco branch of Bank of America. The rewards need not be monetary. The simple act of recognition and peer support within an organization for weight loss or participation in a program, with awards of T-shirts, jogging shoes, or time off for such activities, can be equally effective. Whatever the incentive chosen, it is necessary. The intent is to provide an individual and an organization with positive feedback and rewards for health promotion to offset, if not overcome, the negative incentives which are so pervasive and often unrecognized.

Finally, partial or total financing of health promotion programs can be provided by trimming excessive costs in present medical coverages or by reallocating some money away from disease treatment to health promotion. Under this approach there are a variety of cost-saving strategies enumerated by corporate consultant and publisher Jere Daniel:

> . . . create and finance new medical delivery systems—particularly the Health Maintenance Organizations . . . to promote out-patient medical care—one-day surgery, pre-hospital admission diagnostic tests, emergicenters, home care, second opinions for surgery . . . form coalitions—cooperative efforts . . . with enough muscle to persuade the care providers to hold down prices . . . rate doctors and hospitals by cost effectiveness and negotiate discounts . . . encourage and train executives and line employees to serve on boards of hospitals and shape up their inefficient business practices . . . build health planning agencies (as the Feds phase out) to fight waste in hospitals . . . work with labor, which cooperates on cost cutting with a wary eye against cuts in hard-won benefits. (*Daniel, 1982*)

Each of these efforts can contribute to a small amount of time and money which can be freed up from excessive medical costs to be used in the financing of modest health promotion programs. All of the above efforts can be enhanced by another of Daniel's points, which emphasizes employee responsibility and involvement in all aspects of the medical benefits package by "sometimes increasing employee contributions but rewarding them for staying healthy and using doctors less; or by offering 'cafeteria' plans that let employees select medical benefits to fit their needs (less when single and more when raising a family, for instance)" (Daniel, 1982).

After an extensive consideration of these issues, Jane Bryant Quinn concluded, "Employers believe that corporate welfare will continue to expand in the years ahead. . . . They'll [company executives] fix a price that the company wants to spend on employee benefits—and let *you* allocate the dollars to suit yourself" (1982). In keeping with these and other guidelines being formulated with greatly increasing frequency, a recent article in the *New England Journal of Medicine* proposed a system of rating an individual's health insurance premiums by known risk factors. The particular instance cited by physician Joseph Stokes III of the Boston University Medical Center was heart disease. His proposal would permit employees at a certain risk level to pay a premium based upon his or her efforts, or lack of efforts, to raise or lower their risk level. Presumably, high-risk workers would wish to lower their risk and would be "encouraged by offering a system of cash rebates on health and life insurance premiums. . . . For example, if a person was eligible for an 8 percent premium reduction upon initial assessment, but one year later had an index that made him or her eligible for a 28 percent reduction, 20 percent of the annual premium would be rebated as a cash payment. Such a system should scrupulously avoid any meddling in patients' private lives, and compliance should be entirely voluntary. . . . those who might not wish to undergo risk rating would not be denied life insurance, their premiums would merely be set at the same level as for those found to be at maximum risk. One purpose of the system should be to encourage people to take more responsibility for their health" (Stokes, 1983). All of these strategies point toward individuals becoming more well-informed and active consumers of medical care by exercising concern for cost and quality.

Consultation in cost-saving measures and reallocation of funding is the basis for a highly successful company, the U.S. Administrators Incorporated (USA). Based in Los Angeles, the company has been able to cut medical costs by 15 percent to 30 percent by processing claims through four computerized screenings for its clients. Claims are examined on the basis of: "length of stay . . . ancillary services —to make sure there's no overuse of hospital services . . . model treatment . . . and ambulatory treatment—whether treatments during visits to the doctor's office fit the patient's welfare—or the doctor's" (Daniel, 1982). Based on this screening, as much as one fifth of charges are found to be unnecessary. One "memorable" hospital bill of $77,000 had $40,000 in "questionable" expenses. Individuals and organizations can save money on medical expenses through such strategies and reassessment. When that step is taken, the next possible action is to reallocate these resources toward health promotion programs and positive incentives for individuals and their companies to create sustained health and productivity.

CORPORATE HEALTH MAINTENANCE ORGANIZATIONS (HMOs)

One successful and conservative means of financing health benefits has been for a company to establish its own Health Maintenance Organization. Industrialist Henry J. Kaiser began the HMO concept in the early 1940s when he retained a physician to provide prepaid health care for employees of his shipbuilding empire.

In 1945, the Kaiser-Permanente health plan began accepting outside members and today provides services to over 4.2 million members throughout the United States, and projections are that there will be over 25 million members by 1990. Two significant events in this astounding growth of HMOs occurred in 1973 and 1976. During 1973 a law authorized federal funding for HMOs, and the number jumped from 33 to over 277 similar plans now in existence. Then, in 1976, the R. J. Reynolds Company in Winston-Salem, North Carolina, started a highly successful and popular HMO for its 15,000 employees and followed that with an equally successful dental plan in 1978 for over 36,000 members. This highly visible and often studied HMO prompted other major corporations to initiate such programs, and HMOs are continuing to grow at a significant rate. As one example, there are now seven successful HMOs in the Minneapolis–St. Paul area serving Honeywell, Control Data, General Mills, and 3M. For many of these companies, a third or more of their workers, and at General Mills more than three out of four, are members. Substantial savings have resulted to all of the companies involved.

According to estimates by Joseph A. Califano, Jr., "Big business could have saved up to $150 million last year if just 5% of the employees of Fortune 500 companies belonged to HMOs" (Lublin, 1978). For corporations and health professionals interested in such a system, the United States Chamber of Commerce provides a 250-page guide addressing HMOs and related areas of health promotion. This guide is the product of a committee of twenty-two leaders from business, labor, insurance, and health care. Through the use of charts and references the report details:

. . . how to set up health-promotion programs; steps businesses can take to get the local Chamber of Commerce involved in health care; ways in which companies can make more demands on their insurance carriers; methods for emphasizing economy, quality, and accessibility of care; and procedures for becoming involved in health planning. (Medical World News, *1978*)

Another useful overview of the structural elements and functions of an HMO is a brief article entitled "Feasibility of Simulation of Health Maintenance Organizations," by A. Taher Moustafa and David W. Sears (1974) of the University of Massachusetts. Three major corporations, Goodyear, Firestone, and B. F. Goodrich, who have adopted such programs under the rubric of "self-insurance" (*Business Week,* 1976), have reported substantial reductions in health care costs.

Other corporate giants involved in such programs are General Motors, Deere and Company, and Ford Motor Company. The latter noted that health care was the single most expensive fringe benefit, costing the company "an estimated $520 million this year and $600 million next year, up from $450 million in 1977 despite no increase in coverage" (Lublin, 1978). With such figures at stake the provision of more cost-efficient health care is a point of agreement between labor unions and management. At the present time "Ford is saving $2 million from HMO participation by 10,000 employees, or just 4% of its U.S. work force" (Lublin, 1978). A 1979 Report of the President's Council on Wage and Price Stability described 126 HMO programs developed in cooperative efforts between employers and unions since 1973. At the present time the Kaiser-Permanente Medical Group in Oakland, California, is conducting an "Employee Health Promotion Demonstration Project" (Squyres, 1983) at two Kaiser facilities. One immediate goal is to develop an effective health promotion program for employees, followed by a long-term goal of providing such a program for the HMO corporate subscribers in addition to the medical benefits plan. Such an innovative program accompanied by its own in-house evaluation, will help further the utilization of combined HMO and health promotion programs. With insurance costs rising, these plans of self-insurance and HMO facilities are viable alternatives. For this reason alone, it would be prudent for insurance carriers to begin seriously to consider measures which they can undertake in health promotion not only for their clients but for their own economic viability.

Virtually all of the corporations which have adopted voluntary HMO systems have noted financial benefits such as: (1) an increased ability to pinpoint irregularities or excessive fees for services. This results from a regular review of claims to be sure that "doctors and hospitals don't overcharge, keep patients in hospitals longer than needed, or bill for unnecessary and sometimes unperformed services" (Daniel, 1982); (2) by avoiding the use of an outside insurance carrier, the saving of taxes on premium reserves and insurance company profits. Under such plans the companies often pay the providers directly and can exert more control over their expenditures and realize a direct return in savings; and (3) reductions of 3 percent to 5 percent of their previous health benefit expenditures. One major impediment to the further effectiveness of an HMO approach is not the corporations' willingness but "acceptance by employees." Charles S. Ryan, who is director of health and safety at Sun Company, has noted that since his company began its own HMO in Pennsylvania several years ago, "only 433 of Sun's more than 32,000 employees have so far enrolled" (*Business Week,* 1978). This has been an issue with all voluntary HMO programs and points up the necessity of providing education and incentives. Initially, organized medicine fought the development of HMOs, but the American Medical Association now concedes that HMOs do provide high-quality care.

A more striking departure from traditional pathology management is seen in the number of corporate programs offering an HMO approach plus health promotion and physical fitness facilities as a means of promoting optimum health. Programs such as these have been characterized by physician Lorenz K. Y. Ng of the National Institute on Drug Abuse as "Health Promotion Organizations" or HPOs. This is an extremely important concept. It is described in an excellent article by Ng and his colleagues (Ng, Davis, and Manderscheid, 1978) and considered at length in Chapter II of *Longevity* (Pelletier, 1981). Health Promotion Organizations have proved viable in corporate, state government, hospital, and private sectors and mark a significant trend for the future.

PREFERRED PROVIDER ORGANIZATIONS (PPOs)

Partially in response to the success of HMOs, companies have also developed some further alternatives for providers of medical services. One major innovation has been the development of Professional Standards Review Organizations or PSROs. These committees were initially established in hospitals to focus primarily upon whether or not a patient's length of hospitalization was excessive. Most committees were not very active until the Nixon administration directed the PSROs to be sure that Medicare and Medicaid patients were hospitalized only when necessary. However, the biggest change in PSROs came when private corporations contracted with them to oversee and evaluate the medical care and hospitalization received by their employees.

At the same time that the PSROs were being developed, an experimental program was initiated by the Martin E. Segal actuarial company in 1967. This innovation came to be known as the Preferred Provider Organization or PPO. The reason PPOs have a broad appeal to both corporations and medical providers is that they provide companies with a degree of review and control while preserving an employee's right to choose his or her own doctors and hospitals from a limited selection. According to *Business Week*, PPOs work in this fashion:

A company, union trust fund or insurer negotiates a contract with certain doctors or hospitals to provide medical services. The providers may offer to discount those services or set up special utilization review programs to control medical expenses, or they may do both. In return, the company, fund, or insurer promises prompt payment and increased patient volume. It delivers the volume by offering employees breaks on co-payments and deductibles if they use the preferred providers, but all employees retain the option of staying with traditional insurance or an HMO. (*1982*)

Essentially, insurance companies or actuarial firms which manage a company's medical benefits can now negotiate with groups or individual medical providers for reduced rates in exchange for the company's turning over most of its medical care to them. Employees are not required to use the preferred providers, but they must pay any difference between what their company allows and the cost of their personal physician's fees. Actually, the State of California adopted a similar legislative action which required all hospitals in California to negotiate contracts with the state for the treatment of MediCal patients on a competitive cost basis. As a result, some hospitals were not awarded contracts in what Chancellor Julius R. Krevans, of the University of California School of Medicine in San Francisco, has termed "a modified, if not revolutionary, health delivery system" (1982). This new market has provided both headaches and opportunities for medical providers who see possibilities of creating alternatives to HMOs, which function on a "closed panel" basis and exclude nonmember physicians from providing services.

In the atmosphere of PPOs, some physicians are forming independent practice associations where groups of doctors treat patients in their own offices for one fixed premium that is usually all-inclusive and paid by the patients or by contracting employers. Such a system preserves a modified private practice model, ensures that patients will have a wider range of choices, and meets many of the criteria for cost-containment which have made the HMOs so successful. In fact, one California executive has stated, "We see PPOs as the best thing we have to look forward to in terms of reducing health care costs" (*Business Week,* 1982). Among the model programs are the Physicians Health Plan developed by the Hennepin County Medical Society in Minneapolis and the Quad Cities Health Plan in Moline, Illinois, which was initiated by Deere and Company. It seems that PPOs may provide even more cooperation between corporate and medical organizations for the provision of medical services. There are clear indications that PPOs are very effective in terms of cost containment. The seven-hospital Lutheran Hospital Society of California is marketing such an approach based on its own experience as both a provider and employer and has saved "a considerable amount of money —$300,000 to $400,000 a year so far" (*Business Week,* 1982). Among the other promising examples are MED Network with 18 hospitals and 1,300 physicians in southern California which reported a 15 percent increase in costs compared to overall increases of 30 percent for comparable services in 1981; Rohr Industries Incorporated of Chula Vista, California, reported saving $300,000 after its first year of a PPO which it negotiated with hospitals in its area and obtained a 4 percent to 25 percent reduction on typical fees from six hospitals (*Business Week,* 1982).

Although preferred provider systems appear to be promising, they are very new and are subject to considerable problems. For instance, in a recent decision in *Arizona* v. *Maricopa County Medical Society,* the Supreme Court ruled that physicians who agreed on the maximum fees covered by certain insurance plans were guilty of price fixing. As a result, the Federal Trade Commission will carefully monitor PPOs to ensure that they remain competitive. Critics of medical providers point out that the alliance of medical providers and corporate health planners is an uneasy alliance. Willis Goldbeck is one business leader who doubts such cooperation and points out, "We're talking about shifting economic resources around, and when that happens someone will lose" (Daniel, 1982). An even more blunt concern has been expressed by John S. Harding, corporate benefits administrator of Bourns Incorporated, who predicts, "Any spirit of cooperation that now exists is going to evaporate when we really get down to cutting the cost of medical care . . . insurance has prostituted the entire system because we have separated the person receiving the service from most of the financial consequences of using this system. . . . In simple language, the medical providers to us, the payors, are nothing more than vendors and should be treated like any other vendor that a company deals with. . . . When the real changes in health plan design by employers that will change the system come into place, the employers will be standing alone . . . the real mover in the system is going to be money" (1982). Strong observations such as these are becoming more frequent as debate and choices are now being made which will have profound social and economic impact. Questions remain about the long-term effectiveness of PPOs, but there is no question about the fact that such concerns are becoming a number-one priority for employers, medical practitioners, and state as well as national government.

QUALITY CIRCLES AND HEALTH PROMOTION

A trend toward active participation and interaction between employees and top management is closely related to the development and success of health promotion programs. This emerging trend in management makes it more likely that any worker, at any level in the organization, has the potential for significant input and influence upon the company working conditions and health benefits. Personal health promotion activity (Sphere I) may directly interact with corporate policy (Sphere III). Among the many mechanisms which have evolved in response to this participatory mode are "self-managed" work teams, labor and management steering committees, "core" or "problem-solving" groups, "design committees" that combine human and technological needs in designing the workplace, and the "quality circles" which were developed in Japan and are becoming more pervasive in the United States. For a complete consideration of quality circles within the correct context of Japanese cultural and corporate values, *The Art of Japanese Management* (1981) by Richard Tanner Pascale and Anthony G. Athos is unsurpassed. As we mentioned earlier, they put great emphasis upon the uniqueness of the American workplace and the need to adapt any management approach to these particular circumstances. "Every firm has to evolve its own way of being good at all the S's, and their fit to one another. Mechanistic, programmatic 'solutions' that do not change what executives do and, indeed, to some degree who they are, are likely to fail. The task is not to imitate cosmetically, but to evolve organically. And each company like each individual, has to develop in its own way." This vital requirement is especially true for health promotion programs.

Quality circles, or "QC," are groups of approximately ten workers, foremen, and managers who meet several times a month to identify and find solutions to production problems in their area. Richard Tanner Johnson and William G. Ouchi of Stanford University School of Business point out the need to adapt this concept to our culture. "Differences are especially pronounced in the Japanese and American attitudes toward individuality and self-sufficiency" (1974). Due to these essential, cultural differences, the quality circle concept has evolved into a form unique to the American workplace (Holden, 1980). In some variations, one person acts as a leader; in a group of eight to twelve people, an overall coordinator or facilitator keeps the group progressing; brainstorming is encouraged in early meetings while constructive solutions are the focus in later sessions. These procedures are more directive than the Japanese methods. In the U.S. versions, recommendations are often presented to top management by the group as a whole with the agreement that an immediate yes or fully justified no will follow. With such a system there can be problem areas, such as shop workers being unfamiliar with such responsibilities or managers becoming too controlling (Patchin, Novak, and Dotlich, 1981). Despite the problems of adaptation to an American situation, results have been impressive.

Among the most effective programs are Honeywell with 350 quality circles involving 4,000 employees or 5 percent of their total work force. Bolivar implemented a program in the mid-1970s and closely evaluated it over fifty-six months. After deducting program costs, the benefit for the company amounted to $3,000 per hourly worker. Shaklee Corporation of San Francisco adopted "self-managed" work teams and found that they were "producing the same volume at 40 percent of the labor costs" with two thirds of that due to the change in management style (*Business Week*, 1981). One of the most outstanding and best-known programs is the Quality of Worklife program by General Motors in 95 of its 130 plants. President of General Motors F. James McDonald is highly in favor of the program, which has improved management and union relationships and improved employee morale. In a recent interview McDonald noted, "In our Quality of Worklife programs, we've got some grand successes that indicate that we can change worker attitudes. I'm excited about these possibilities" (Witzenburg, 1981).

As in health promotion programs, the attitude changes and morale improvement are the core issue. If improved profits are the only goal of quality circles or health programs, the programs are doomed to failure. With greater worker participation, a new respect for all employees emerges. "Most work innovation experts say that the diversity of worker needs must be respected. People should not be pressed into innovative work relationships against their will. . . . If a work improvement aims only at improving productivity, it quickly loses worker support. But a program that has only a vague plan of making workers feel better about themselves is likely to collapse for lack of business perspective. 'Improved job satisfaction and improved productivity go hand in hand'" (*Business Week*, 1981). This last point emerges again and again and is a key factor in planning comprehensive health promotion programs.

Although quality circles have primarily addressed production areas, they have established an important procedure and precedent for employees to become more involved in issues of personal and organizational health care. As the growth of quality circles and health promotion programs converges, there is fertile ground for innovation.

The mutuality needed in both these efforts is an effective rebuttal to critics of corporate health promotion programs who dismiss them as exploitation of employees for greater productivity and profit, or "elitist." One aspect of health programs frequently cited as elitist is "eligibility restrictions." When resources are limited, many programs start with top executives in the corporate headquarters, but not always. Sometimes salaried employees are admitted prior to hourly-wage earners, as in the Kimberly-Clark program. High-risk groups can have priority, as in the Ford Motor Company cardiovascular risk screening in the Dearborn, Michigan, world headquarters. Few programs include dependents or retirees. Limited. resources will always force some restrictions, for business organizations are not primarily in the health care business. Nevertheless, within the inevitable financial restraints, the programs cited here constitute sincere and effective efforts to improve individual and organizational health in the workplace for mutual benefit. Although scientific inquiry usually proceeds by examining the average results of numerous studies, the study of unique or exemplary case histories is useful in a new area such as health promotion programs. At these early stages of a rapidly evolving field the study of unique programs may yield guidelines for future programs. In an area of inquiry far removed from organizational health promotion programs, astronomer Halton Arp has stated, "Any number of cases may obey the red shift distance relationship, but only one case is necessary to establish the existence of a new phenomenon." Studying coal will yield only limited information about diamonds, and observing piano teachers tells us little about concert pianists. Even if only one corporate program, and there are many more than that, yields a new direction in individual and organizational health, it needs to be respected and watched.

NATIONAL POLICY: AT THE OUTER LIMITS

Personal health, health in the workplace, and organizational health policies are embedded in larger cultural, political, and environmental issues. In Chapter I we saw these issues as Sphere IV. Since the variables here are virtually infinite, we can address only a few determinants which have a direct impact upon the workplace. Among these influences are national and state government legislation regarding occupational health and safety, toxic substance exposure, and environmental impacts; enforcement of these same laws; overall fluctuations in the economy; legal precedents and lawsuits; and the renewed and growing menace of nuclear armaments. Clearly, these issues undergo a wide range of fluctuation and are generally not amenable to individual or even organizational influence except through the voting and legislative process. For these reasons such determinants are only briefly considered, as a measure not of their importance but of their magnitude.

During 1980, Julius B. Richmond, Assistant Secretary for Health and the Surgeon General, issued an extremely important document entitled *Promoting Health—Preventing Disease: Objectives for the Nation.* In the preface to this document, Richmond stated: "Our national strategy for achieving further improvements in the health of Americans was established in *Healthy People,* a document that notes our accomplishments in prevention, identifies the major health problems, and sets national goals for reducing death and disability. This volume sets out specific and measurable objectives for fifteen priority areas that are key to achieving our national health aspirations." Among the fifteen areas he enumerated were "Toxic Agent Control," "Occupational Safety and Health," and "Accident Prevention and Injury Control." For each of these major categories the report cites the existing statistics, projects trends, states the necessary preventive measures and objectives for the year 1990, and cites the specific national and state agencies and programs designed to achieve these ends. If anyone thinks that the case for prevention and health promotion through improvement of behavioral and environmental conditions in the workplace has been overstated, even a cursory reading of this document will convince the reader otherwise. For example, under the section on "Occupational Safety and Health," the report states: "Each year 100,000 Americans die from occupational illnesses; nearly 400,000 new cases of occupational diseases are recognized annually . . . occupational exposure . . . can produce various problems such as lung disease, cancers, sensory loss, skin disorders, degenerative diseases in a number of vital organ systems, birth defects or genetic damage . . . increase the frequency of stillbirths, spontaneous abortions, reduced fertility, and sterility." Even these appalling statistics are based upon "the presently inadequate reporting of occupational disease." While the statistics are clear, the proposed measures to curtail them are not. On the positive side is the unequivocal support of the former Secretary of Health and Human

Services Richard S. Schweiker for "making wellness instead of sickness our top priority." Recently, Schweiker proposed the creation of an Office of Preventive Health Applications of Research (Sun, 1982) to conduct applied research in disease prevention. Whether or not that office will ever be created depends largely upon political pressures, and attitudes among scientists about basic versus applied research. On the negative side are the biases of the current administration and the weakening and dismantling of OSHA and other programs.

Although the objectives stated in *Promoting Health—Preventing Disease* are laudable, their actual implementation is precarious at best. For anyone concerned about the enormous impact of national and state legislation upon overall health and health in the workplace, this document is essential reading. Priorities and programs have been stated but whether or not they will be carried out will be determined by individuals and organizations acting in concert through elected representatives. Legislative action is often frustrating but it is vital if efforts in the other three spheres—individual, group and corporate— are not to be undermined. Only concerted education will equip workers and the groups which speak for them to influence public policy. Lawrence W. Green, director of the U.S. Office of Health Information, Health Promotion and Physical Fitness and Sports Medicine in Washington, D.C., writes of the need for an informed citizenry:

> Now what benefits do people want in life? This is where values come to play so prominently and where I think it is so dangerous for national government in particular or any federal or highly centralized government to try to make these decisions for people. This is where I believe health education has its largest role to play: helping people to understand risk-benefit ratios, helping young children to think in probabilistic terms, helping people to sort out the competing risks and competing values that they have to assess in making decisions in their daily lives. (*Green, 1979*)

The vital element here is active participation by individuals and organizations based upon informed choice.

National policy regarding toxic exposures has become increasingly less stringent. Overall, the Environmental Protection Agency has pursued a policy which "will tolerate a higher cancer incidence and create a framework that will allow much greater risks in the future" (Marshall, 1982b). A statistical risk of cancer in 1 per 10,000 people rather than the previous level of 1 per 1,000,000 people has been allowed in many cases. Several recent court decisions have indicated that this national policy has resulted in the relaxing of standards for fungicides used widely on fruits, vegetables, grains, nuts, and other edibles; the use of an ant poison with a half-life of twelve years and reaching high proportions in meat and milk; introduction of an insecticide formerly used on cotton which will allow for a "500 percent expansion of the permethrin market" and which will be found in meats, milk, eggs, broccoli, brussel sprouts, cabbage, lettuce, pears, potatoes, and many other foodstuffs; and a pesticide which is concentrated in Great Lakes fish to the point where "the cancer risk from exposure to toxaphene through eating fish in the Mississippi Delta is greater than 1 in 100" (Marshall, 1982b). The same article, in *Science,* concluded, "To the critics, these policies amount to a shift from a preventive stance to one of limiting damage after it has appeared. They refer to the emphasis on human data as 'counting dead bodies.' This is a poor way to deal with carcinogens . . . for 20 years may elapse between exposure to a carcinogen and the appearance of the disease."

National policies such as these will increase the likelihood of another Love Canal incident. There is increasing concern over the EPA easing of regulations on lead exposure. This is alarming because "the accumulating evidence suggests that lead has a devastating effect on the central nervous system at concentrations that only 20 years ago were thought safe" (Marshall, 1982a). Most alarming is the effects upon children. Several researchers have suggested that the lead from automobile exhausts contributes to a "silent epidemic" of lead toxicity. In the midst of EPA firings and political complexities these issues will not be readily resolved and can be influenced by groups of individual voters, environmental organizations, and corporations which can exert influence in this process.

Despite the laxity of national health policies, individual workers and groups of employees are not helpless, especially when they resort to legal action through the courts. Drawn from the cases of the Public Citizen Health Research Group in Washington, D.C., are numerous instances in which aggregates of workers did successfully impact upon national and corporate policies through active participation in the proceedings of the Occupational Safety and Health Review Commission:

1. The American Cyanamid plant in Fort Worth, Texas, manufactured chemicals which are used in the production of gasoline. Many of the chemicals used at this plant are known to be hazardous to worker health. . . . In 1977, the Oil, Chemical and Atomic Workers International Union and its Local 4-208 filed a complaint with OSHA on behalf of the workers at the plant. Upon inspection of the plant OSHA found that the vanadium oxide dust levels in the plant violated the OSHA standard. This was deemed a serious violation because the exposure represented an imminent danger to the workers . . . the case clearly exemplifies that worker participation is essential if the health and safety hazards of workplaces are to be eliminated.

2. The Ford Motor Company metal-stamping plant in Chicago Heights, Illinois, produces car parts. On March 6, 1973, OSHA inspectors issued a citation to Ford charging that noise levels in the plant were above the OSHA standard and presented a hazard to employees. (Excessive noise can cause loss of hearing, mental and emotional disturbances, and neurologic damage.) . . . the Commission set a two-year abatement period. Without worker involvement, however, no abatement period would have been set.

3. The General Electric Company has a large industrial complex in Schenectady, New York. On March 22, 1973, the Steam Turbine–Generator Products Division was cited by OSHA inspectors for a number of safety violations involving lack of eye protection for workers, unsafe ladders, and dangerous elevated work platforms. . . . In proceedings before the Commission, employees were able to prove that General Electric had knowledge of the hazards and had committed them previously. Based on employee evidence of this type, the Commission raised the penalties from $1650 to $7400. (*Goldberg et al., 1981*)

Each of these cases demonstrates that group action can have a clear impact upon corporate practices and, through the review and judiciary process, can alter the implementation of national policies. Lawsuits by over 16,500 workers exposed to asbestos resulted in the

Manville Corporation's declaring bankruptcy. Litigation is ongoing in this instance, but it is a clear indication that group action can affect a major corporation, one which ranked 181 among the Fortune 500 with a net worth of greater than a billion dollars.

In 1982, the Office of Technology Assessment (OTA) in Washington, D.C., released testimony indicating that fifty-nine major corporations were planning to start some form of "genetic testing" of employees in the near future, with six of them already engaged in such practices. Genetic screening seeks out genetic deficiencies that render individuals vulnerable to certain chemicals. At this point there are only a few definitive instances, such as the sickle cell trait which occurs primarily among minority groups. The use of such assessment has stirred a host of legal, ethical, and national policy issues. According to a report in *Science,* "Although companies are by no means rushing into the business of genetic screening, many critics believe they are attracted to it as an alternative to cleaning up the workplace" (Holden, 1982). This proposed practice of weeding out susceptible workers rather than taking the necessary steps to improve environmental safety is a dangerous trend. Toxicologist Samuel Epstein of the University of Illinois has observed, "Companies nowadays are getting very interested in preventive medicine and trying to educate workers on the dangers of alcohol, smoking, overeating, and lack of exercise. But some see this as evading their real responsibilities and trying to 'blame the victim'" (Holden, 1982). Genetic screening is a means of eliminating the victim. Most observers agree that genetic screening is not likely to be widespread primarily because it would make companies susceptible to lawsuits by workers. Compounding the scientific controversy are issues of confidentiality, the proper use of such data, possible discrimination in the workplace, and the use of human subjects in research. These issues are matters of national policy and legal precedent and cannot be solved within one company.

Although present national policy tends toward decreasing environmental protection and increasing toxic exposure in the workplace, one recent court decision has had a positive impact. On May 14, 1982, the U.S. Court of Appeals of the District of Columbia handed down a decision with a "revolutionary impact" upon environmental law. That decision was in a case involving the residents of Three Mile Island, who pressed a suit to prevent starting up an idle nuclear reactor on TMI. The U.S. Court of Appeals supported their suit and said that the Nuclear Regulatory Commission (NRC) must "view psychological stress among Three Mile Island residents as a form of nuclear power pollution" (Marshall, 1982b). This lawsuit was brought by a group of citizens entitled People Against Nuclear Energy (PANE) who based their suit upon the public's perception of the nuclear dangers rather than on the usual analysis of the physical dangers. Also, PANE rejected the argument that expert estimates of risk should outweigh popular feelings. On both counts, PANE won its case and the results of this decision have far-reaching implications for national policy and legal proceedings concerning environmental hazards. Such a decision represents the first time that the National Environmental Protection Act was interpreted to cover "psychological health." The majority opinion of the court rejected the NRC position of discounting the stress arguments, noting that such a stance "ignores the simple fact that effects on psychological health are effects on the health of human beings. . . . We conclude that in the context of EPA, health encompasses psychological health" (Marshall, 1982b). Furthermore, the court did try to distinguish between "true psychological stress" such as found at TMI and the instances of "socioeconomic anxieties" that have been traditionally considered in cases involving federal housing projects and prison construction. They defined stress as "post-traumatic anxieties, accompanied by physical effects and caused by fears of recurring catastrophe" (Marshall, 1982b). That definition could and will be applied to instances in the workplace involving toxic substance exposure, since the court ruled that the EPA is now required to "assess how people perceive and react to the risk . . . a standard will depend largely on how much fear is worked up, from whatever source, rather than how serious the danger actually is" (Marshall, 1982b). Actually the dissenting opinion was not in disagreement over the basic court decision but objected that the decision did not go far enough. Predictably, the NRC and the TMI utility company have appealed the decision, and the final judgment is far from over.

Unemployment is another area where health can be influenced by national policy. The human impact has been drawn by Studs Terkel in *Hard Times* (1978):

True, there was a sharing among many of the dispossessed, but, at close quarters, frustration became, at times, violence, and violence turned inward. Thus, sons and fathers fell away, one from the other. And the mother, seeking work, said nothing. Outside forces, except to the more articulate and political rebels, were in some vague way responsible, but not really. It was a personal guilt.

During periods of economic slump there is a marked increase in murder, suicide, mental illness, heart disease, alcoholism, divorce, domestic violence, family fights, and child abuse. M. Harvey Brenner, sociologist at Johns Hopkins University, has predicted from his research that, "at least 100,000 Americans will die from social stress caused by this recession . . . every 1% jump in the unemployment rate is associated with an additional 36,887 total deaths (20,440 from cardiovascular diseases, 495 from cirrhosis of the liver, 920 suicides, 648 homicides) and 4,227 first admissions to state mental hospitals, and 3,340 admissions to state prisons" (Brenner, 1979). On a more individual basis, Brenner noted that "The suddenly-idle hands blamed themselves, rather than society. True, there were hunger marches and protestations to City Hall and Washington, but the millions experienced a private kind of shame when the pink slip came. No matter that others suffered the same fate, the inner voice whispered, 'I'm a failure'" (1973). The tie between unemployment and suicide is so evident that the nation's suicide rate is probably the single most important sign of economic trouble. A study by Stanley Cobbon of Brown University and Stanislav Karl of Yale University indicated a suicide rate thirty times the national average in communities hard hit by layoffs (1980).

Brenner's work drew criticism on a number of scores, primarily objections about flawed methodology. However, over the last decade a consensus has emerged that ". . . no doubt remains that [Brenner's] fundamental hypothesis . . . that there is an association between macro-economic change and change in the aggregate measures of social pathology . . . has been validated. There is absolutely no debate . . . that unemployment provokes or uncovers physical and mental illness" (Ferman, 1982). This point is important because unemployment is not so much the direct cause of disease and disability as it is the "straw that breaks the camel's back" and aggravates or intensifies existing disorders. One startling study of laid-off workers indicated that men who got new jobs but later underwent repeated layoffs and rehiring actually fare worse in mental and physical health than those who never "succeeded" in finding other employment.

Long-term, chronic, unresolvable stress elicits feelings of helplessness which compound the initial stress to dangerous levels. From a series of interviews with medical directors of community mental health centers, a professional journal found a clear link between periods of recession and numerous forms of psychological and physical illness, at all economic levels (*Behavioral Medicine,* 1980b). *Clinical Psychiatry News* predicts that "the coming decade will be marked by escalating conflict among the demands of personal, family, and work life" and furthermore that the link between workplace stress and subsequent illness becomes "more apparent in recessions" (1980).

Women are equally at risk under an adverse economy. Preliminary data based upon the long-term Framingham Study and data from National Heart, Lung and Blood Institute (Haynes and Feinlieb, 1980) indicate that working mothers are most adversely affected by economic recession, and show an increased incidence of heart disease. Finally, it appears that Mondays are hazardous to your health: Canadian researchers at the University of Manitoba reviewed the cases of 4,000 men with medical histories dating back to 1948. Of the 63 men who died suddenly of a heart attack, 22 of them, or one third, died on a Monday. Moreover, a full 75 percent of deaths from all causes occurred on Mondays. Reviewing these findings, physician Simon W. Rabkin noted that, "Reintroductions to occupational stress, activity, or pollutants after a weekend respite may be factors precipitating the arrhythmias that are the presumed basis for sudden death" (Rabkin, Mathewson, and Tate, 1980). Economic and psychobiological fluctuations interact, with a profound and immediate impact upon health in the workplace.

When uncontrollable factors such as these penetrate to the individual, then personal health practices as well as social and workplace support groups become more rather than less important. It is well documented and therefore predictable that unemployed individuals with few social supports are more likely than other people to develop minor and major illness. Of primary importance is the social support of that person's immediate family. Through interviews, several researchers have found that workers who managed their unemployment well, always reported that regular, open communication with other family members helped them the most. Since the family itself is frequently under great strain, this resource may not be available for many unemployed people and some measure of professional counseling can be helpful for individuals and groups of employees prior to layoff as well as during several identifiable crisis periods following the loss of a job. Several crisis points where assistance is possible have been identified by Louis Ferman of the University of Michigan:

1) *The Job Loss Period;* where counseling, job-seeking services and possibly therapy will be required, 2) *The Exhaustion of Benefits Period;* where the real crisis for many workers begins, characterized by interpersonal distress in the family, 3) *The Intensive Job-Seeking Period;* frequently the most traumatic period, when the worker faces the reality of his / her relative value in the labor force; 4) *Dropping Out of the Labor Force;* many workers choose to exit the job market at this point, and 5) *The Adjustment of the New Job;* at least half of those reemployed will take jobs at lower pay and status than their former jobs, requiring a lifestyle adjustment. (*Adapted from Ferman, 1982*)

At each of the five stages of the unemployment cycle, there are many available services including individual counseling, family casework, job search and placement services, medical care, retraining and skill development programs, and social support systems among unemployed workers. Clearly the best stage in which to initiate such services is prior to termination, where employers could initiate a job phase-out with time allocated to the above services. Such an approach is consistent with some ongoing models of preretirement programs and acknowledges the human values amid economic fluctuations. However, even though such measures can alleviate some of the negative impact, that does not lessen the profound responsibility of our political representatives when unemployment is part of a deliberate policy to curb inflation; the toll in disease and disability must be weighed into the decision.

Every modern nation is subject to these pressures, which are reflected in the health of their populations. Recently there are indications of a sharp rise in coronary heart disease and deaths in the Soviet Union. Similar trends have been noted in China and Japan as well. In an editorial letter following an excellent article on "Rising Death Rates in the Soviet Union" in the *New England Journal of Medicine* (1981), physician Richard Cooper suggests some underlying causes. After examining his statistics, Cooper ventured into social commentary: "The economic forces that encourage production for profit rather than production for need also present obstacles to progress in public health. Despite some moderate improvement in recent years, the tobacco, alcohol, and food industries—not to mention the automobile industry, occupational hazards, and environmental pollution—are the major forces for ill health in our society. Is not the same thing happening in the Soviet Union?" (Cooper, 1981b). Issues such as these turn on the question of values once again. General Motors may need to question whether their Quality of Worklife program is contradicted by their lobbying for the abandonment of certain environmental protection measures, or the R. J. Reynolds Company of Winston-Salem may need to look at their excellent Health Maintenance Organization facilities in North Carolina next to their lobbying efforts which try to deny the unequivocally lethal consequences of cigarette smoking.

These concerns may be indicative of the emergence of a new epoch. Those individuals and organizations which remain flexible and adapt will survive, those that do not will perish. Modern philosophers, historians, and scientists have speculated that the current crises in energy, economics, geopolitics, corporations, planetary ecology, and social systems are indicative of the disintegration of an ancient order at the emergence of the twenty-first century. For many individuals and organizations, only the chaos and disintegration is evident, but that may be the shortsighted view. Among the multitude of manifestations of this emergence into the twenty-first century is the major cultural phenomenon of the women's movement, the emergence of the Southern Hemisphere nations with a demand to develop in their own indigenous manner, a renewed antinuclear movement with Helen Caldicott decrying nuclear arsenals and inefficient nuclear power stations. Each of the separate elements of this next century have not coalesced into a coherent scientific or cultural perspective, but the trend is inexorable. As a consequence of the magnificent achievement of the Industrial Revolution emerged the image of workers as interchangeable and disposable parts of a great machine. This image is being replaced by the emerging, holistic model of dynamic, interconnected systems. In the words of physicist James Jeans, "the universe begins to look more like a great thought than a great machine." Within this context, the interdependence of ecological, human, and workplace environments needs to be respected and enhanced for the mutual benefit of individuals and organizations.

CHAPTER V

Healthy People in Healthy Places

Good health is good business. Health promotion programs in the workplace are not a panacea, but the weight of evidence is that such programs improve both the health and productivity of individuals and organizations. The most fundamental element in any program is the voluntary participation of each individual who wishes to extend his or her personal health promotion practices into the workplace, where people spend most of their adult lives. Health promotion must extend into many areas beyond the medical care system. According to Richard L. Pyle of the University of Massachusetts, "It is unrealistic to expect significant progress given the statistics of the very limited time of exposure doctors have with patients and the excessive demands on them for the traditional services they provide. . . . The shift in emphasis toward better lifestyles and away from remedial medicine must be led by other factions of society than the medical field" (1979b). Willis Goldbeck and his colleagues have concluded, "While it is fair to characterize the United States medical system as the world's best, it is also fair to say that it was not designed to keep any of us healthy. Therefore, many large employers are in the forefront of the health promotion movement as their recognition grows that disease prevention, a healthy workforce, and responsible cost management are inextricably linked" (Weinberg, Kiefhaber, and Goldbeck, 1980). Due to the pressures of exorbitant medical costs to large organizations, this relatively straightforward equation has been recognized and acted upon with significant success.

HEALTH AND THE BOTTOM LINE

Historically, the involvement of large organizations in the health care of their employees has been minimal and has consisted largely of their investment in "health" insurance. The cost of this, however, was not minimal. It was estimated to be $42 billion in 1978 by the United States Commerce Department. There are a few instances of more direct, corporate involvement in medical care, but these have been considered as anomalies. Following World War II, industrialist Henry J. Kaiser began to develop the first Health Maintenance Organization, a prepaid group practice, and this has emerged as the largest private, nonprofit, direct service program in the world, providing care to over four million people. Similarly, the Gillette Company began a health care program for its employees more than thirty years ago. With these few exceptions, most organizations have limited their involvement to treating work-related accidents. Even this effort was mainly in response to the labor union movement. This situation is changing. During a 1981 speech to the National Industry Council for HMO Development, Robert Burnett, the chief executive officer of the $400-million-a-year Meredith publishing company, stated, "What's the average CEO's information quotient on the subject of health-care costs? Somewhere in the area of 0 to 5 on a scale of 100." A somewhat more optimistic assessment was given by David A. Winston, chairman of a Health and Human Services task force: "On a scale of 1 to 100, I would rank corporate interest in health policy issues 25, but moving up rapidly" (Iglehart, 1982). It is this trajectory which is most encouraging.

There are two driving forces behind this trend. Most evident is the economic imperative. In a recent issue of the *New England Journal of Medicine,* Willis Goldbeck stated, "It is very important to recognize that you can purchase health care in precisely the way you purchase any other product . . . tough policy and value decisions need to be made, and economic leverage must be brought to bear . . . remember that you are using your stockholders' money, and your profits to pay for health care that is not really needed. That's what it really comes down to, and in this era of limited resources none of us can afford that kind of waste" (Iglehart, 1982). Later in the same article, Robert Burnett reflected upon his involvement in launching an HMO in Des Moines for his company. That effort failed largely due to resistance of the medical community, but it is clear that Burnett and other top executives recognize the necessity of such reforms and intend to pursue them further. According to Burnett, "the tragedy is that I can make more money for the corporation and its stockholders in the next three or four or five years . . . by doing something effective in the way of cost control than I can by selling . . . every dollar of health care cost that's saved goes to the bottom line." More and more organizations will be compelled to take a serious role in health promotion for their own economic interests.

This trend is of great significance for providers of health care, although the implications are frequently overlooked. One observer has drawn a fascinating analogy between the railroad business and the medical care business. In the early 1900s the railroads were at a peak of efficiency with solid investments and a national system of effective transportation. Now the railroads consist of abandoned lines and empty stations, and are essentially bankrupt. Although many factors contributed to this downfall, Gary J. Adamson of the Swedish Medical Center in Colorado has hypothesized that "one major element that is the root cause of the railroads' demise: railroads came to see themselves as being in the railroad business rather than in the transportation business" (1981). As new transportation developed and cultural styles shifted, the railroads failed to adapt and suffered the fate of the survival of the fittest. By analogy, Adamson observes that "the medical field today is precisely in the same position that the railroads were during the early 1900's." Unless health professionals realize that individuals, corporations, and organizations are becoming more concerned about the business of health than the business of disease, it is very likely that they will occupy a much less predominant position in the future. This is particularly true in light of the fact that any work organization is more concerned about its product. Disease management or health promotion per se is not their concern except as it affects performance and productivity. In some communities the organizations and corporations which employ large numbers of people could emerge in the future as the most potent providers of health resources.

Within a corporate framework, health promotion programs must confront certain basic financial realities. "Simple economic realities must also be considered when confronting the approach for 100,000 employees averaging $10,000 annually as against 100 executives averaging annual salaries of $100,000. This is not to be interpreted as less concern for the well-being of lower level personnel—their not having private offices does not reflect less concern, but rather a different status and function" (Pyle, 1979a). Whether or not health promotion programs are a voluntary gesture of sincere social conscience and responsibility, they must also meet the rigors of private enterprise economics. They must be at least self-sustaining, and even profitable, if they are not to disappear. It is highly unlikely that health promotion programs will be spontaneously generated from within the medical care system, national or state government, or the already overburdened school systems, and that leaves only a few other settings such as universities and the private business sector. Although there are excellent university-based programs at the Universities of Wisconsin, Minnesota, North Carolina, and California at Berkeley, they do not represent the range of ages and occupations as in business and industry.

However, within the business environment, health promotion programs must meet the same criteria for support and continuation that all other budgets must meet. Richard L. Pyle has suggested a way of evaluating the cost / benefit results of such programs. This is done in three stages: (1) short-term measures of "primary value to individual participants" (3 to 4 months) including physiological measures such as blood pressure, coronary risk factors such as smoking cessation, and health hazard appraisals or lifestyle questionnaires; (2) intermediate measures (1 year) of "primary value to the management of the department involved" including absenteeism, attitude, and morale of group, self-confidence and self-image of individuals, plus longer-term monitoring of the previous short-term measures; and (3) long-term (minimum 3 to 5 years) changes of value to corporate management, such as impacts upon medical costs, insurance factors, productivity indicators, and overall organizational effectiveness (Pyle, 1979b). Many efforts at health promotion and wellness programs have failed because of their neglect of these very real concerns. If health promotion is to move beyond individual efforts and emerge as a priority in organizational and governmental settings, then these factors need to be taken into account. From business, health promotion programs can learn a great deal about goal setting, management by objectives, performance assessment, and structured efforts toward a specific goal. From health promotion programs, business can learn to respect attitudes, morale, fitness, job satisfaction, and the human dimension of any goal.

In the future we might see a health-status accounting as an integral part of the corporations' fiscal statement. These "health accounts" would:

> . . . specify how much each firm is paying for health benefits, what the corporation spends on occupational health and safety

programs, on physical fitness activities and on employee and community health education and what the corporation does about smoking on the job and about vending machines with junk food, cigarettes, or soft drinks. (*Ng et al., 1978*)

Such an accounting system would serve to keep the goal of health promotion and its costs and benefits in clear view. It is increasingly ineffective to isolate health care to the health department of a corporation. Most of the existing programs are relatively isolated from the entire context of the corporation. The result is that "coffee breaks," with their deleterious effects of excessive caffeine upon the central nervous system and cardiopulmonary functions, exist side by side with jogging programs; stress-provoking working conditions and faulty interpersonal communications compete with stress management programs; corporate dining rooms and vending machines supplying excessive amounts of refined carbohydrates undercut both dietary and exercise programs; and so on. Because of such contradictions, isolated and limited programs are less effective, cost more, and result in fewer savings than comprehensive programs which subtly alter the overall organization in many dimensions.

MODEL HEALTH PROMOTION PROGRAMS

The following descriptions are not intended to be program evaluations. There are little if any data currently available, and most evaluations to date are little more than impressionistic opinions. There is one excellent publication entitled *Managing Health Promotion in the Workplace: Guidelines for Implementation and Evaluation* (1982), by Rebecca S. Parkinson and her associates from various government and private organizations. There are brief descriptions of seventeen programs, some of which are discussed here, as well as background papers and guidelines for the development of health promotion programs in the workplace. For any individual or organization seriously considering the implementation of such a program, this book offers professional and exacting state-of-the-art preparation. Systematic evaluations by organizations themselves as well as outside agencies, such as the Washington Business Group on Health or Metropolitan Life, are currently under way and will provide a future basis for soundly based evaluations, but results are years away.

XEROX CORPORATION

Perhaps the most frequently cited example of a comprehensive health promotion program is that of Xerox Corporation. Among the many influences which gave rise to this health promotion program was the knowledge that Xerox spends more than $58 million annually on insurance and medical premiums. It estimates the loss of an executive who suffers a fatal heart attack at age 49 costs the company $600,000. Xerox announced its program called the Xerox Health Management Program (XHMP), which is presently under the direction of George Pfeiffer, program manager in Webster, New York. Since its inception in 1967, the facilities have grown in range from 4,000 square feet to over 35,000 square feet in response to different employee population sizes and facility usage. All of the centers are equipped with a range of exercise equipment from bicycle ergometers to rowing machines. At the more elaborate centers are full gymnasiums, swimming pools, and racquetball courts. Administratively, each center is usually under the management of personnel services and an "annual participation fee" is required of all employees ranging from $80 to $200. In addition to these facilities, the Xerox Employee Assistance Program (XEAP) provides counseling and referral services to both employees and family members in areas such as marital counseling, substance abuse, and financial counseling.

From the program description, it is "a preventive-maintenance approach to fitness through regular aerobic exercises and common-sense lifestyle. It does not offer any new exercises, diets, gimmicks, mail-order gadgets or shortcuts to fitness and health. . . . We view the . . . program as a way to keep both our employees and our company in top shape" (Pfeiffer, 1983). This is not a departure for the company, for Xerox has a reputation for a long-standing commitment to the idea that a fit employee is more productive (Arnold, 1978). There are now eleven fitness centers in the United States and one abroad. Also, the program has been introduced with reduced facilities at twenty Xerox facilities. At present the largest facility is a $3.5 million complex in Leesburg, Virginia. Another active branch is in Rochester, New York, under direction of Jim Post, who is the program director of their Executive Fitness Program. In an open letter Post described the program as "one major step on behalf of our employees and their families toward the holistic concept to better health" (1980).

The Xerox Health Management Program is primarily oriented toward self-help and uses health education to promote a healthy lifestyle through a health promotion packet which is detailed below, audiovisual presentations, special events, and periodic workshops. This program is designed to address over 67,000 employees and family members and has proved to be successful in meeting that objective. One of the strongest dimensions of the program is that XHMP has trained over 250 volunteer team leaders, who act as facilitators within their own work group at local worksites. According to the program description, "Team Leaders volunteer twelve hours a month to promote and organize activities within their local office. For example, a Team Leader may organize fun runs, guest speakers on stress and nutrition, schedule CPR training, besides disseminating information provided by the XHMP staff. In turn, XHMP attempts to establish a relationship with established community agencies (i.e., American Heart Association, American Red Cross, American Cancer Society, and American Lung Association) to help the local Team Leader in local programming" (Pfeiffer, 1983). Use of available community resources is an important aspect of any successful health promotion program. Furthermore, the Xerox program is completely voluntary and has taken basic health information and presented it in an "upbeat" manner with the theme "Take Charge of Your Life." The basic message is that quality of life may lead to quantity as well. As a model of future corporation-based Health Promotion Organizations, the Xerox undertaking is an excellent prototype.

Under the Xerox health program the voluntary participants are given three booklets: *Take Charge of Your Life: The Road to Better Health and Happier Lifestyles; Fitbook;* and the book *Take Care of Yourself* (Vickery and Fries, 1976), which addresses the medical self-care dimension. Although there is overlap in the content of each booklet, each of them emphasizes one aspect of optimum health. *Take Charge of Your Life* introduces the program and provides specific assessments and forms for participants to evaluate their current health status, particularly cardiovascular risk factors. Included are an excellent self-administered series of evaluations including: (1) a cardiovascular disease risk-factor estimate based on numerical values for certain answers to a series of fifteen questions resembling a credit card application form; (2) a "step test" modeled after the aerobic approach of Kenneth Cooper; (3) a self-administered body composition test to determine the percentage of body weight which is fat; and (4) a joint flexibility exercise and evaluation. Each is clearly described, with illustrative photographs and practical record-keeping forms. The booklet is undoubtedly the result of a great deal of research and organization, and the results are most impressive. Also, the simplicity and lack of gimmicks are a refreshing departure from the plethora of "how to" books currently being marketed. In the health promotion field, most of the necessary information is known; what remains is its unequivocal presentation and implementation, and that is precisely what the Xerox program accomplishes. *Take Charge of Your Life* emphasizes warm-up exercises with illustrations for seven basic stretching exercises. Additionally, the brochure provides practical information concerning heart-rate protocols for endurance training, instructions for cool-down periods, a list of "Six Do's and Don'ts of a Good Workout," and information regarding personal athletic equipment. Again each potentially complex topic is covered clearly and without exaggerated claims.

Of all the program materials, *Fitbook* is the most comprehensive. It includes a sequence of four "modules." Module one concerns the warm-up exercises previously noted in *Take Charge of Your Life*. Module two focuses on the "target pulse protocol" and the basic principles of aerobic exercise. In module two are specific instructions for the safe development of an aerobic exercise program in jogging, cycling, swimming, and rope skipping. Module three contains "developmental exercises" which are designed to develop strength, flexibility, and endurance for major muscle groups. Module four contains illustrations of exercises appropriate for a five-minute cool-down period as well as seven exercises specific to strengthening and preserving the integrity of the back. Among the other topics addressed in the booklet are smoking, drugs and alcohol, caffeine consumption, nutrition and weight control, and relaxation exercises. The section on stress and relaxation is quite comprehensive. It contains relaxation procedures similar to those detailed in *Mind as Healer, Mind as Slayer* (Pelletier, 1977). Overall, the program is comprehensive and presented with extraordinary clarity. Many elements of the program are drawn from the *Canadian Fit Kit* (1980), which is a 33⅓ rpm record and exercise charts illustrating an aerobic exercise program.

Recently the Xerox program has been revised and expanded. According to George Pfeiffer, "The *Fitbook* has been expanded in a number of areas: aerobic alternatives, environmental considerations, and injury index" (1983). Under the heading of "aerobic alternatives," the descriptions of the activities, their benefits, and potential sources of injury have been extended to include cross-country skiing, Alpine skiing, racquetball, handball, squash, skating, dancing, rowing, and even basketball and tennis, which are more limited in aerobic conditioning due to their sporadic pacing. Under "environmental considerations" are topics such as heat versus cold, and a discussion of heat exhaustion and heat stroke. The most significant addition to the program is the inclusion of a "Why Risk It" health risk evaluation, with self-administered assessments enabling an individual to determine his or her above-average health risk and reduce that risk accordingly. Such assessments are based upon the Health Hazard Appraisal System detailed in *Holistic Medicine* (Pelletier, 1979) and upon later commercial forms including the program of Control Data Corporation discussed later in this chapter. Essentially the risk assessment is a series of questions which an individual answers to obtain information on his or her present health status. Results are then compared with those of other people of comparable age, sex, and race to create tables which project expected mortality rates in the next ten years from automobile accidents to cancer and heart disease. A person is given an "appraised health age" which reflects this greater or lesser health risk.

Beyond the risk assessment the Xerox "Why Risk It" program includes two excellent components in the form of: "(1) personalized strategy sheets which give you basic 'how to's' and resources to help you achieve your health targets; and (2) goal contracts: a systematic approach to help you prioritize your goals and set realistic schedules for achieving them" (Pfeiffer, 1983). Even though these assessments and strategy sheets are not unique to the Xerox program, they are particularly clear and well done to make them accessible to employees at all levels. Finally, the basic program has been extended to family members through an excellent newsletter entitled *Take Charge*. Issues of the newsletter have focused upon stress, overeating, and psychological problems, to name but a few areas. Although budget cuts have eliminated home mailings, the payroll stuffers and posters remain as a "coordinated promotion / education process at a low cost" (Pfeiffer, 1983). Overall, the continued growth and comprehensive diversification of the Xerox program is a testimony to its success. Any organization can learn a great deal from the experience and excellent materials comprising the Xerox Health Management Program. Xerox is involved in participation on industry health boards such as the Fairfield-Westchester Business Group on Health, which is a coalition of twenty-one businesses. This coalition employs 4.5 million people nationwide and its "overall goal is to discover successful models that can be introduced worldwide" (Crowley, 1981). With these numbers involved, the impact of a successful model such as the Xerox program cannot be overestimated.

KIMBERLY-CLARK CORPORATION

Kimberly-Clark Corporation of Neenah, Wisconsin, created a $2.5 million facility in 1977 with thirty-five full- and part-time health care personnel including physicians, nurses, counselors, secretaries, and exercise specialists. This facility is a major part of their comprehensive Health Management Program. All of the 2,400 employees at its headquarters building are eligible, and more than 60 percent of those eligible have signed up to take part in the program. Prior to entry into the program, potential participants undergo an extensive, computerized medical history, multiphasic screening, physical examination, and an exercise stress test. After these results are completed, there is a health review with specific recommendations for that individual's program. The medical examinations alone turn up many problems. "Heart disease requiring surgery in five persons. Cancer was detected in six employees. Abnormal treadmill tests, indicating possible risk for heart attack, occurred in about 10 percent of employees" (Dedmon et al., 1979). Similar assessments are an integral aspect of the Xerox program, and in the Johnson & Johnson program discussed in the next section. Of particular interest are cardiovascular risk factors and one medical department screening found "22.6% of males and 14.4% of females had two cardiovascular risk factors, and 4.6% of males and 1.8% of females had three" (Beery, 1981). It appears that virtually every company program has found that at least 10 percent of their employees do have two or more coronary risk factors. When figures reach over 36 percent, as in this instance, the potential benefit to human life and cost-effectiveness begins to become clear. For employees entering the exercise program, the "exercise prescription" is based upon the employee's age, treadmill capacity, the presence of risk factors or known cardiovascular disease, and any orthopedic abnormalities. A special summary form was developed to communicate these results and recommendations to the employee's personal physicians. This is an example of how these programs can reach out into the larger community. According to the results of these assessments and the health review, employees enter various levels of a moderate aerobic exercise program with a diversity of aerobic activities including running on a 100-meter track, swimming in the facility's pool, stationary cycling, aerobic dancing, and water exercise. The facilities are open from 5:00 A.M. to 9:00 P.M., Monday through Friday, and 8:00 A.M. to 5:00 P.M. on Saturday. Ready and convenient access to health facilities is an important dimension of any program. There is also a special program of cardiac rehabilitation using a *Coronary Risk Handbook*. One participant is Steven Samu, a 44-year-old research scientist, who runs 3 miles per day after undergoing open-heart surgery and quips, "Instead of saying goodbye at 48, I may say goodbye at 68. It's a good deal all around—for me and for the company" (Lublin, 1978). That sentiment is echoed many times over throughout Kimberly-Clark and other corporations which have recognized that the health and longevity of their employees are synonymous with corporate health. Kimberly-Clark's program includes other health education programs and activities, including nutrition counseling, smoking control, exercises for low back pain, diet management, and a series under the heading of "self-instruction classes" for the areas of obesity, breast self-examination, and relaxation skills. In the obesity control a significant weight reduction was maintained up to one and a half years after the program was initiated for one high-risk group. Finally, there is an ongoing Employee Assistance Program which has helped "362 employees and 199 family members, a total of 561 persons. Forty-four percent of these were alcohol or drug-related problems, and the rehabilitation rate is 65 percent which should improve" (Beery, 1981). These figures could be translated into savings in lives as well as monetary values.

To date, some limited evaluations have been conducted of the Kimberly-Clark program, and the results are encouraging. In measuring successful outcome there is no widespread agreement as to which yardsticks are to be used. Richard L. Pyle's concept of progressive assessments helps to clarify this confused area. Potential outcome measures include those listed earlier including cost benefits, reduction of risk factors or accidents, less absenteeism, and even basic measures of adherence and continuity of the health promotion programs themselves. For the Kimberly-Clark program, medical director Robert E. Dedmon and his staff have focused primarily upon "short-term" measures of physiological functions. On the first-time retesting of twenty-five employees in the aerobic exercise program for twelve to eighteen months, Dedmon found a reduction in systolic and diastolic blood pressure, in serum triglycerides, and improved treadmill time. Other risk factors such as weight, percentage of body fat, and cholesterol showed no significant changes. Among the less tangible benefits, Dedmon has cited the fact that the "Health Management Program has enhanced Kimberly-Clark's public reputation and has assisted in corporate recruiting efforts" and that for individuals, the physical exercise "significantly improves a subjective sense of well being" (Dedmon et al., 1979). Some critics of health promotion programs imply that economic motivations and benefits to the companies involved are of paramount concern. The preliminary data from the Kimberly-Clark program do not yet support this position. Based upon data, the cost per employee is estimated at $435, including the comprehensive medical examination. Given these figures, Dedmon notes, "Our projections indicate that the overall break-even point for our program will be about 9.5 years (three years for the Employee Assistance Program, and about 6.5 years for the risk factor reduction portion of the program). In about ten years significant annual savings should be achieved" (Dedmon et al., 1979). Health promotion programs do not guarantee short-term or even long-term benefits for the employer, although pilot studies are encouraging. However, there are almost immediate and recognizable benefits to individuals and to company morale.

In looking toward the future of the Kimberly-Clark program and other comparable efforts, Dedmon has come to the same conclusion as many other program directors and researchers. The key problem is not money, or facilities, or even a lack of data but the question of effective motivational efforts to elicit and maintain ongoing involvement. "This [motivational effort] is probably the greatest challenge facing those responsible for these efforts. A variety of incentives have [sic] been tried, including money, achievement awards, health hazard appraisals, insurance premium reductions, subsidized YMCA memberships, films, lectures, seminars, newsletters, and exercise breaks at the worksite. Exercise groups also help reduce attrition by engaging participants in an ongoing activity where they can experience relatively immediate positive results. However, like the fountain of youth, the successful formula has yet to be discovered. Success will probably be achieved only if these programs evolve into cultural changes in eating, exercise, and other habits" (Dedmon et al., 1979). He has also noted that "Indications are such company programs can have significant effect, particularly in view of the increasing age of the work force over the next 20 years" and that "Effectively helping people achieve their normal life expectancy as healthy, motivated and productive citizens is really the bottom line" (Beery, 1981). Programs such as these indicate a genuine concern for the health of individuals in the workplace. Substantial investments have been made with a guarantee of future returns, although that is a realistic and reasonable expectation.

JOHNSON & JOHNSON

Among the programs in major corporations is Johnson & Johnson's Live for Life program. Based in the corporate headquarters in New Brunswick, New Jersey, the program represents one of the most comprehensive worksite health programs in the country. According to Lloyd C. Arnold, the director of the program with a doctorate in education, the program "is a health promotion effort intended eventually for all Johnson & Johnson employees worldwide" and is "designed to encourage employees to follow lifestyles which will result in good health" (1981).

There are several unique characteristics of the program. Employees from all levels of the company participated in a variety of planning committees and surveys to design the program. This vital element of voluntary, participatory involvement in planning and implementation is clearly evident in the results. On that basis alone, employees reported an unprecedented increase in employee morale and job satisfaction. Also, the program not only includes the customary health promotion components such as smoking cessation, stress, weight reduction, and others but goes much further to include environmental changes in the workplace. A company smoking policy has been established and efforts are ongoing to improve the quality of foods in the company cafeteria.

Outlined in a colorful brochure entitled *Live for Life,* the program components include "exercising for life," "eating for health," "kicking the habit" (a smoking-cessation program using support groups as well as a carbon monoxide monitor to measure the effects of this noxious gas), "coping with stress" through yoga, clinical biofeedback, and stress reduction tapes, and "learning about health," which is a broad area including safety in the home, cardiopulmonary resuscitation (CPR) training, as well as a resource center of books and audiovisual materials on health promotion.

Once management support has been clearly committed for the Live for Life program, it is undertaken in a manner which actively involves the employees. As of July 1981 there were approximately 8,000 employees involved in ongoing programs, and that number is increasing. For the program itself, employee participation is voluntary and free of charge. Programs have been initiated at several company offices in Pennsylvania and New Jersey. With few exceptions the time in the program is off company time. Although physical exercise is a major part of the program, there appears to be a refreshing emphasis upon the other major areas of health promotion as well. Entry into the program is based upon a physical examination and lifestyle questionnaire similar to the procedure outlined for the Kimberly-Clark program. After completion of this phase, employees are "invited to attend an entertaining and informative seminar . . . the profile describes your current health status and defines changes you should make to improve your health . . . you have the opportunity to sign up for an action group that concentrates on a specific change in lifestyle . . . as you complete one action group you may sign up for another" (*Live for Life,* 1980).

Johnson & Johnson has undertaken a two-year study to evaluate the cost-effectiveness of these programs. For purposes of the study, four branches of the company are using the complete Live for Life program while five other branches serve as control groups by offering only the initial health screening to their employees on an annual basis. Comparable data in the following areas are being collected from all nine groups on an annual basis after baselines have been determined: (1) "biometric (e.g., blood lipids, blood pressure, body fat, weight, and estimated maximum oxygen uptake)"; (2) "behavioral (e.g., smoking, alcohol use, physical activity, nutrition, healthy heart behavior pattern, job performance and human relations)"; and (3) "attitudinal measures (e.g., general well-being, job satisfaction, company perception and health attitudes)" (Arnold, 1981). Approximately 4,000 employees are involved in the epidemiological study with an equal number of individuals in the program and control sites.

Upon completion of the study it is planned to introduce the full program at the control site and replicate the effective program components. Finally, a systematic cost / benefit analysis is possible since Johnson & Johnson is a self-insured company. Any substantial decrease in "illness care claims" attributable to a positive health program will be of great importance to the employees and company. Among the other measures to be analyzed are "absenteeism, turnover rates, accident rates, and a host of employee and management attitudes toward themselves, their work and one another. It is felt that this is pioneering work in an area where potential benefits have been difficult to measure with existing systems and methods" (Arnold, 1981). Once again it should be pointed out that programs have been undertaken before results are in.

Of all the major health promotion programs, Johnson & Johnson's is one of the few which has released significant though preliminary evaluation data. Results of a one-year study indicate that the participants consistently show greater improvements in major lifestyle areas than controls. These changes include "increases in general well being, as well as increased morale and job satisfaction, and fewer sick days; among the important findings is a substantial reduction (32%) in elevated blood pressure among participants in this nonmedical intervention" (Brown, 1981). Such evaluations will be invaluable as feedback to correct and refine future directions and developments. Since these evaluation efforts are inextricably bound up with controversies such as the diet-heart link, exercise benefits questions, and other concerns which have yet to be definitely resolved despite decades of sophisticated research, it is highly unlikely that these questions will be quickly resolved.

CONTROL DATA CORPORATION

Perhaps the most sophisticated and widespread health promotion program is the StayWell program implemented and marketed by the Life Extension Institute, which is the health care service component of Control Data Corporation in Minneapolis, Minnesota. This program is offered for the employees of Control Data Corporation but is also marketed as a service to other companies and organizations that wish to create a similar program. There are three major components: (1) "StayWell," which is a health self-management program including health screening and assessment, health education, and supervised group activities; (2) "Employee Assistance Programs," which have been used at CDC for over six years to help employees with issues of family problems, sexual difficulties, mental health, financial questions, and a twenty-four-hour telephone hotline; and (3) "Occupational Health Service" addressed to the "problems of maintaining a safe and healthful working environment" through a computer-based system which collects and tracks data on medical and exposure information for individual employees. Overall the stated goal of the StayWell program is to focus "on promising good health and good habits, rather than just subsidizing the costs of illness-related care." Since most of the potential subscribers to such a program are in business, the approach has a management orientation:

> The StayWell program is designed to help you make the most of your health, by managing factors which could adversely affect it. Like all good management techniques, health and lifestyle management requires an understanding of the potential and real problems you face, their short-term and long-term impact, and an action plan to help you solve those problems. And, like all good management plans, health management requires follow-up, evaluation and measurement to assure long-term success. (*Control Data Corporation, 1983*)

These highly structured goals, objectives, and action plans borrowed from management science, enhance the appeal of the program.

Access to the program is available to both employees and spouses. There are four steps: First, applicants complete a "Health Risk Profile" questionnaire which is followed by a "20-minute health screening," which is not synonymous with a physical examination. This Health Risk Profile is a variation of the Health Hazard Appraisal or HHA which was detailed and discussed in Chapter IV of *Holistic Medicine* (Pelletier, 1979) with a sample printout in the Appendix. Many commercial assessments have been marketed based on the early HHA prototype. For individuals who are interested in such assessments, one of the best is available to individuals or organizations at nominal cost from General Health Corporation in Washington, D.C., under the title of *Personal Risk Profile* (Elliott, 1982).

For the second step, a lifestyle consultant compiles the assessment data and meets with the individual employee, with his or her spouse, or in employee groups for approximately one hour to discuss and interpret the profile. At the third phase, a second interview is scheduled with the consultant, in which the habits and lifestyle factors which bear on the identified risks are the focus. It is at this point that the employee and consultant "plan a course of action to accomplish these changes as new and sustained lifestyle habits." This program consists primarily of education in fitness, nutrition and weight control, safety, smoking cessation, stress management, and quality of life. Finally, the employee's progress is the subject of a fourth meeting. Periodic reports help the employee measure his or her progress. Each year, enrolled employees are invited to repeat the Health Risk Profile in order to "objectively help you measure your achievements and provide information to help you plan your goals for the following year." Overall, the StayWell approach is clearly committed to a preventive approach:

> We believe that preventing illness is a sound, sensible, and effective alternative to remedial care. . . . We hope that a strong health promotion program that encourages our employees and their families to do something to keep themselves healthy every day will pay off by helping us all control escalating health care costs caused by avoidable illnesses. (*Control Data Corporation, 1983*)

Up to this point the thrust of the StayWell program falls within Sphere I, which is concerned primarily with individual health promotion activities. Fortunately the program proceeds beyond this limited stage. The StayWell approach provides a clear structure for influencing the overall organization. There are six steps for implementing the program among groups: (1) "Organization Planning," which selects and prepares the resources in a particular workplace; (2) "Data Collection and Evaluation Planning"; (3) "Program Initiation," which involves orientation meetings for management, physicians, and employees to discuss the Health Risk Profiles and screening procedures; (4) "Social Support Initiation," which develops peer support and team building to enhance and sustain individual efforts; (5) "Education and Behavior Change Activities" where groups learn new lifestyle skills in areas such as stress management and nutrition; and (6) "Social Support Activities" to establish networks in the workplace for coordination of groups at each worksite to guide overall implementation.

Two other programs within the Life Extension Institute address the visible hazards of occupational safety, with a particular emphasis upon toxic substance control. Under the title of "Occupational Health Services," one program "helps organizations to detect and respond to problems that may result from increasingly complex technology, regulations, and potentially toxic materials." The other program is the "Compliance Assistance Services" which "gather and organize medical and exposure information concerning each employee and the work environment." This latter program is quite sophisticated and is built around a computer-based record-keeping and surveillance system, tailored to meet the needs of both small and large business environments. Given the fact that Control Data Corporation is essentially a computer firm, the means to conduct such studies are well within their reach. They will be of great significance since the interventions are fairly structured, uniform within settings, and yet conducted in a variety of organizations. Outcome studies based upon such a data base will be increasingly important in the development of health promotion programs in the workplace.

Clearly the StayWell program of Control Data Corporation is a sophisticated and well-developed approach to health promotion and one which addresses the multiple levels within organizations. Even within such a comprehensive approach, however, there are limits since some companies find that the structure is helpful but too rigid to address their particular needs. Health promotion programs in a bank have important differences from those conducted for a tire manufacturer. No matter how well-developed a program is, it must be adapted as much as possible to individual employees and employers. A number of analysts have found the Control Data program to be overly medical in its orientation and too dependent upon the annual physical. In developing a truly comprehensive program it is important to include educational programs concerning hazardous lifestyles, health profiles based on the Health Hazard Appraisal, computer-based dietary assessments, and stress management through biofeedback or deep-relaxation methods. When corporate health programs either grow predominantly out of the medical departments or fall predominantly in their jurisdiction, the results are likely to result in highly technological, instrumentation-laden programs tending to emphasize physical or medical approaches to preventing specific disorders such as cardiovascular disease. While such efforts are commendable, they narrow the scope of health promotion to pathology prevention. Health is not a subspecialty of medicine. The diagnosis and treatment of disease is one limited aspect of health promotion.

This is an extremely important distinction since it will govern the nature, cost, and overall effectiveness of any given program. Programs of health promotion for corporations can be greatly enhanced, and overhead greatly reduced, by placing any approach in its proper perspective alongside the other diversified components.

GENERAL DYNAMICS CORPORATION

Among the more recent health promotion programs to be developed is the Wellness in the Workplace program of General Dynamics Corporation. This was created by the mutual efforts of a local community, the state government, and a private business. Sponsors of the program included the American Association of Fitness Directors in Business and Industry (AAFDBI), the American Heart Association, the California Governor's Council on Wellness and Physical Fitness, and General Dynamics. Beginning in 1979, General Dynamics initiated their efforts in cooperation with the San Diego Heart Association by offering a hypertension screening for 2,800 employees. Enthusiasm for such efforts grew from high-risk identification to health promotion, in a series of steps culminating with the opening of the Health-Fitness Center in 1981. As with the previous programs, physical fitness is a mainstay, but there are also educational classes covering the major areas of health promotion. Although the setting or content is not unique, this program is a significant one since General Dynamics has made a concerted and effective effort to involve both national and community organizations.

IBM

One last example of a program which stands in contrast to all of the previous ones is that of IBM. This program was initiated in February 1981 under the title of "A Plan for Life" and contains the familiar health promotion components. However, one unique feature is that IBM deliberately avoided building elaborate and expensive facilities for physical fitness. By contrast, the IBM program at Armonk, New York, has made use of the existing facilities of the local YMCA. This is in keeping with a recommendation of the Washington Business Group on Health that "even the largest firms go to great lengths to avoid duplicating or competing with existing community facilities and programs." When community resources are available, use of them brings the additional benefit of having the company become more integrated with the community as a whole. Health promotion programs provide a perfect opportunity for companies to work closely with local organizations and governments to effect an improvement in the health of the total community. In the IBM program, all courses and activities are conducted before or after working hours and eligibility is for "regular and part-time IBM employees and their spouses . . . as are retirees and their spouses" (IBM, 1982). Any of the regular courses are offered free to these eligible individuals and, additionally, there is a program of "tuition assistance" where the company pays an amount ranging from $10 to $75 toward the cost of a community commercial program. Among the areas designated for such assistance are exercise, smoking cessation, and stress management, to cite a few. There are specific exclusions in areas of hypnosis, behavior modification, yoga and meditation, as well as "skill" courses such as swimming or golf. Such a program has clear limitations, but at least it is not locked into a large, corporate gymnasium which dictates that physical exercise remain a priority by virtue of the financial commitment alone.

SCHERER BROTHERS LUMBER COMPANY

If there is any question about whether or not a relatively small company or a single individual can create an effective health promotion program, the example of Scherer Brothers Lumber Company in Minneapolis should put that to rest. During the summer of 1979, Gregg Scherer, one of the company's owners as well as an avid rugby player and marathon runner, developed a model health promotion program for its 135 employees. In deciding to do so, he was greatly influenced by witnessing three valuable workers die prematurely. One company foreman who was overweight, had hypertension, and exhibited a "driving" personality died of a massive heart attack at 45 years of age. Another yard worker, who often took unnecessary chances around heavy equipment, was crushed to death in a preventable yard accident. Finally, an employee of 25 years suffered headaches and dizziness due to arteriosclerosis in the brain and was forced into retirement. Lack of family support and loss of his driver's license left him alone, immobile, and in financial difficulties. One night he hanged himself at home with his belt. According to Gregg Scherer, "Three good employees, three lives lost, three deaths which could have been prevented through a program of active intervention. . . . These situations are not isolated, they happen in all corporations. . . . When reduced to simplistic terms we were dealing with factors such as poor nutrition, lack of exercise, inability to control stress, poor safety habits, and bad financial planning; all factors which take these tragedies out of the realm of fate and put them squarely in the arena of corporate responsibilities" (Scherer, 1983). Scherer Brothers decided to do something about these occurrences. Out of this concern the company has created a low-cost, highly effective health promotion program which is an excellent prototype.

This family-owned lumber company, with yearly sales of over $30 million, has a long history of concern for its employees, which proved to be an invaluable asset in the program being taken seriously and utilized. When the company was founded fifty years ago by Gregg Scherer's father and uncle, they instituted a "free lunch" program for office employees that continues to this day. Now the midday meals for thirty-nine office workers are prepared by a staff nutritionist and feature chef's salads and whole-grain breads, with no high-fat foods, butter, or salt, and no red meats. Plans are under way to expand the free-meal program to all ninety-six yard workers. As if this was not surprising enough, the Scherer Brothers' program has progressed even further to include such measures as: (1) all cigarette machines were removed and the junk food in the vending machines was replaced with yogurt and granola bars; (2) all employees have choices of free fresh fruit; (3) in the soft-drink machines there are choices such as iced tea, lemonade, noncarbonated fruit drinks, and one cola drink; and (4) the company installed a free popcorn machine and popcorn breaks are encouraged instead of coffee and sweet rolls. This measure is based upon the fact that 15 to 18 ounces of popcorn each day provide the body with enough crude fiber to reduce the risk of both cardiovascular disease and gastrointestinal cancer. A small note on the machine reminds employees of this finding.

In addition to these dietary measures, the company undertook other health-related measures, including: (1) blood pressure monitoring; (2) the reduction of noise levels in several work areas; and (3) the addition of a Health Maintenance Organization (HMO) insurance option to the existing medical insurance plan. Furthermore, the company offers positive incentives to encourage physical fitness and weight control by providing financial rewards to those employees who pledge a certain goal and attain it. Families of the employees are encouraged to use the recreational and exercise facilities which the company provides, without cost. Employees also receive "wellness pay" and there is no "sick leave." For each month that an employee is not sick from work, he or she receives two hours of extra pay. According to Gregg Scherer, "When one or two weeks' sick leave is allowed a year, it's amazing how many people get sick exactly five or ten days" (*Congressional Record,* 1980). An employee who misses work for illness also misses his or her pay, although the company does provide medical insurance. The only absences allowed are vacations, holidays, funerals, or jury duty. Eight on-the-job back injuries were reported in 1979, due to lifting shingles. In response to this, management bought a new $65,000 lift truck and there was only one back injury in 1980, which saved time, money, and human suffering for all concerned. Collectively, these measures have created an exemplary model of a true holistic health promotion program.

These specific aspects of the program are not the most important or impressive dimensions. Gregg Scherer points out that, "Wellness takes commitment . . . it's not throwing away salt and butter." When the program was started, the first action consisted of establishing a company "Wellness Committee" consisting of a cross section of the company ranging from top management to yard workers. Over a four-week period in the summer of 1979, the committee distributed printed information to the employees explaining the concept of "holistic health." One must remember here that this is not a high-tech corporation on the West Coast or in the Northeast nor a university community but a midwestern lumber company addressing a range of employees found in virtually any corporation. Emphasis in the holistic program is upon individual awareness and voluntary involvement:

> Self-responsibility is important because of one paramount reason. The medical community as we know it today is, of necessity, designed not so much to promote health as to alleviate illness. Its task is to return us from a condition of sickness to the midpoint of what we call the death to immortality continuum. It is *our* job as individuals to move off that midpoint into the positive area of active health promotion. This is not a criticism of doctors because the doctors are not responsible for feeding us, do not lay out our gym shorts and Adidas for us and don't fasten our seat belts for us when we enter our automobiles. . . . So we

came to understand the term "holistic" as applied to health promotion. (*Scherer, 1983*)

Self-responsibility is a key factor throughout the program.

After the initial education period, questionnaires were circulated to all employees for a "lifestyle profile." Questions ranged from how many stairs they climbed daily, to the nature of their diet and what kind of music they enjoyed. This information was collected and followed by another questionnaire asking the employees to help choose programs in which they would be willing to participate. Again the emphasis was upon self-responsibility. Nothing was forced upon the employees. In 1980 a newspaper article concerning the program was read into the *Congressional Record* of the 96th United States Congress, which quoted Scherer: "What we've done is educate people on what the program is all about, and give them the conviction to do it for themselves, to show them that they're responsible for their own health. . . . Buying in is a matter of commitment, a personal decision. We have some people who participate vigorously, and we have a few who vigorously tend to ignore the program" (1980). At this point the Wellness Committee remains as a six-member group which meets monthly to decide upon which areas of holistic health will be the focus for that month. As one example, the company recently completed a three-month program on back safety which included a series of back- and stomach-muscle tests for each employee with follow-up three months later. Although the program has found the white-collar workers to be more receptive than the blue-collar workers, overall involvement has been very high. The program is a good example of the attempt to extend and enhance individual efforts at health promotion into the workplace. The psychological involvement of employees has been encouraged throughout and positive incentives have been provided for those who participate so that benefits are shared by both the individual and the organization.

Benefits of the new program have been substantial, even though it is admittedly "sketchy, embryonic, and unstructured." Results have not been methodically evaluated, but some observations are very encouraging. There were fifteen to twenty smokers in the main office before the program began, now there are only six who still smoke. Employee absences and lateness dropped from 31 out of 135 employees to 3 out of 135 within a few months of beginning the program. At this point the corporation's absenteeism rate of .3 percent is well below the usual 3 percent to 4 percent reported for comparable industries. A number of people have lost up to twenty pounds of excess weight, and enthusiasm for the program is very high.

At this point the company is beginning to collect more structured information on two levels of evaluation. One level is "financial data" such as lower compensation claims, reduced absenteeism and health costs, as well as reduced equipment maintenance and replacement costs. A second level is "psychological data" including number of program participants, frequency of participation, knowledge gained, and general trends in weight reduction, smoking cessation, and exercise involvement. Together these two types of data should begin to provide some objective measures. However, as Gregg Scherer points out, this is a holistic approach rather than a cause and effect issue: "Insurance costs, reduced absenteeism and lowered workmen's compensation claims can be translated into dollars with reasonable accuracy but even these are subject to a variety of different factors. Within any comprehensive holistic health program it is difficult, almost impossible to determine which programs resulted in which benefits" (Scherer, 1980). The hope of a quick economic fix for uncontrollable medical costs through a health promotion program is a poor motivation at best. Surprisingly, the program has cost a modest $10,000 per year, showing that an effective, holistic program does not have to be expensive or require elaborate facilities. It is more important to build support than buildings.

This $10,000 per year is offset by present and potential savings. One area where the company hopes to save from $25,000 to $30,000 per year is in the area of workmen's compensation. That is a realistic goal since a significant reduction in lumberyard injuries has led to a reduction in hospitalization costs and earned the company a $16,500 insurance rebate from its medical insurers. The company's property insurance assessor inspected the lumberyard and found the work conditions to be safe enough to reduce the company's insurance premium by $7,500. Although these are impressive figures, Scherer Brothers recognizes that health promotion programs are not a panacea and that the question of "cost-effectiveness" is far from answered. The program's overall value is difficult to assess. "There are so many trade-offs," says Scherer, "it's really hard to tell. We're going to give it five years before we really sit down and ask is it worth it because it might take that long to figure it out." Scherer Brothers' program has attracted a great deal of well-deserved national attention, with its emphasis upon employee health education and willingness to examine its own total environment in terms of health hazards, incentives, and overall policy and structure. "We've had letters from people all around the country about this program. Some of the people who wrote said it's a shame that something like this is a novelty instead of the norm. The fact that it's unusual for an employer to be concerned about his employees is pretty sad" (Covert, 1980). Finally, the most important observation is from Gregg Scherer himself, who acknowledges that it would be wonderful if every company had a health promotion program. But even more significantly, he has mused that "What would be even better would be wellness in the workplace without wellness programs" (*Congressional Record*, 1980). Ultimately, that is the essence of healthy people in healthy places.

A NEW WORK ETHIC

Underlying any consideration of the individual in his or her work environment is the concept of "work ethic." Two of the most frequently cited problems afflicting the workplace are that productivity is stagnant and that the work ethic has deteriorated. Stagnation is an evident fact, but it may be symptomatic of a more profound shift in work ethic which social analyst Daniel Yankelovich has defined as "endowing work with an intrinsic moral worth and believing that everyone should do his or her best possible job irrespective of financial reward" (1982). At the heart of hard economic statistics is a set of psychological and philosophical beliefs held by individual employees and reflected in certain collective behaviors. While cynics often point to the deterioration of this work ethic, there are clear indications from numerous surveys that this philosophical ideal is alive, well, and growing stronger. In fact, a 1980 Gallup poll for the United States Chamber of Commerce indicated "a widespread commitment among U.S. workers to improve productivity . . . there are large reservoirs of potential upon which management can draw to improve performance and productivity." If the work ethic remains strong and there is an apparent commitment by individuals to that ideal, why has actual job performance slackened? According to Daniel Yankelovich, "the answer lies . . . in the deeply flawed reward system, both psychological and financial" (1982). To illustrate this point, approximately 82 percent of workers polled have indicated "some degree of discretion and control" over their "work efforts" and 88 percent had control over the "quality of the work or service they performed," but only 16 percent, or one in five, use this power to improve their performance. This is the heart of the matter since the real issue is not the work ethic per se but a growing perception that workers simply do not gain any benefits from such efforts. Rewards accrue to the remote realm of management, other consumers, or stockholders. "The question of who benefits from increased productivity, and how, are the critical factors, not the work ethic. . . . Why should workers make greater effort if: (a) they don't have to and (b) they believe that others will be the beneficiaries of such efforts. It is ironic that a political administration so finely tuned to encouraging the business community should pay such scant attention to stimulating the average American to work harder" (Yankelovich, 1982). Actually this may not be so much a matter of political policies as it is an anachronistic world view characteristic of the Industrial Revolution, where workers were seen as interchangeable parts and were thought to work because it was a necessity and nothing more. Failure to understand the newly evolving work ethic with its new emphasis on psychological fulfillment is a serious oversight.

Perhaps this is a startling insight to United States employers, but it has been a long-standing and highly effective characteristic of the Japanese workplace, which recognizes the necessity of giving individuals both monetary and psychological incentives and rewards for their efforts. Business management, state and national government, professional economists, and even labor unions who supposedly represent workers have missed a critical point. They "do not have a firm grasp of the soft factors and how they interact with the hard ones. Unwittingly, most 'experts' hold an obsolete image of the work force as a pool of 'labor' responsive solely to economic imperatives, driven by the fear of unemployment, and inspired by the promise of consumer goods—the familiar carrot-and-stick psychology that worked in the past when workers and work were different" (Yankelovich, 1982). In the realm of health promotion programs, the active, voluntary involvement of each individual is the key to success for individuals and organizations. Any approach to health promotion in the workplace which does not provide psychological and monetary incentives for those involved will and should fail. Workers have changed and the workplace needs to adapt to these "tens of millions of well-educated Americans, proud of their achievements, zealous of their freedoms, motivated by new values, with substantial control over their own production, and ready to raise their level of effort if given the proper encouragement" (Yankelovich, 1982). Approaches to health promotion which fail to acknowledge the new work ethic and the dignity of the new employee are doomed as Band-Aid remedies.

Recently a group of 550 California aerospace workers organized both within and among their companies to "humanize the world of work" (*Leading Edge,* 1981). Among the companies involved are General Dynamics, Xerox, Singer, Bendix, TRW, Hughes Aircraft, Teledyne, and Prudential Insurance Company. Some groups are sanctioned by management and others are not, but all are proceeding. These employee networks have been named the "Making a Difference" clubs, and their primary goal is to work together more productively and have a greater impact upon working conditions. According to the newsletter the clubs intend to "change the aerospace industry so that people do not feel that they are small cogs in the massive government / aerospace industrial machine but rather that each person knows that he or she truly makes a difference." Although the groups are diverse in their activities, they all emphasize personal health as well as "right-brain learning" approaches and cooperation rather than competition, and they express a new work ethic, new philosophy and values.

In a *Newsweek* editorial describing these new values, Carolyn Lewis reflected upon her "unprodigal sons" and realized that "Plainly, what my sons want and need is something different—something smaller, simpler and more manageable. They march to a different drummer, searching for an ethic that recognizes limits, that scorns overbearing competition and what it does to human relations, and says simply and gently, enough is enough. Is my sons' solution to the complexity and seeming intractability of modern problems the answer for everyone? Of course not, but to choose small places, modest ambitions and values that are tolerant and loving is surely an admirable alternative. It may in the end be the only alternative we have to an urban culture in which we have created so much ugliness, and where we seem to inflict so much pain on each other through neglect, selfishness and failure of will" (1982). Emphasis here is upon the quality of life rather than numbers on a financial statement. Such a philosophy is neither liberal nor conservative and marks an evolving, apolitical trend.

Surveys conducted by the Stanford Research Institute have indicated that aggregates of such individuals are rapidly becoming a major force in the decade of the 1980s. As such, they will influence the nature of the products and services in demand as well as the nature of the workplace which delivers these services. SRI projections suggest that a "socially conscious" group of individuals made up of more than 47 million people will comprise more than one quarter of the United States population by 1990. Overall, they are projected to be of low as well as high incomes, mostly under 50, relatively well-educated, and sharing certain values defined as "societal responsibility, environmentalism, global philosophy, smallness of scale, inner growth, and simple living" (Dietz, 1980). Of particular importance in these values is an emphasis upon individual freedom and involvement in decision making. Out of this will emerge a new work ethic and environment where strategic decisions will still be made by a limited executive board but employees will expect to have and will have a greater role in deciding their working conditions and procedures. Perhaps the greatest change will be a marked reduction in the numbers of middle-management personnel, who will become obsolete in a future of "participatory management."

A great deal has been written about a uniquely Japanese style of management which appears to be more consistent with the revitalized work ethic. Beyond the superficial aspects of quality circles, lifetime employment, corporate anthems, and exercise programs is an implicit reliance upon individuals working together for mutual benefit. Recent evidence is mounting that a major failure in the United States workplace is not the employees but the middle-management obsession with unbridled competition. "If a manager knows something a colleague or competitor doesn't, the manager has an edge" (Shay, 1981). Among the instances where this error has been successfully corrected is in a Sears Warwick TV manufacturing operation which had a very poor record for quality control and a poor return on its assets. Finally, Sears sold the company to Sanyo. Within a few months Sanyo resolved virtually all of the difficulties by employee involvement. Interestingly, Sanyo did not fire a single factory worker but did dispense with over 300 middle-management jobs. Similar findings are evident in Motorola's Quasar operation after it was purchased by Matsushita. Donald E. Petersen, president of the Ford

Motor Company, has espoused a "new spirit of working together" at Ford with an emphasis upon "the people factor." At Ford, an innovation has been introduced that will provide "lifetime job protection" to 80 percent of the work force. Along the same lines is an observation by Sony Chairman Akio Morita, who believes that American workers are "excellent" but the "problem in the United States is management" (Shay, 1981). The changes at Sanyo, Motorola, and Ford do not result from a wholesale importing of a Japanese workplace model like Toyota's or Sony Walkman's, but an adaptation of a new workplace philosophy and ethic to the United States work environment and employees. Behind these changes is an evolution of values led by "unprodigal sons and daughters." Profound changes are under way, and the workplace and the health programs of the future will reflect new values.

Nobel prize winner Roger W. Sperry of the California Institute of Technology has written about how a "science of values" will revolutionize the way we look at our lives, work, and health:

Introduction of mental phenomena into the causal sequence of brain function means, among other things, that values of all kinds, even aesthetic, spiritual and irrational, must now be recognized as positive causal factors in human decision making . . . our present interpretation goes far to restore to human nature the personal dignity, freedom of choice, inner creativity, and other humanistic attributes of which it has been long deprived by the behavioristic and materialistic movements. . . . A separate science of values becomes theoretically feasible, and a matter of top priority today considering the critical control role played by the human factor in determining world crisis conditions. (*Sperry, 1976*)

These observations derived from research into the human brain are consistent with the visionary philosophies of the late E. F. Schumacher. In *Small Is Beautiful* (1973) he suggested a "Buddhist economics" which rejected the old values and ideals which saw the world in an image of exponential growth, the ethic of "more is better," environmental exploitation, and the "people of the forward stampede" whose guiding principle is "a breakthrough a day keeps the crisis at bay!" At the center of Schumacher's vision of a future of voluntary simplicity is the Buddhist concept of "right livelihood" which is a socially creative, ecologically sound, and cooperative mode of work for both individuals and organizations.

For both Sperry and Schumacher these values were not idle abstractions but causative agents in determining the nature of future planetary conditions. Concern over these critical choices is at the core of a series of future scenarios produced by the Stanford Research Institute in the form of "Seven Tomorrows." Each scenario was written as if the researchers were looking back from the year 2000, and together they portrayed a range of possible futures, from an "Apocalyptic Transformation" just short of a nuclear war to a "Mature Calm" scenario which involves a slow adaptive evolution consistent with "small is beautiful" and a new ethical orientation. After reviewing "Seven Tomorrows," Harold Gilliam concluded, "Whether we follow the scenarios of disaster or of hope depends on how well we learn the new rules, whether we choose to adapt to the new circumstances or to continue living by the rules of the past" (1982). Between the close of this century and the unfolding of the twenty-first century lie these and other extraordinary challenges: exploring the capacity of the mind to release powerful chemicals whose existence was not even suspected a few years ago; understanding the body's immune system and the process by which an individual can "die of a broken heart"; planning for a society in which an unprecedented number of people live beyond 100 years old; and fostering the emergence of a post-material age with a renewed emphasis upon transcendent values.

Such revolutionary trends cannot be reduced to accounting department ledgers yet ultimately have a profound impact upon those indicators as well. For the individual, these changes will mean new empowerment and choice. The model health promotion programs we have examined are the first steps in introducing a new work ethic, based upon cooperation, empowerment of the individual, and nondestructive lifestyles, into our major corporations and thus Western society at large. Healthy people at all levels are demanding healthy places in which to spend their half century of working life. Considerations such as these might remain visionary speculations if our very survival did not depend upon the answers.

APPENDIX A

Health Promotion Resources

This resource guide was created in response to many requests for information concerning health promotion programs for individuals and organizations. These organizations should be able to provide accurate and current information in their respective areas. This list is not comprehensive or definitive; it is only a representative sample of resources. Most of the organizations or publications listed offer their services at no cost or at low fees. Many private organizations offering such services have not been listed. When possible, the listings have been annotated based upon the organization's own program descriptions and announcements.

I. PROFESSIONAL ORGANIZATIONS AND AGENCIES

American Association of Fitness
  Directors in Business and Industry
  (AAFDBI)
400 Sixth Street, S.W.
Washington, D.C. 20201
  This organization sponsors conferences, offers a placement service for fitness directors, and works to heighten awareness among corporations on the value of physically fit employees.

American College of Preventive
  Medicine
1015 15th Street, N.W.
Suite 403
Washington, D.C. 20005
  A clearinghouse for information on health promotion programs. Information is available concerning model programs in the workplace.

The American College of Sports
  Medicine
1440 Monroe Street
Madison, Wisconsin 53706
  Information on endurance testing and certification of exercise leaders.

American Heart Association
7320 Greenville Avenue
Dallas, Texas 75231
  Businesses are advised to contact their local heart association; services vary depending on availability of resources in different locations, but may include written materials, screening programs, and / or educational programs taught by training teams.

American Hospital Association Center
  for Health Promotion
American Hospital Association
840 North Lake Shore Drive
Chicago, Illinois 60611
  Offers a comprehensive selection of

materials—including bibliographies, reprinted articles, pamphlets and films—
on health promotion.

American Occupational Medical
   Association
150 North Wacker Drive
Chicago, Illinois 60606
   Conducts educational conferences in
occupational medicine and is the largest society of physicians in industry,
government, and academia who promote the health of workers in industry.
Services include surveillance of harmful substances, alcoholic rehabilitation,
and employment referral for physicians interested in occupational medicine.

American Public Health Association
1015 18th Street, N.W.
Washington, D.C. 20036
   Devoted to the promotion of public
health for its members (50,000 plus)
and the concerned public. Sets standards for solving health problems,
sponsors large public-awareness cam-
paigns about specific health dangers,
and disseminates information about the
latest developments in public health to
its members and others.

The California Governor's Council on
   Wellness and Physical Fitness
The Sun Building
717 K Street, #222
Sacramento, California 95814
   The Governor's Council is dedicated
to promoting health as an achievable
goal for all Californians. The objective
is to stimulate wellness activities such
as stress management, nutritional
awareness, environmental sensitivity,
physical fitness, and self-responsibility
(including smoking cessation, weight
control, and drug reduction) in all sectors of the society.

California NEXUS Foundation
2152 Union Street
San Francisco, California 94123
   Conducts intensive workshops with
senior management from corporations,
government, and universities. Emphasis is on the role of leadership in organizations. Also maintains an ongoing
data base of organizational health promotion programs and consults in the
design, implementation, and evaluation of such programs.

Center for Medical Consumers and
   Health Care Information
237 Thompson Street
New York, New York 10012
   Free health library including medical textbooks and publications and lay
tests for members and nonmembers as
well as free phone-in library (Tel-Med,
which has a hundred tapes). Also has
educational program of lectures and
workshops on self-care, vision problems, back problems, etc., twice a
year and publishes *Health Facts,* a
bimonthly consumer bulletin on
health problems. Encourages memberships ($5 per year) but makes its ser-
vices available to all.

Office of Health Information and
   Health Promotion
Department of Health and Human
   Services
Washington, D.C. 20203
   A national clearinghouse for health
information.

Health Insurance Institute
1850 K Street, N.W.
Washington, D.C. 20006

Health Policy Institute
Boston University
53 Bay State Road
Boston, Massachusetts 02215

Minnesota Coalition on Health Care
   Costs
Health Associations Center
2221 University Avenue, S.E.,
   Suite 440
Minneapolis, Minnesota 55414

National Center for Health Education
30 East 29th Street
New York, New York 10016
   Created over a decade ago as the
result of a recommendation of the
President's Committee on Health Education, the center is an independent
not-for-profit organization. Among its
excellent projects are a comprehensive
health education program for elementary and secondary level schools, an
ongoing study of health education in
the workplace, a hypertension and
education program, smoking cessation
programs, and numerous others in this
unique and important organization.

National Health Information
   Clearinghouse (NHIC)
P. O. Box 1133
Washington, D.C. 20013
   Established to provide consumers
with a number of valuable referral
services. NHIC has also produced a
publication which lists and summa-
rizes federal and federally supported
resources on a broad spectrum of
health-related issues and topics.

President's Council on Physical Fitness
   and Sports
400 Sixth Street, S.W.
Room 3030
Washington, D.C. 20201
   Informs and assists the public in becoming physically fit. The council issues numerous publications including
the *Physical Fitness Research Digest*
and a newsletter, which are available
through the U.S. Government Printing
Office.

Washington Business Group on Health
922 Pennsylvania Avenue, S.E.
Washington, D.C. 20003
   Provides publications, research reports, legislation trends, and consulta-
tions to individuals and organizations
in the area of health promotion programs in occupational settings. Represents and conducts research in health
promotion for major corporate clients
and is one of the most reliable and
accurate sources of information.

II. STRESS MANAGEMENT

ABC Learning Resources
Stress: Are We Killing Ourselves?
1330 Avenue of the Americas
New York, New York 10019
   One of the best, brief videotape
overviews of stress and its effects upon
psychological and physical disorders.
Narrated by Jules Bergman and origi-
nally prepared as a series for the
ABC World News.

American Institute of Stress
124 Park Avenue
Yonkers, New York 10703
   This institute is devoted to the multidisciplinary study of the relationship
between stress and illness. It acts as a
clearinghouse of information and programs in the areas of stress and wellness. A newsletter is planned and other
informational material is offered to the
public.

National Clearinghouse for Mental
   Health
National Institute of Mental Health
Room 11A33
Parklawn Building
5600 Fishers Lane
Rockville, Maryland 20857

Time / Life Video Program
*Stress Management: A Positive
   Strategy*
1230 Avenue of the Americas
New York, New York 10020

An excellent series of five half-hour-long videotapes focused upon stress management in the workplace. It is based upon following the employees of a fictitious company through a variety of commonly stressful situations. Commentaries are provided by experts in the field. Videotapes are used in conjunction with a workbook for both participants and the group leader.

Western Center for Behavioral and
   Preventive Medicine
208–125 East 13th Street
North Vancouver, British Columbia
   V7L 2L3
Canada

With an international board of advisors, the center has compiled a computer-based, annotated bibliography on stress and behavioral medicine. Also has published an excellent series of practical booklets on stress management as well as a periodic newsletter, *Behavioral Medicine and Stress Management News*. These research resources are available upon request at nominal cost.

III. PHYSICAL FITNESS

National Jogging Association
919 18th Street, N.W.
Suite 830
Washington, D.C. 20006

A nonprofit association of joggers, the association publishes a newsletter and *The Jogger's Flash*, a listing of publications concerning jogging.

Participation
Director of Marketing
80 Richmond Street West, Suite 805
Toronto, Ontario M5H 2A4, Canada

An exceptional organization which provides a packet of materials entitled *Fitness: The Facts*, a six-part series of colorful and accurate brochures on physical fitness. They have a prominent name recognition in Canada and recently produced a series on fitness, especially for organizations.

President's Council on Physical Fitness
   and Sports
400 Sixth Street, S.W.
Room 3030
Washington, D.C. 20201

IV. TOXIC SUBSTANCE CONTROL AND ENVIRONMENTAL PROTECTION

American Institute of Architects
1735 New York Avenue, N.W.
Washington, D.C. 20006

American Planning Association
1776 Massachusetts Avenue
Washington, D.C. 20036

American Society of Landscape
   Architects
1900 M Street, N.W.
Washington, D.C. 20036

Center for Labor Research and
   Education
Occupational Safety and Health
   Project
Institute of Industrial Relations
9244 Bunche Hall
University of California
Los Angeles, California 90024

In recent years the Labor Center has dealt with such issues as automation and technology, the changing nature of work, social welfare programs, the need to reach into new organizing fields, civil rights, opportunities for minorities and women, and economic dislocation. Occupational health and safety is the newest area of major emphasis by the Labor Center.

Chicago Area Committee on Occupational Safety and Health (CACOSH)
542 South Dearborn Street
Chicago, Illinois 60605

CACOSH is the first and one of the most successful of the COSH groups. A coalition of trade unions and health and legal workers, it provides a variety of organizing functions for trade unionists and unorganized workers. A list of twenty or so COSH groups nationwide can be acquired from CACOSH. It publishes *Health and Safety News* at $3 per year.

Citizens for Clean Air
32 Broadway
New York, New York 10004

Conservation Foundation
1717 Massachusetts Avenue
Washington, D.C. 20036

Consumer Information Catalog
Consumer Information Center
Pueblo, Colorado 81009

The center lists, on a quarterly basis, booklets from almost thirty agencies of the federal government about consumer health and information.

Defenders of Wildlife
1244 19th Street
Washington, D.C. 20036

Departments of Occupational Health
Found at most major university medical centers, these departments are primarily for research and training of physicians. However, if pressed, they can provide technically advanced clinical help to workers who get no satisfaction elsewhere.

Environmental Action
1346 Connecticut Avenue, N.W.
Washington, D.C. 20036

Environmental Defense Fund
1525 18th Street, N.W.
Washington, D.C. 20036

Environmental Sciences Laboratory
Mount Sinai School of Medicine
100th Street and Fifth Avenue
New York, New York 10029

An occupational health research center which is helpful for large problems or research questions.

Friends of the Earth
208 West 13th Street
New York, New York 10011

Health Policy Advisory Center
17 Murray Street
New York, New York 10007

Publishes information on occupational and environmental health issues.

Public Citizen, Inc.–Health Research Group
2000 P Street, N.W.
Suite 708
Washington, D.C. 20036

Information on toxic substances, food, drugs, health care, occupational safety.

International Association of Machinists (IAM)
Health and Safety
1300 Connecticut Avenue, N.W.
Washington, D.C. 20036

This large trade union publishes an excellent and readable *Guide for Safety and Health Committees.*

International Union for Conservation of Nature and Natural Resources
CH–1196
Gstaad, Switzerland

Labor Occupational Health Program
2521 Channing Way
Berkeley, California 94720

This project of the University of California Department of Industrial Relations provides some of the best

educational conferences, materials, and
trainings available for a wide variety
of workers. Their *Monitor*, published
bimonthly at $8 a year, focuses on a
different occupational group each issue. Write for a complete list of their
numerous publications.

League of Women Voters of the
  United States
1730 M Street, N.W.
Washington, D.C. 20036

National Audubon Society
950 Third Avenue
New York, New York 10022

National Institute for Occupational
  Safety and Health (NACOSH)
Division of Technical Services Public
  Dissemination
4676 Columbia Parkway
Cincinnati, Ohio 45226
  This is OSHA's research arm. It is
a virtual cornucopia of information on
everything technical in the field. Research that is used to determine standards for a wide variety of toxins and
safety hazards is available free of
charge. Its ten regional offices are
listed under U.S. Department of Labor OSHA.

National Parks and Conservation
  Association
1701 18th Street, N.W.
Washington, D.C. 20009

National Resources Defense Council
1725 I Street, N.W.
Washington, D.C. 20006

National Wildlife Federation
1412 16th Street, N.W.
Washington, D.C. 20036

National Women's Health Network
224 7th Street, S.E.
Washington, D.C. 20003

New York Committee for Occupational Safety and Health (NYCOSH)
Box 3285
Grand Central Station
New York, New York 10017
  An active and successful East Coast
COSH group with strong ties to the
labor community. Particularly active
and knowledgeable on legislative issues and on the activities of COSH
groups around the country.

Oil, Chemical and Atomic Workers
  International Union (OCAW)
P. O. Box 2812
Denver, Colorado 80201
  One of the best unions on the health
and safety issue. Publishes *Lifelines*
monthly, the best union health and
safety newsletter, $5 per year to the
general public. Also available for sale
($125) or rental through OCAW:
"Asbestos, Fighting a Killer," an excellent forty-five-minute slide show
with cassette tape.

Planned Parenthood–World
  Population
515 Madison Avenue
New York, New York 10022

Sierra Club
530 Bush Street
San Francisco, California 94108

Toxic Project Clearinghouse
Environmental Action Foundation
724 Dupont Circle Building
Washington, D.C. 20036
  Publishes information on toxic sub-
stances and exposure.

U.S. Department of Labor
Occupational Safety and Health
  Administration (OSHA)
Publications
Room N-3423
200 Constitution Avenue, N.W.
Washington, D.C. 20210
  This federal standards and enforce-

ment agency is the one to call with a complaint against an employer leading to workplace inspection. It also publishes a variety of free booklets, posters, and pamphlets on your rights under the law, including *Workers' Rights Under OSHA* (a summary). Will send multiple copies of any of its publications. OSHA has ten regional offices listed in the phone book under U.S. Department of Labor, and about half the states have their own OSHAs. Contacting the office in your locale is best for other than general information.

Water Pollution Control Federation
2626 Pennsylvania Avenue, N.W.
Washington, D.C. 20037

Wilderness Society
1901 Pennsylvania Avenue, S.E.
Washington, D.C. 20003

World Wildlife Fund
1601 Connecticut Avenue, N.W.
Washington, D.C. 20009

Zero Population Growth
367 State Street
Los Altos, California 94022

V. ACCIDENT PREVENTION

National Institute for Occupational
  Safety and Health
5600 Fishers Lane
Rockville, Maryland 20857
Prepares technical reports on the effects and control of hazardous substances, and has a catalog of publications available. Can supply experts in particular areas to businesses with special concerns. Also will search the medical literature for information on given topics for business or other clients.

National Safety Council
444 North Michigan Avenue
Chicago, Illinois 60611

Offers educational materials, brochures, and posters (some bilingual) on off-the-job safety through more than seventy-five chapters nationwide. Offers several types of memberships; dues for businesses are based on number of full-time employees.

VI. ALCOHOL AND CHEMICAL ABUSE

National Institute on Alcohol Abuse
  and Alcoholism
Public Health Service
5600 Fishers Lane
Rockville, Maryland 20857
These agencies were established by the federal government to initiate research and prevention programs concerning alcoholism and drug abuse. NIAAA's current goal is the treatment of alcoholism within the mainstream of our nation's health care delivery system. Activities include research, treatment, rehabilitation, and training.

National Institute on Drug Abuse
Public Health Service
5600 Fishers Lane
Rockville, Maryland 20857

VII. HIGH BLOOD PRESSURE CONTROL

American Heart Association
205 East 42nd Street
New York, New York 10017
Businesses are advised to contact their local heart association; services vary depending on availability of resources in different locations, but may include written materials, screening programs, and / or educational programs taught by training teams.

National High Blood Pressure
  Education Program
120/80 National Institutes of Health
Bethesda, Maryland 20014
  Offers a work-setting kit especially
for industry which includes instructional materials and information for
distribution; also has consultants and
other resources available.

VIII. WEIGHT CONTROL

Overeaters Anonymous
World Service Office
2190 190th Street
Torrance, California 90504
  A worldwide nonprofit fellowship
designed to help people obtain and
maintain normal weight. They offer
literature and the book *Overeaters
Anonymous* as well as group meetings.

Weight Watchers
800 Community Drive
Manhassett, New York 11030
  This group offers a four-step plan:
(1) *Food plan*—a complete nutrition
and variety of maintenance plans to
guide members in keeping weight off;
(2) *Personal action plan*—designed to
help participants change eating behaviors in positive ways; (3) *Personal exercise plan*—two optional ways to stay
fit; and (4) *Group support*—weekly
group meetings to provide an atmosphere of mutual sharing, encouragement, and understanding.

IX. SMOKING CESSATION

American Lung Association
1740 Broadway
New York, New York 10019
  The goal of the Lung Association
is the prevention and control of lung
diseases. They offer patient services,

school programs, educational materials
and teacher-training workshops. Offered free to the public are a vast
array of quit-smoking kits, pamphlets,
buttons, and brochures.

National Cancer Institute
9000 Rockville Pike
Bethesda, Maryland 20205
  Established in 1937 as part of the
Public Health Service, this is the federal government's principal agency for
cancer research and prevention programs. The institute's goal is the reduction and eventual elimination of
cancer as a major health problem.

X. PUBLICATIONS

Building a Healthier Company
Available from Blue Cross / Blue
  Shield, President's Council on
  Physical Fitness and Sports, and
  AAFDBI.

Cardiovascular Primer for the Workplace
U.S. Department of Health and
  Human Services
Public Health Service
National Institutes of Health
NIH Publication No. 81-2210
January 1981

Consumer Guide to Health Care Costs
California Health Facilities
  Commission
555 Capitol Mall, Room 525
Sacramento, California 95814
  A national and California review of
health care costs and cost containment
efforts.

Employee Fitness
Printing and Publishing
Supply and Services, Canada
Ottawa, Canada K1A 0S9

Employee Fitness: The How To's
Irene Korgul
Ontario Ministry of Culture and
  Recreation
Sports and Fitness Branch
Toronto, Ontario, Canada
  Proceedings of 1979 Ontario Employee Fitness workshop. An extremely informative book (190 pages) dealing with rationale, programming, facility considerations, fitness testing, and financing.

Employee Health and Fitness
  Newsletter
American Health Consultants
67 Peachtree Park Drive, N.E.
Suite 116
Atlanta, Georgia 30309
  A monthly newsletter for people who run employee fitness programs.

Fitness in the Workplace: A Handbook on Employee Programs
President's Council on Physical Fitness and Sports
Washington, D.C. 20201

Medical Self-Care
P. O. Box 717
Inverness, California 94937
  This quarterly magazine is designed to give the public a broader access to health tools.

A National Health Care Strategy
The National Chamber Foundation
1615 H Street, N.W.
Washington, D.C. 20062
  Five health action plan booklets written primarily for corporate managers. Strongly oriented toward cost containment, but many good ideas on employee wellness.

Physical Activity in the Work Place
  and
Physical Activity Patterns in Ontario
Irene Korgul

Ontario Ministry of Culture and
  Recreation
Sports and Fitness Branch
  Two research reports from the Ministry of Culture and Recreation.

Practical Planning Guide for Employee Health Promotion Programs
Health Planning Council, Incorporated
310 Price Plaza, Suite 206
Madison, Wisconsin 53705
  Emphasizes resources in Wisconsin, but can be used nationally. Detailed information on creating a program, evaluations, benefits, legal considerations, and financial issues.

Proceedings of the National Conference on Health Promotion Programs in Occupational Settings
Superintendent of Documents
U.S. Government Printing Office
Washington, D.C. 20402
  Order #017-001-00424-3/$3.25.

Promoting Health: Source Book
U.S. Office of Health Information and
  Promotion
National Health Council and National
  Center for Health Education
211 Sutter Street, 4th Floor
San Francisco, California 94108

Recreation Management
National Industrial Recreation
  Association
20 North Wacker Drive, Station 2020
Chicago, Illinois 60606
  Official journal of NIRA, a non-profit organization, dedicated to the principle that employee recreation, fitness, and services programs are essential to effective personnel management.

XI. HEALTH ASSESSMENTS

General Health Corporation
1046 Potomac Street, N.W.
Washington, D.C. 20007

Health Action Plan
Preventive Medicine Institute—Strang
  Clinic
55 East 34th Street
New York, New York 10016

Medical Datamation
Southwest and Harrison
Bellevue, Ohio 44811

XII. UNIVERSITY HEALTH PROMOTION PROGRAMS

Southern Illinois University
Student Wellness Resource Center
Carbondale, Illinois 62901

University of California
Picture of Health
Student Health Service
Cowell Memorial Hospital
Berkeley, California 94720

University of South Carolina
Office of Health Promotion
School of Public Health
Thomson Student Health Center
Columbia, South Carolina 29208

University of Wisconsin
University Health Service and Lifestyle
  Improvement Program
Stevens Point, Wisconsin 54481

APPENDIX B

Organizational and Corporate Health Promotion Programs

The following corporations and organizations have health promotion programs, ranging from a single-factor approach to comprehensive programs. This list is not definitive or exhaustive. All of the organizations listed in this table participated in a study which I conducted of "Corporate Health Promotion Programs" under the auspices of the California Health and Medical Foundation and the California NEXUS Foundation. There is some emphasis upon workplace health promotion programs in California since these organizations were more geographically accessible. Funding for this study was provided by The Minneapolis Foundation, the Ruth Mott Fund, and The San Francisco Foundation. Their support is gratefully acknowledged.

CORPORATION ADDRESSES

Acurex
485 Clyde Avenue
Mountain View, California 94042

Advanced Micro Computers
3340 Scott Boulevard
Santa Clara, California 95051

Aetna Life & Casualty
151 Farmington Avenue
Hartford, Connecticut 06156

The Allied Corporation
P. O. Box 2245R
Morristown, New Jersey 07960

Allis Chalmers Corporation
P. O. Box 512
Milwaukee, Wisconsin 53201

Allstate Insurance Company
Allstate Plaza
Northbrook, Illinois 60062

Alpha Therapeutic Corporation
5555 Valley Boulevard
Los Angeles, California 90032

Amalgamated Clothing and Textile
  Workers Union, AFL-CIO
Social Services Department
770 Broadway
New York, New York 10003

American Cyanamid
One Cyanamid Plaza
Wayne, New Jersey 07470

American Telephone and Telegraph
  Company
195 Broadway
New York, New York 10007

ARMCO Incorporated
703 Curtis Street
Middletown, Ohio 45042

Atlantic Richfield Company
515 South Flower Street
Los Angeles, California 90071

Avantek, Inc.
3175 Bowers Avenue
Santa Clara, California 95051

Bank of America
555 California Street
San Francisco, California 94104

Bekins Company
777 Flowers Street
Glendale, California 91201

The Bendix Corporation
Bendix Center
Southfield, Michigan 48037

Bristol-Myers Corporation
345 Park Avenue
New York, New York 10022

Campbell Soup Company
Campbell Place
Camden, New Jersey 08101

Carter Hawley Hale Stores, Inc.
550 South Flower Street
Los Angeles, California 90071

Champion International Corporation
One Champion Plaza
Stamford, Connecticut 06921

The Chase Manhattan Corporation
Cardiovascular Fitness Laboratory
One Chase Manhattan Plaza
New York, New York 10081

Chemical Bank
20 Pine Street
New York, New York 10005

Chubb and Son, Inc.
15 Mountain View Road
P. O. Box 1615
Warren, New Jersey 07078

Citicorp
399 Park Avenue
New York, New York 10043

Clark Oil and Refining Corporation
8530 West National Avenue
Milwaukee, Wisconsin 53227

Clorox
1221 Broadway
Oakland, California 94612

Colgate-Palmolive Company
300 Park Avenue
New York, New York 10022

Connecticut General Life Insurance
Company
Hartford, Connecticut 06152

Connecticut Mutual Life Insurance
Company
140 Garden Street
Hartford, Connecticut 06115

Control Data Corporation
Life Extension Institute
8100 34th Avenue, South
(Mailing Address: Box O)
Minneapolis, Minnesota 55440

Corning Glass Works
Houghton Park
Corning, New York 14830

Country Companies Incorporated
1701 Towanda Avenue
Bloomington, Illinois 61701

Crocker National Corporation
79 New Montgomery Street
San Francisco, California 94105

Crown Zellerbach Corporation
One Bush Street
San Francisco, California 94104

Deere and Company
John Deere Road
Moline, Illinois 61265

Delta Air Lines
Atlanta International Airport
Atlanta, Georgia 30320

Diamond International Corporation
733 Third Avenue
New York, New York 10017

Eaton Corporation
100 Erieview Plaza
Cleveland, Ohio 44114

El Paso Electric Company
P. O. Box 982
El Paso, Texas 79960

Equitable Life Assurance Society of
the United States
1285 Avenue of the Americas
New York, New York 10019

Exxon Corporation
1251 Avenue of the Americas
New York, New York 10020

Farmers Home Mutual Insurance
Company
1550 East 78th Street
Richfield, Minnesota 55423

Fluor Corporation
3333 Michelson Drive
Irvine, California 92730

First National Boston Corporation
100 Federal Street
Boston, Massachusetts 02110

Flick-Ready Corporation
15 York Road
Bensenville, Illinois 60106

Ford Motor Company
900 Parklane Towers West
Dearborn, Michigan 48126

General Dynamics Corporation
Health and Fitness Center
Convair Recreation Association
5001 Kearny Villa Road
San Diego, California 92138

General Electric Company
3135 Easton Turnpike
Fairfield, Connecticut 06431

General Foods Corporation
250 North Street
White Plains, New York 10625

General Mills, Inc.
Health and Safety Department
9200 Wayzata Boulevard
Minneapolis, Minnesota 55440

General Motors Corporation
767 Fifth Avenue
New York, New York 10153

General Telephone and Electronics
Corporation
One Stamford Forum
Stamford, Connecticut 06904

Getty Oil Company
3810 Wilshire Boulevard
Los Angeles, California 90010

The B.F. Goodrich Company
500 South Main Street
Akron, Ohio 44318

Government Employees Insurance
Company
Government Employees Insurance
Operations Building
Medical Division, GEICO Plaza
Washington, D.C. 20076

Great Western Financial Corporation
8484 Wilshire Boulevard
Beverly Hills, California 90211

Greyhound Corporation
Greyhound Tower
Phoenix, Arizona 85077

GTE (Sylvania)
100 Ferguson Drive
Mountain View, California 94042

Hewlett-Packard Company
11000 Wolfe Road
Cupertino, California 95014

Home Life Insurance Company of
New York
253 Broadway
New York, New York 10007

Honeywell Inc.
Honeywell Plaza
Minneapolis, Minnesota 55408

H. R. Textron, Inc.
25200 West Rye Canyon Road
Valencia, California 91355

International Business Machines
Corporation (IBM)
Corporate Health and Safety
Old Orchard Road
Armonk, New York 10504

Inter-Community Medical Centers
303 North Third Avenue
Covina, California 91723

Johns-Manville
Ken Caryl Ranch
Denver, Colorado 80217

Johnson & Johnson
317 George Street
New Brunswick, New Jersey 08903

Kimberly-Clark Corporation
North Lake Street
Neenah, Wisconsin 54956

Levi-Strauss and Company
1155 Battery Street
San Francisco, California 94106

Liberty National Life Insurance
Company
2001 Third Avenue, South
Birmingham, Alabama 35233

Eli Lilly and Company
307 East McCarty Street
Indianapolis, Indiana 46285

Lincoln National Life Insurance
Company
1300 South Clinton Street
Fort Wayne, Indiana 46801

Lockheed Corporation
2555 Hollywood Way
Burbank, California 91503

Manufacturers Hanover Corporation
350 Park Avenue
New York, New York 10022

Manufacturers National Corporation
Manufacturers Bank Tower
Detroit, Michigan 48243

Memorex Corporation
San Tomas at Central Expressway
Santa Clara, California 95052

Metropolitan Life Insurance Company
One Madison Avenue
New York, New York 10010

Miller Fluid Power Corporation
7 North York Road
Bensenville, Illinois 60106

Minnesota Mining and Manufacturing
Company
3M Center
St. Paul, Minnesota 55101

Monsanto Company
800 North Lindbergh Boulevard
St. Louis, Missouri 63166

Mutual Benefit Life Insurance
Company
520 Broad Street
Newark, New Jersey 07101

National Bank of Detroit
611 Woodward Avenue
Detroit, Michigan 48226

National Semiconductor Corporation
2900 Semiconductor Drive
Santa Clara, California 95051

NCR Corporation
1700 South Patterson Boulevard
Dayton, Ohio 45479

New England Electric System
25 Research Drive
Westborough, Massachusetts 01581

New York Telephone
Medical Department—Room 2565
1095 Avenue of the Americas
New York, New York 10036

Northern States Power Company
414 Nicollet Mall
Minneapolis, Minnesota 55401

Northrop Corporation
1800 Century Park East
Los Angeles, California 90067

Northwestern Mutual Life Insurance
   Company
720 East Wisconsin Avenue
Milwaukee, Wisconsin 53202

Northwestern National Life Insurance
20 Washington Avenue, South
Minneapolis, Minnesota 55440

Pacific Gas and Electric Company
77 Beale Street
San Francisco, California 94106

Pacific Anchor Chemical Corporation
6055 East Washington Boulevard,
   Suite 700
Los Angeles, California 90040

Pacific Motor Trucking Company
1766 El Camino Real
Burlingame, California 94010

Pacific Mutual Life Insurance
   Company
700 Newport Center Drive
Newport Beach, California 92660

Pacific Telephone
140 New Montgomery Street,
   Room 800
San Francisco, California 94105

Panhandle Eastern Pipe Line Company
P. O. Box 1642
Houston, Texas 77001

Paul Monroe Hydraulics, Incorporated
1701 West Sequoia Avenue
Orange, California 92668

PepsiCo, Inc.
Anderson Hill Road
Purchase, New York 10577

Phillips Petroleum
B 66 Adams Building
Bartlesville, Oklahoma 74004

Pillsbury Company
3146 Pillsbury Center
Minneapolis, Minnesota 55402

Pittsburgh National Bank
Fifth Avenue and Wood Street
Pittsburgh, Pennsylvania 15265

Plantronics, Inc.
1762 Technology Drive
Suite 225
San Jose, California 95110

Polaroid Corporation
750 Main Street
Cambridge, Massachusetts 02139

Press Enterprise Company
3512 14th Street
Riverside, California 92501

Prudential Insurance Company of
   America
Employee Health Service
Prudential Plaza
213 Washington Street
Newark, New Jersey 07101

Public Service Electric and Gas
   Company
80 Park Place
Newark, New Jersey 07101

Quaker Oats Company
Merchandise Mart Plaza
Chicago, Illinois 60654

The Rand Corporation
1700 Main Street
Santa Monica, California 90406

Reynolds Industries, Inc.
5005 McConnell Avenue
Los Angeles, California 90066

Rockwell International
600 Grant Street
Pittsburgh, Pennsylvania 15219

San Diego Transit Corporation
100 16th Street
P. O. Box 2511
San Diego, California 92112

Scherer Brothers Lumber Company
9 Ninth Avenue, N.E.
Minneapolis, Minnesota 55413

SCM Corporation
299 Park Avenue
New York, New York 10171

Security Pacific Corporation
333 South Hope Street
Los Angeles, California 90071

The Sentry Corporation World
   Headquarters
Employee Health and Fitness Program
1800 North Point Drive
Stevens Point, Wisconsin 54481

Smith Tool
17871 Von Karman
Irvine, California 92714

Southland Corporation
2828 North Haskell Avenue
Dallas, Texas 75204

Sperry Univac, Inc.
Information Storage Systems
3333 Scott Boulevard
Santa Clara, California 95051

Standard Brands, Inc.
625 Madison Avenue
New York, New York 10022

Standard Oil Company
Midland Building
Cleveland, Ohio 44115

State Mutual Life Assurance Company
   of America
440 Lincoln Street
Worcester, Massachusetts 01605

Tandem Computers
19333 Vallco Parkway
Cupertino, California 95014

Teledyne, Inc.
1901 Avenue of the Stars
Los Angeles, California 90067

Tenneco Inc.
P. O. Box 2511 TEC-826
Houston, Texas 77001

The Travelers Corporation
One Tower Square
Hartford, Connecticut 06115

TRW Inc.
23555 Euclid Avenue
Cleveland, Ohio 44117

Tosco Corporation
10100 Santa Monica Boulevard
Los Angeles, California 90067

U.S. Bancorp
309 S.W. Sixth Avenue
Portland, Oregon 97204

U.S. Fidelity and Guaranty
100 Light Street
Baltimore, Maryland 21202

Union Mutual Life Insurance
   Company
2211 Congress Street
Portland, Maine 04122

Union Oil Company of California
Union Oil Center
Los Angeles, California 90017

Ventura Coastal Corporation
2325 Vista del Mar Drive
Ventura, California 93001

Wells Fargo Bank
525 Market Street
San Francisco, California 94104

Western Bankcorp
707 Wilshire Boulevard
Los Angeles, California 90017

Western Electric Company
222 Broadway
New York, New York 10038

Weyerhaeuser Company
Tacoma, Washington 98477

Xerox Corporation
800 Philips Road, Building 337
Webster, New York 14580

Bibliography

ABDEL-HALIM, A. A. Employee effective responses to organizational stress: Moderating effects of job characteristics. *Personnel Psychology,* Autumn 1978, *31*(3), 561–579.

ABDEL-HALIM, A. A. Effects of role stress–job design–technology interaction and employee work satisfaction. *Academy of Management Journal,* June 1981, *24*(2), 260–272.

ABURDENE, P. Beyond executive stress: Board responsibility for CEO mental health. *Directors and Boards,* Summer 1977, *2*(2), 27–40.

ACADEMY OF FAMILY PHYSICIANS. *A report on lifestyles / personal health care in different occupations.* Kansas City: The Academy of Family Physicians, 1979.

The Accountant. Joys of jogging. August 21, 1980, *183*(5506), 311. (a)

The Accountant. Burning off calories. August 21, 1980, *183*(5506), 312. (b)

ACHTERBERG, J., and LAWLISS, F. G. *Imagery of cancer.* Champaign, Ill.: Institute for Personality and Ability Testing, 1978.

ACREE, K. H. Worksite health promotion demonstration. Draft submitted to California Governor's Council on Wellness and Physical Fitness, October 1, 1981.

ADAMS, J. D. Improving stress management. *Social Change,* 1978, *8*(4).

ADAMS, J. D. Guidelines for stress management and life style changes. *The Personnel Administrator,* June 1979, *24*(6), 35–38.

ADAMSON, G. J. Health promotion and wellness: A marketing strategy. *Group Practice Journal,* May / June 1981, 17–22.

ADER, R. (ed.). *Psychoneuroimmunology.* New York: Academic Press, 1981. (a)

ADER, R. The little black box for the body's defenses. *Psychology Today,* August 1981, 92. (b)

AKABAS, S. H., and BELLINGER, S. Programming mental health care for the world of work. *Mental Health,* Spring 1977, *61*(1), 4–8.

AKABAS, S. H., KURZMAN, P., and KOLBEN, N. *Labor and industrial settings: Sites for social work practice.* New York: Industrial Social Welfare Center, Columbia University School of Social Work, 1979.

ALBRECHT, K. *Stress and the manager: Making it work for you.* Englewood Cliffs, N.J.: Prentice-Hall, 1979.

ALDERMAN, M. H. Detection and treatment of high blood pressure at the work place. *Proceedings of the National Conference on High Blood Pressure Control in the Worksetting,* October 1976.

ALDERMAN, M., GREEN, L. W., and FLYNN, B. S. Hypertension control programs in occupational settings. *National Conference on Health Promotion Programs in Occupational Settings.* Washington, D.C.: Office of Health Information and Health Promotion, U.S. Department of Health, Education, and Welfare, January 17–19, 1979.

ALLEN, R. F. Changing lifestyles through changing organizational cultures. *Proceedings of the Society of Prospective Medicine,* St. Petersburg, Florida, October 1978.

ALLPORT, S. Sharpening doctor's awareness of "vague" occupational disease. *Medical Tribune,* August 26, 1981, 4.

ALTORFER, O. Emotional job fitness: The Education of the Heart. *Personnel,* September / October 1975, *52*(5), 32–37.

AMERICAN MEDICAL ASSOCIATION. *Stress, work, health* (booklet). November 19, 1980.

American Medical News. Many employers jump aboard employee fitness bandwagon. January 5, 1979, 3.

American Medical News. Brain cancer incidence found high at refineries. September 5, 1980, 7. (a)

American Medical News. Lifestyle held exaggerated as cancer cause. November 7, 1980, 14. (b)

American Medical News. Job-linked stress topic of book. February 6, 1981, 10. (a)

American Medical News. Women's health on decline, report says. March 27, 1981, 24. (b)

American Medical News. AMA urges caution on cancer-environment ruling. July 31, 1981, 8. (c)

American Medical News. AFL-CIO, government plan cancer screening. September 4, 1981, 22. (d)

American Medical News. New business attacks on costs seen. November 6, 1981, 23. (e)

ANDERSON, C. R. Stress, performance, and coping: A test of the inverted-U theme. *Proceedings of Academy of Management,* August 1975, 152–154.

ANDERSON, C. R., HELLRIEGEL, D., and SLOCUM, J. W., JR. Managerial response to environmentally induced stress. *Academy of Management Journal,* June 1977, *20*(2), 260–272.

ANDERSON, J. *The effect of EMG feedback and relaxation training on police personnel responses to occupational stress.* University Microfilms, Ann Arbor, Michigan, 1975, 76-711.

ANDERSON, R. R. Personal communication. April 7, 1981.

ANDERSON, R. R. Observations from the private / business sector in America. Transcription of an undated lecture.

ANTONOVSKY, A. *Health, stress, and coping.* New York: Jossey-Bass, 1979.

ARBOSE, J. Home truths about stress. *International Management,* February 1979, *34*(2), 42–43.

ARDELL, D. B. *High-level wellness.* New York: Bantam, 1977.

ARENDS, J. How to cope. *Security Management,* September 1980, *24*(9), 104–105.

ARNOLD, L. C. *Live for life—technical overview.* New Brunswick, N.J.: Johnson & Johnson, June 18, 1981.

ARNOLD, W. B. Cardiovascular health program. *Recreation Management,* April 1973, 14–15.

ARNOLD, W. B. The physical treatment of a company of good minds. *Recreation Management*, November 1974, 6–8.

ARNOLD, W. B. Before you start a fitness program. . . . *The Journal of Employee Recreation, Health, and Education*, July 1976, *19*, 10.

ARNOLD, W. B. Before you start a fitness program . . . take time to analyze your approach. *Recreation Management*, July 1976, *18*, 10–12.

ARNOLD, W. B. Organization profile: Xerox international center for training and management development. *Recreation Management*, January 1978, *20*, 30–32.

ARNOLD, W. B. Employee fitness in today's workplace. In L.K.Y. NG and D. L. DAVIS (eds.), *Strategies for public health*. New York: Van Nostrand Reinhold, 1981, 342–355.

ARP, H. Red Shift: Stars. *Omni*, February, 1982, 148.

ASHFORD, N. *A crisis in the workplace*. Cambridge, Mass.: M.I.T. Press, 1976.

ASPY, D., and ROEBUCK, F. *A lever long enough*. Washington, D.C.: The National Consortium for Humanizing Education, 1976.

Association Management. Coping with stress: An interview with Dr. James J. Gallagher. February 1979, *31*(2), 95–99. (a)

Association Management. Cope with stress by learning your body's early-warning signs. October 1979, *31*(10), 56–59. (b)

Association Management. Coping with stress. Leadership, Special Issue, November 1979, 54. (c)

Association Management. How do you handle pressure on the job? May 1980, *32*(5), 56–61.

Association Management. Executive health. January 1981, *33*(1), 58–61, 63.

BAINES, D. Nine steps toward beating executive stress. *Armed Forces Comptroller*, May 1980, *25*(2), 6–9.

BALLENTINE, R. (ed.). *Theory and practice of meditation*. Honesdale, Pa.: Himalayan International Institute of Yoga Science and Philosophy, 1976.

Banking. How fit are your executives? June 1974, *66*(12), 32–35, 88.

BARBER, T. X., (ed.). *Biofeedback and self-control*. Chicago: Aldine-Atherton, 1976.

BARNES, J. Health aspects of the woman executive. *The Accountant*, January 25, 1979, *180*(5426), 98–100.

BARTOL, K. M. Professionalism as a predictor of organizational commitment, role stress, and turnover: A multidimensional approach. *Academy of Management Journal*, December 1979, *22*(4), 815–821.

BARTRAM, P. Taking the stress out of keeping fit. *Director*, April 1980, *32*(10), 116–117.

BECK, A. C., and HILLMAR, E. D. *A practical approach to organization development through MBO*. Reading, Mass.: Addison-Wesley, 1972.

BEEHR, T. A. Work-role stress and attitudes toward co-workers. *Group and Organization Studies*, June 1981, *6*(2), 201–209.

BEEHR, T. A., and NEWMAN, J. E. Job stress, employee health, and organizational effectiveness: A facet analysis, model, and literature review. *Personnel Psychology*, Winter 1978, *31*(4), 655–699.

BEERY, C. A. *Good health for employees and reduced health care costs for in-*

dustry. Washington, D.C.: Health Insurance Institute, 1850 K Street, N.W., 20006, 1981.

Behavior Today. Pacific Mutual: Behavioral research + maintenance = lower health costs. December 25, 1978, 2–4.

Behavior Today. Career burnout—or, inhumanity in the human service. October 6, 1980, 4–7. (a)

Behavior Today. Job "isolation" special stress for judges. September 14, 1980, 6. (b)

Behavioral Medicine. Inflation continuing to affect mental health, alcoholism, drug abuse patterns. November 1980, 27. (a)

Behavioral Medicine. Significant proportion of chief executives believe job pressures affect health. October 1980, 3. (b)

BEHLING, O., and HOLCOMBE, F. D. Dealing with employee stress. *MSU Business Topics,* Spring 1981, *29*(2), 53–61.

BELL, A. D., JR. The PSE: A decade of controversy. *Security Management,* March 1981, *25*(3), 63–73.

BENEDICT, D. S. A generalist counselor in industry. *Personnel and Guidance Journal,* June 1973, 717–722.

BENSAHEL, J. G. The importance of privacy at work. *International Management,* June 1976, *31*(6), 49–50.

BENSON, H. A simple, cost-free, and comfortable way to combat job tension. *Nation's Business,* December 1976, *64*(12), 29–36.

BENSON, H., and ALLEN, R. L. How much stress is too much? *Harvard Business Review,* September / October 1980, *58*(5), 86–92.

BERKMAN, L. F., and SYME, S. L. Social networks, host resistance, and mortality: A nine-year follow-up study of Alameda County residents. *American Journal of Epidemiology,* 1979, *109*(2), 186–204.

BERLINER, H. S., and SALMON, J. W. The holistic health movement. *Socialist Review,* January / February 1979, *4*(1), 31–52.

BERMAN, D. *Death on the job.* New York: Monthly Review Press, 1979.

BERNSTEIN, D. A., and BORKOVEC, T. D. *Progressive relaxation training: A manual for helping professions.* Champaign, Ill.: Research Press, 1973.

BETTNER, J. Using common sense to avoid heart attacks. *Business Week,* April 7, 1980, 99.

BISHOP, J. E. Stress of American life is increasingly blamed for emotional turmoil. *The Wall Street Journal,* April 2, 1979.

BJURSTROM, L. A., and ALEXIOU, N. G. A program of heart disease intervention for public employees—a five year report. *Journal of Occupational Medicine,* August 1978, *20*(8).

BJURSTROM, L. A., and ALEXIOU, N. G. *A program of physical fitness / heart disease intervention for public employees: A five year report.* Albany, N.Y.: State Education and Civil Service Departments, AAFDBI Abstract, 1979.

BLACKBURN, G. L. et al. *Analysis of fitness using a multidisciplinary treatment program.* Boston: Cancer Research Institute, AAFDBI Abstract, 1979.

BLAIR, S. N., PATE, R. R., HOWE, H. G., BLAIR, A. E., ROSENBERG, M., and PARKER, G. M. Leisure time physical activity and job satisfaction. *Medicine and Science in Sport,* 1979, *11*(1), 105. (Abstract)

BLAKESLEE, S. Study of Japanese-Americans indicates stress can be a major factor in heart disease. *The New York Times*, August 5, 1975, 8.

BLALACK, R. O., DAVIS, H. J., and RUBIN, H. W. Sources of job stress for the FLMI: A comparative analysis. *Journal of Risk and Insurance*, June 1979, *46*(2), 123–137.

BLANCHARD, L. G. Getting health-care costs under control. *EXXON Newsletter*, Houston, Texas, 1982, 8–11.

BLAU, G. An empirical investigation of job stress, social support, service length, and job strain. *Organizational Behavior and Human Performance*, April 1981, *27*(2), 279–302.

BLOT, W. J., BRINTON, L. A., FREUMENIG, J. F., JR., and STONE, B. J. Cancer mortality in U.S. counties with petroleum industries. *Science*, October 7, 1977, *198*, 51–53.

Blue Cross / Blue Shield of California. President's Council on Physical Fitness and Sports and the American Association of Fitness Directors in Business and Industry. *Building a healthier company*, 1982. (Pamphlet)

BOBELE, H. K., and BUCHANAN, P. J. Taking the stress out of change. *Director*, September 1978, *31*(3), 60–61.

BOFFEY, P. M. Reassessing the cancer threat. *This World*, May 2, 1982, 22.

BOLONCHUCK, W. W. *Exercise intervention into a normal lifestyle*. Grand Forks, N.D.: Human Nutrition Research Laboratory, AAFDBI Abstract, 1979.

BORONSON, W. The myth of the unhealthy executive. *Across the Board*, February 1978, *15*(2), 10–16.

BRADFORD, L. P. Can you survive your retirement? *Harvard Business Review*, November / December 1979, *57*(6), 103.

BRAMEL, D., and FRIEND, R. Hawthorn, the myth of the docile workers, and class bias in psychology. *American Psychologist*, August 1981, *36*(8), 867–878.

BRANCHINI, C. *Broadening the concept of industrial health*. Presented at the Annual Meeting of the American Public Health Association.

BRENNER, M. H. *Mental illness and the economy*. Cambridge, Mass.: Harvard University Press, 1973.

BRENNER, M. H. Unemployment, economic growth, and mortality. *The Lancet*, March 24, 1979.

BREO, D. L. Is it worth dying for? *American Medical News*, May 15, 1981, 24–26.

BRESLOW, L. A policy assessment of preventive health practice. *Preventive Medicine*, June 1977, *6*(2), 242–251.

BRESLOW, L. A positive strategy for the nation's health. *Journal of the American Medical Association*, November 9, 1979, *242*(19), 2093–2095.

BRESLOW, M. D., and SOMERS, A. R. The lifetime health-monitoring program. *New England Journal of Medicine*, March 17, 1977, *296*, 601–608.

BRIEF, A. P. How to manage managerial stress. *Personnel*, September / October 1980, *57*(5), 25–30.

BRISCOE, D. R. Learning to handle stress—a matter of time and training. *Supervisory Management*, February 1980, *25*(2), 35–38.

BRODEUR, P. *Expendable Americans*. New York: Viking Press, 1974.

BRODEUR, P. *The zapping of America: Microwaves, their deadly risk and the cover-up*. New York: Norton, 1977.

BROOKS, P. P. Industry-agency program for employee counseling. *Social Casework*, July 1975, 56(7), 404–410.

BROWN, B. *Stress and the art of biofeedback*. New York: Harper & Row, 1977.

BROWN, B. B. Obstacles to treatment for blue-collar workers. *New dimensions in mental health*. Report from the Director, National Institute of Mental Health, Washington, D.C., June 1976.

BROWN, E. G., JR. *Preventing a toxic tomorrow*. State of California: Office of the Governor, September 10, 1980.

BROWN, J. Turning health care around. *East West Journal*, February 1980, 30–43.

BROWN, J. *Wellness in the workplace*. State of California: Office of the Governor, 1981.

BRUNNER, B. C. Personality and motivating factors influencing adult participation in vigorous physical activity. *The Research Quarterly for Exercise and Sport*, 1969, 40(3).

BURCK, C. G. Working smarter. *Fortune*, June 15, 1981, 68–73.

BURNS, D. W. Management of stress. *The Accountant*, August 21, 1980, 183(5506), 292–296.

Business Week. Executives on an exercise kick. June 3, 1972, No. 2231, 44–45.

Business Week. The new Rx for better health. January 5, 1974, 91–96.

Business Week. The skyrocketing costs of health care. May 17, 1976, 144–147.

Business Week. Using cancer's rates to track its cause. November 14, 1977, 69–75.

Business Week. How companies cope with executive stress. August 21, 1978, No. 2548, 107–108. (a)

Business Week. Unhealthy costs of health care. September 4, 1978, 58–68. (b)

Business Week. Executive stress may not be all bad. April 30, 1979, No. 2583, 96–103. (c)

Business Week. Coping with anxiety at AT&T. May 28, 1979, No. 2587, 95–106. (a)

Business Week. The corporate attack on rising medical costs. August 6, 1979, 54–56. (b)

Business Week. Living with chronic illness. March 3, 1980, 88–92.

Business Week. The new industrial relations—special report. May 11, 1981, 84–98.

Business Week. A new cure for health-cost fever. September 20, 1982, 117.

Business Week. Wellness programs paying dividends. September 21, 1981, 1, 36, 37.

CALABRESE, E. J. *Nutrition and environmental health: The influence of nutritional status on pollutant toxicity and carcinogenicity*. Vol. 1: *The Vitamins*. New York: Wiley-Interscience, 1980.

CALDWELL, F. Business invests in employee fitness. *The Physician and Sportsmedicine*, December 1976, 4, 81–88.

CALIENDO, M. A. *Nutrition and preventative health care*. New York: Macmillan, 1981.

California Department of Health Services. *Health promotion in the public and private sectors*, April 1981.

CANNON, W. Stresses and strains of homeostasis. *American Journal of Medical Science*, 1935, *189*, 1–14.

CARLSON, R., and FULLARTON, J. *Wellness in the workplace*. Demonstration project and position paper prepared for the California Governor's Council on Wellness and Physical Fitness, 1981.

CARLSON, R., and GOLDBECK, W. *Health promotion in the marketplace*. Mill Valley, Calif.: Health Resources and Communications, Inc., 1979.

CARPENTER, D. C., JR. *The health promotion and fitness center: A new effort for hospitals*. Salt Lake City: Intermountain Health Care, AAFDBI Abstract, 1979.

CARPENTER, M. Physicians' lifestyles appear to be healthier than lawyers', and their work more satisfying. *Medical Tribune*, November 12, 1980, 3.

CARRINGTON, P. Phone company workers offered meditation for stress. Reported in *Brain / Mind Bulletin*, January 7, 1980, *5*(4), 1–3.

CARROLL, S. J. Psychological needs as moderators of reactions to job enrichment. *Proceedings of Academy of Management*, 38th Annual Meeting, August 1978, 55–58.

Center for Disease Control. *Proportional allocation of the contributing factors of premature mortality to the four elements in the health field; ten leading causes of death among the total population 1+ years of age rank by number of years of life lost by age 65, USA, 1975*. Atlanta: Georgia Center for Disease Control, 1978.

CHASE, M. Ounce of prevention is worth a pound of cure, or so say proponents of the "wellness" movement. *The Wall Street Journal*, September 15, 1981, 11.

CHASSIE, M., and BHAGAT, R. S. Role stress in working women: Differential effect on selected organizational outcomes. *Group and Organization Studies*, June 1980, *5*(2), 224–233.

CHEW, G., GELL-MANN, M., and ROSENFELD, A. Strongly attracting particles. *Scientific American*, Fall 1964, *210*, 74–83.

CLARY, T. C., and CLARY, E. W. Managing stress before it manages you. *Governmental Finance*, February 1977, *6*(1), 22–23, 26–29.

CLEMONS, N. Physical fitness or corporate fitness? *Journal of Applied Management*, September / October 1980, *5*(5), 11–15.

CLEVER, L. H. Personal communication, January 1, 1982.

Clinical Psychiatry News. Poverty key psychosomatic disorder risk factor. March 1979, 1.

Clinical Psychiatry News. Work, mental health link more apparent in recession. July 1980, *8*(7), 1.

Clinical Psychiatry News. Companies can cut stress by accounting for "human factor." October 1981, *9*(10), 17. (a)

Clinical Psychiatry News. Vulnerability, lack of support can lead to work stress. October 1981, *9*(9), 25. (b)

CLUTTERBUCK, D. Executive fitness aids corporate health. *International Management*, February 1980, *35*(2), 19–22.

CLUTTERBUCK, D. Corporate outcasts. *International Management*, July 1981, *36*(7), 14–15+.

COBBON, S. Social support as a moderator of life stress. *Psychosomatic Medicine*, September / October 1976, *38*(5), 300–314.

COHEN, S. R. Another look at the in-plant occupational health program. *Journal of Occupational Medicine*, November 1973, *15*(11), 869–873.

COLLINS, M. L. *Employee fitness*. Ottawa: Ministry of State for Fitness and Amateur Sport, 1977.

COLLINS, R. T. *Managing stress on the job*. Blue Cross of Northern California, 1974, 48–53.

Commerce Today. Fitness movement seen curbing high cost of illness to U.S. industry. February 3, 1975, *5*(9), 11–14.

COMMONER, B. *The closing circle*. New York: Alfred A. Knopf, 1971.

COMMONER, B. *The poverty of power*. New York: Alfred A. Knopf, 1976.

COMMONER, B. *The politics of energy*. New York: Alfred A. Knopf, 1979.

The Conference Board. *Industry roles in health care*. New York: 1974.

Congressional Record. A wellness program. May 5, 1980, *126*(71).

CONRAD, C. C. Why your organization should consider starting a physical fitness program. *Training*, February 1979, *16*(2), 28–31.

COOPER, C. L. Cumulative trauma and stress at work. *Accounting, Organizations and Society*, September 1980, *5*(3), 357–359.

COOPER, C. L. Stress contagion in industry. *Employee Relations*, 1980, *2*(1), 25–26.

COOPER, C. L., and MARSHALL, J. An audit of managerial (DI) stress. *Journal of Enterprise Management*, 1978, *1*(3), 185–196.

COOPER, D. F. On the design and control of crisis games. *Omega*, 1978, *6*(5), 460–461.

COOPER, D. F. The superior commander: A methodology for the control of crisis games. *Journal of the Operations Research Society*, June 1979, *30*(6), 529–537.

COOPER, P. D., KEHOE, W. J., and MURPHY, P. E. (eds.). *Marketing and preventing health care: Interdisciplinary and interorganizational perspectives*. Chicago: American Marketing Association, 1978.

COOPER, T., and EDSON, L. Stress stress stress. *Across the Board*, September 1979, *16*(9), 10–19.

CORRIGAN, D. L. et al. *Effect of habitual exercise on total health as reflected by non-accidental insurance claims*. West Lafayette, Ind.: Purdue University, AAFDBI Abstract, August 1979.

CORROLL, V. A. Employee fitness programs—an expanding concept. *International Journal of Health Education*, 1980, No. 1, 35–41.

COVERT, C. This lumber company's building health. *Prevention*, October 1980, 74–78.

COX, M. H., and SHEPARD, R. J. Employee fitness, absenteeism, and job satisfaction. *Medicine and Science in Sports*, 1979, *11*(1), 105.

CRANTON, E. M. Holistic medicine. *Newsletter of the AHMA*, November 1981, 1.

CROWLEY, D. Four top health care executives speak out. *World*, Spring 1981, 11–12.

CSIKSZENTMIHALYI, M., and GRAEF, R. Feeling free. *Psychology Today*, December 1979, *13*(7), 84–99.

CUMMINGS, N. A. The anatomy of psychotherapy under national health insurance. *American Psychologist*, September 1977, *32*, 711–718.

DADAKIS, C. S. Executive perquisites. *Conference Board Record*, July 1976, *13*(7), 50–56.

DANAHER, B. S. Smoking cessation in occupational settings: State of the art report. *National Conference on Health Programs in Occupational Settings*. Washington, D.C.: Office of Health Information, and Health Promotion, Department of Health, Education, and Welfare, January 17–19, 1979.

DANIEL, J. An offer your doctor can't refuse. *American Health*, November / December 1982, 68–83.

DANIELS, C. E. *Correlates of Type A coronary prone behavior in a middle / upper management population.* Third Annual Meeting, Society of Behavioral Medicine, March 3–5, 1982.

DAVIDSON, M. J., and COOPER, C. L. Executive stress in women. *The Accountant*, August 21, 1980, *183*(5506), 297–299. (a)

DAVIDSON, M. J., and COOPER, C. The extra pressures on women executives. *Personnel Management*, June 1980, *12*(6), 49–51. (b)

DAVIDSON, M. J., and COOPER, C. What women managers face. *Management Today*, February 1981, 80–83.

DEBATS, K. E. Industrial recreation programs: A new look at an old benefit. *Personnel Journal*, August 1981, *60*(8), 620–627.

DEBOARD, R. The anxious organization. *Management Today*, December 1978, 58–61+.

DEDMON, R. E. et al. An industry health management program. *The Physician and Sportsmedicine*, November 1979, *7*(11), 57. (a)

DEDMON, R. E. et al. *Outcome evaluation and accountability in corporate fitness programs.* Neenah, Wis.: Kimberly-Clark Corporation, AAFDBI Abstract, August 1979. (b)

DEDMON, R. E., and KUBIAK, M. K. The medical director's role in industry. *The Personnel Administrator*, September 1981, *26*(9), 59, 61+.

DICKSON, P. *The future of the workplace: The coming revolution in jobs.* New York: Weybright and Talley, 1975.

DIBNER, K. Guidelines for establishment of physical fitness facilities in federal space. *Federal Register*, December 1978, *43*(244).

Dietary goals for the United States. U.S. Congress, Senate Select Committee on Nutrition and Human Needs, 95th Congress, 1st Session, 1977. Washington, D.C.: U.S. Government Printing Office, Document #Y4.N95:D56.

DIETZ, D. New markets, new strategies. *San Francisco Examiner & Chronicle*, May 25, 1980, Section C, 11.

Directory of on-going research in smoking and health. U.S. Department of Health, Education, and Welfare, Public Health Service, Center for Disease Control, Bureau of Health Education, National Clearinghouse for Smoking and Health. Washington, D.C.: U.S. Government Printing Office, Document #HE20, 70195:976.

DONOGHUE, S. The correlation between physical fitness, absenteeism and work performance. *Canadian Journal of Public Health*, May / June 1977, *68*.

DONWAY, W. Work in America is hazardous to your health. *Private Practice,* April 1980, 31–62.

DOUGLASS, M. E. Stress and personal performance. *The Personnel Administrator,* August 1977, *22*(6), 60–63.

DRIVER, R. W. *Analysis of a model depicting employers' perceptions of benefits for the organization which accrue from company-sponsored physical fitness programs.* Norman: University of Oklahoma, Division of Management, 1980.

DUBOS, R. *The mirage of health.* New York: Harper, Colophon, 1979.

DUEMER, W. C., WALKER, N. F., and QUICK, J. C. Improving work life through effective performance planning. *The Personnel Administrator,* July 1978, *23*(7), 23–26+.

DUGGAR, B. C., and SWENGROS, G. The design of physical activity programs for industry. *Journal of Occupational Medicine,* June 1969, 322–329.

DUNHAM, B. How to commit suicide slowly . . . American style. *Supervision,* August 1981, *43*(8), 5–8.

Dun's Review. What kills executives? March 1975, *105*(3), 35–39.

Dun's Review. Executive dilemma: Work vs. family. November 1980, *116*(5), 120–122.

DU PONT, R. L. The control of alcohol and drug abuse in industry. *National Conference on Health Promotion Programs in Occupational Settings.* Washington, D.C.: Office of Health Information and Health Promotion, Public Health Service, Department of Health, Education, and Welfare, January 17–19, 1979.

DURBECK, D., et al. *The NASA-USPHS health evaluation and enhancement program* (monograph). Washington, D.C.: Division of Occupational Medicine, Headquarters, National Aeronautics and Space Administration.

DURBECK, D. C. et al. The National Aeronautics and Space Administration—United States Public Health Service health evaluation and enhancement program. *American Journal of Cardiology,* November 1972, *30*(7), 784–790.

DUVAL, M. K. *Ongoing study of the National Center for Health Education,* San Francisco, 1982.

EADS, D. What, me worry? *Supervisory Management,* April 1981, *26*(4), 36–39.

EDELWICH, J., and BRODSKY, A. *Burn-out: Stages of disillusionment in the helping professions.* New York: Human Sciences Press, 1980.

EDWARDS, S. E., and GETTMAN, L. R. The effect of employee physical fitness on job performance. *The Personnel Administrator,* November 1980, *25*(11), 41–44, 61.

ELLIOTT, D. *Personal risk profile.* Washington, D.C.: General Health Corporation, 1046 Potomac Street, N.W., 20007, 1982.

ELSON, P. R. Teaching management and fitness. *Sales & Marketing Management,* May 18, 1981, *126*(7), 78–79.

Employee Health and Fitness Newsletter. American Health Consultants, September 1979, *1*(1), 1–16.

Employee Benefit Plan Review. General Mills forum focuses on stress, mental illness. August 1980, *35*(2), 40+.

Employee Benefit Plan Review. Now, out of your swivel chairs and into the pool. October 1980, *3*(4), 34, 36.

Environmental Defense Fund and Boyle, R. *Malignant neglect*. New York: Alfred A. Knopf, 1979.

ETTLIE, J. E. An evaluation of training for technological change. *Training and Development Journal*, July 1979, *33*(7), 22–26.

Euromoney. The nightmare stress of a bond dealer. May 1980, 17–29.

EVERETT, M. D. *The economics of exercise, physical fitness, and health*. Hattiesburg: University of Southern Mississippi, AAFDBI Abstract, 1978. (a)

EVERETT, M. D. *Strategies for physical fitness in business and industry: An economic analysis*. Johnson City: East Tennessee State University, AAFDBI Abstract, 1978. (b)

EVERETT, M. D. Strategies for increasing employees' level of exercise and physical fitness. *Journal of Occupational Medicine*, July 1979, *21*(7).

FABREGA, H. The need for an ethnomedical science. *Science*, 1975, *189*, 969.

FALLOWS, J. American industry: What ails it, how to save it. *The Atlantic*, September 1980, 35–50.

FARIA, I. E. *Cardiac risk factors associated with clinical coronary heart disease in California assemblymen*. Sacramento: California State University, AAFDBI Abstract, 1979.

FARQUHAR, J. *The American way of life need not be hazardous to your health*. New York: Norton, 1979.

FARQUHAR, J. W. *The American way of life need not be hazardous to your health*. Stanford, Calif.: Stanford Alumni Association, 1978.

FARQUHAR, J., MACCOBY, N., WOOD, P., BREITROSE, H., BROWN, B., HASKELL, W., MCALLISTER, A., MEYER, A., NASH, J., and STERN, M. Community education for cardiovascular health. *The Lancet*, June 4, 1977.

Federal Laboratory Consortium—Far West Region. *Stress: A survey of emotional health management programs*, 1980.

FEIN, R. What is wrong with the language of medicine? *New England Journal of Medicine*, April 8, 1982, *36*(14), 863–864.

FERGUSON, T. Contented workaholics. *Medical Self-Care*, P.O. Box 717, Inverness, California 94937, Summer 1981, 20–24.

FERGUSON, T. *Medical Self-Care*, 1982.

FERMAN, L. A. *Some health aspects of unemployment*. Ann Arbor: A public address, University of Michigan, October 1982.

FERRIS, T. *Galaxies*. San Francisco: Sierra Club Books, 1980.

FIELDING, J. E. *Preventive medicine and the bottom line*. Massachusetts Department of Public Health, August 1978.

FIELDING, J. E. Preventive medicine and the bottom line. *Journal of Occupational Medicine*, February 1979, *21*(2), 79–88.

FIELDING, J. E. Health promotion and disease prevention at the workplace. *Wellness Resource Bulletin—California Department of Mental Health*, February / March 1981, *1*(5), 1–12.

FIELDING, J., and BRESLOW, L. "Health Promotion Programs Sponsored by California Employees," U.C.L.A. School of Medicine, May 27, 1982, unpublished.

FIGLER, H. R. Managing stress. *Management Accounting,* August 1980, *62*(2), 22–28.

FILIPOWICZ, C. A. The troubled employee: Whose responsibility? *The Personnel Administrator,* June 1979, *24*(6), 17–22+.

FINEMAN, S. The stressless redundancy? *Management Decision,* 1978, *16*(6), 331–337.

FINEMAN, S. The nature of stress: A case study. *Leadership and Organization Development Journal,* 1980, *1*(4), 3–8.

FINEMAN, S., and PAYNE, R. Role stress—a methodological trap? *Journal of Occupational Behavior,* January 1981, *2*(1), 51–64.

FISHER, D. J. Business buys behavior mod. *Masters in Business Administration,* November 1976, *10*(10), 26.

FISKEL, J. Stress and stability: New concepts for risk management. *Human Systems Management,* April 1981, *2*(1), 26–33.

FLACH, F. F. Your personal management: Coping with depression. *Supervisory Management,* August 1975, *20*(8), 34–38.

FLETCHER, B., GOWLER, D., and PAYNE, R. Exploding the myth of executive stress. *Personnel Management,* May 1979, *11*(5), 30–34.

FLY, R. D. Why rotating shifts sharply reduce productivity. *Supervisory Management,* January 1980, *25*(1), 16–21.

FOGLE, R. K., and VERDESCA, A. S. The cardiovascular conditioning effects of a supervised exercise program. *Journal of Occupational Medicine,* April 1975, 240–246.

FOLLMANN, J. F., JR. *Alcoholics and business.* New York: AMACOM, a division of the American Management Association, 1976.

FOLLMANN, J. F., JR. *The economics of industrial health: History, theory, practice.* New York: AMACOM, 1978.

FOOTE, A., and ERFURT, J. A model system for high blood pressure control in the worksetting. *Proceedings of the National Conference on High Blood Pressure Control in the Worksetting,* October 1976.

FOOTE, A., and ERFURT, J. C. *Occupational employee assistance programs for substance abuse and mental health problems.* Ann Arbor: University of Michigan, Institute of Labor and Industrial Relations, 1977.

FOOTE, A., and ERFURT, J. C. *Cost-effectiveness of occupational employee assistance programs.* Ann Arbor: University of Michigan–Wayne State University, Institute of Labor and Industrial Relations, 1978.

Forbes. Getting a move on. March 1, 1974, *113*(5).

Forbes. The ratings game. January 15, 1976, *117*(2), 46–47.

FORBES, R., SIEGENER, R., TEMPLETON, J., MUTTER, J., and HAGUE, H. Stress-getting loose. *Sales & Marketing Management,* June 18, 1979, *122*(8), 51–82.

FORD, D. L., JR., and BAGOT, D. S. Correlates of job stress and job satisfaction for minority professionals in organizations: An examination of personal and organizational factors. *Group and Organization Studies,* March 1978, *3*(1), 30–41.

FORD, R. C., and HARTJE, J. Biofeedback and management stress. *Human Resource Management,* Fall 1978, *17*(3), 12–16.

FOREYT, J. P., SCOTT, L. W., and GOTTO, A. M. Weight control and nutrition education programs in occupational settings. *National Conference on Health*

Promotion Programs in Occupational Settings. Washington, D.C.: Office of Health Information and Health Promotion, Department of Health, Education, and Welfare, January 13–19, 1979.

FORSBERG, S., HEIKKINEN, E., AUNDOLA, S., PARKATTI, T., RAHKILA, P., SARASTE, M., and VUDRI, L. Physical fitness and exercise among 40–50 year old men in 2 Finnish industrial enterprises. *Scandinavian Journal of Social Medicine,* 1980, *14,* 24–32.

Fortune. Keeping fit in the company gym. *Fortune,* October 1975, *92*(4), 136–143.

FOX, B. H. *Premorbid psychological factors as related to incidence of cancer: Background for prospective grant applicants.* National Cancer Institute, National Institutes of Health, 1976. Reprinted in *Journal of Behavioral Medicine,* March 1978.

FOYLE, J. How better reading skills can cure executive stress. *Canadian Business,* September 1975, *48*(9), 40–44.

FREUDENBERGER, H. J., with RICHELSON, G., *Burnout: The High Cost of Achievement,* New York: Anchor / Doubleday, 1980.

FREW, D. Unstressing the stressed-up executive. *Conference Board Record,* July 1975, *12*(7), 57–60.

FRIEDMAN, M., and ROSENMAN, R. *Type A behavior and your heart.* New York: Alfred Knopf, 1974.

FULLARTON, J. Obesity: A new social policy perspective. *International Journal of Obesity,* 1978, *2,* 267–285.

GAERTNER, J. F., and RUHE, J. A. Job-related stress in public accounting. *Journal of Accountancy,* June 1981, *151*(6), 68–74.

GARAMENDI, J. *Stay-well promotion programs.* Hearing: California Legislature Senate Committee on Health and Welfare, Tuesday, October 7, 1980.

GARDELL, B. Stress research and its implications: Sweden. *Industrial Relations Research Association Proceedings,* 1980, 268–275.

GARDNER, E. W., and HALL, R. C. W. The professional stress syndrome. *Psychosomatics,* August 1981, *22*(8), 672–680.

GARDNER, R. J. An industry on the move. *Dun and Bradstreet Reports,* July / August 1979, *27*(4), 37–43.

GARFIELD, S. "Primary Total Health Care Project." Proposal to Henry J. Kaiser Family Foundation, January 17, 1980, unpublished.

GARMAN, J. F. *Physical fitness, mental health, and job performance: A preliminary report.* Ann Arbor: University of Michigan, AAFDBI Abstract, 1979.

GARRY, W. W. Integrating wellness into learning. *Training and Development Journal,* July 1980, *34*(7), 48–51, 53+.

GASNER, D. B. The creation of stress. *Masters in Business Administration,* October 1975, *9*(9), 42–44.

GEANNETTE, G. Inside the corporate gymnasium. *The American Way,* January 1979, *12*(1), 21–23.

The General Mills American family report, 1978–1979: Family health in an era of stress. Minneapolis: General Mills, Inc., 1979.

GILLIAM, H. A look at "Seven Tomorrows." *This World,* March 14, 1982, 25.

GLASS, D. *Behavior patterns, stress, and coronary disease.* New York: Halsted Press, 1977.

GOLDBECK, W. *Survey of industry sponsored health promotion, prevention, and education programs.* Washington, D.C.: Washington Business Group on Health, December 1978.

GOLDBECK, W. *A WBGH survey on employee mental wellness programs.* Washington, D.C.: Washington Business Group on Health, June 1979.

GOLDBECK, W. *Evaluating corporate health programs (ongoing study of the Washington Business Group on Health).* Washington, D.C.: 1982. (a)

GOLDBECK, W. Transcribed talk to the American Psychological Association Task Force on Promotion and Prevention, March 2, 1982. (b)

GOLDBECK, W. *Industry and its growing responsibility for the health of our nation.* Talk given to AAFDBI Annual Meeting, San Diego, June 1983.

GOLDBERG, I. et al. Effect of a short-term outpatient psychiatric therapy benefit on the utilization of medical services in a prepaid group practice medical program. *Medical Care,* September / October 1970, *7*(5), 419–428.

GOLDBERG, M. et. al. *A worker's guide to winning at the Occupational Safety and Health Review Commission.* Washington, D.C.: Public Citizen Health Research Group, 2000 P Street, N.W., Washington, D.C. 20036, 1981, $5.00.

GOLDBERG, P. *Executive health.* New York: McGraw-Hill, 1978.

GOLIN, M. Physician burnout. *American Medical News,* July 31, 1981, 1–4.

GOULD, D. Executive health. *International Management,* August 1979, *34*(6), 55.

GRAES, S. B. Kicking the tranquilizer habit. *Masters in Business Administration,* October / November 1978, *12*(8), 50–55.

GREEN, L. W. Toward cost-benefit evaluations of health education: Some concepts, methods, and examples. *Health Education Monographs,* 2; Supplement 1, 1979, 34–60.

GREEN, L., KREUTER, M., DEEDS, S., and PARTRIDGE, K. *Health education planning: A diagnostic approach.* Palo Alto, Calif.: Mayfield, 1980.

GREENBERG, J. The stress-illness link: Not "if" but now. *Science News,* December 10, 1977, *112*, 394–398.

GREENBERGER, R. S. How Burnout Affects Corporate Managers and Their Performance. *Wall Street Journal,* April 23, 1981.

GREIFF, B. The history of occupational psychiatry. *Psychiatric Opinion,* December 1978, 10–17.

GROSSE, R. N. Cost benefit analysis of health services. *Annals of American Academy of Political and Social Science,* 1972, *339*, 89–99.

GUENTHER, R. Stress management plans abound, but not all programs are run well. *The Wall Street Journal,* September 30, 1982, 2.

GUNDERSON, E. K., and RAHE, R. H. (eds.). *Life stress and illness.* Springfield, Ill.: Charles C. Thomas, 1974.

GUNN, R. R. *An analysis of the beliefs and policies of companies, businessmen, and medical experts with respect to physical fitness.* Unpublished master's thesis, Salt Lake City, 1970.

GUTSTEIN, W. H., HARRISON, J., PARL, F., KIU, G., and AVITABLE, M. Neural factors contributing to atherogenesis. *Science,* January 27, 1978, *199*, 449–451.

HACKLER, T. The yearly physical: A costly indulgence? *Mainliner*, June 1980, 112–115.

HALENAR, J. F. Doctors don't have to burn out. *Medical Economics*, October 26, 1981, 148–161.

HALES, D. Psycho-immunity. *Science Digest*, November 1981, 12–14.

HAMEL-SMITH, N. The dangers of over managing. *Marketing*, June 10, 1981, 5(11), 24–25.

HANNON, E. L., and GRAHAM, J. K. A cost benefit study of hypertension screening and treatment program at the work setting. *Inquiry*, December 1978, 15, 345–358.

HARDING, J. S. Letter to Russ Coile, Western Consortium for the Health Professions, Inc., September 15, 1982.

HARRIGAN, S. For managers, stress may be an addiction. *The Wall Street Journal*, July 26, 1981, 3. (a)

HARRIGAN, S. For managers, stress may be an addiction. *The Wall Street Journal*, August 26, 1981, 11. (b)

HARRISON, E. Executive stress. *The Accountant*, March 23, 1978, 178(5383), 386–389.

Harvard Medical School Health Letter. Periodic health exams in perspective, July 1980, 1–4.

Harvard Medical School Health Letter. Fitness programs for employees. October 1982, 7(12), 3–4. (a)

Harvard Medical School Health Letter. The war on cancer—where do we stand? April 1982, 7(6), 1–5. (b)

HARVEY, D. How to take stress in your stride. *Director*, September 1978, 31(3), 62–64.

HASKELL, W. L. Physical fitness programs, medical clearance, program design and operation. *Journal of Occupational Medicine*, April 1972, 306–308.

HASKELL, W. L. Physical activity in health maintenance. In D. Sobel (ed.), *Ways of health*. New York: Harcourt Brace Jovanovich, 1979.

HASKELL, W. L., and BLAIR, S. N. The physical activity component of health promotion programs in occupational settings. *National Conference on Health Promotion Programs in Occupational Settings*, Washington, D.C.: Office of Health Information and Health Promotion, Department of Health, Education, and Welfare, January 17–19, 1979.

HAYES, J. J. Biking vs. jogging. *Association Management*, April 1977, 29(4), 88–89.

HAYNES, S., and FEINLIEB, M. Women, work, and coronary heart disease. *American Journal of Public Health*, February 1980.

Health systems plan for southern Wisconsin, 1978–83. Madison, Wis.: Health Planning Council, Inc., April 1978.

HEINZELMAN, F., and BAGLEY, R. Responses to physical activity programs and their effects on health behavior. *Public Health Reports*, October 1970, 85(10).

HENNESSEY, E. Executive health. *Director*, April 1979, 31(10), 105–108.

HERBERT, W. An epidemic in the works. *Science News*, September 18, 1982, 188–190.

HIGDON, H., "How Industry Is Curbing Health Care Costs." *American Medical News*, May 29, 1981, 9–10.

HIGGINS, C. W., and PHILIPS, B. U. How company-sponsored fitness programs keep employees on the job. *Management Review*, December 1979, *68*(12), 53–55.

HILKER, R. J., ASMA, F. E., DAGHESTANI, A. N., and Ross, R. L. A drug abuse rehabilitation program. *Journal of Occupational Medicine*, June 1975, *17*, 351–354.

HILKER, R. J., ASMA, F. E., and EGGERT, R. A. Company-sponsored alcoholic rehabilitation program: Ten year evaluation. *Journal of Occupational Medicine*, October 1972, *14*, 769–772.

HILL, R. Must work success be bought at the cost of private life? *International Management*, November 1980, *35*(11), 21–22, 23.

HOLDEN, C. Behavioral medicine: An emergent field. *Science*, July 1980, *209*, 479–481.

HOLDEN, C. Innovation: Japan races ahead as U.S. falters. *Science*, November 14, 1980, *210*, 751–754.

HOLDEN, C. Looking at genes in the workplace. *Science*, July 23, 1982, *217*, 336–337.

HOLMES, T. Stress: The new etiology. In A. Hastings et al. (eds.), *Health for the whole person*. Boulder, Colo.: Westview Press, 1980.

HOLMES, T., and RAHE, R. The social readjustment rating scale. *Journal of Psychosomatic Research*, 1967, (11), 213–218.

HOLSTI, O. R. Limitations of cognitive abilities in the face of crisis. *Journal of Business Administration*, Spring 1978, *9*(2), 39–50.

HORNE, W. M. Effects of a physical activity program on middle-aged sedentary corporation executives. *American Industrial Hygiene Association Journal*, March 1975, *36*(3), 241–245.

Hotel & Motel Management. Employee satisfaction is good for business. July 1977.

HOWARD, J. H. et al. Coping with job tension—effective and ineffective methods. *Personnel Management*, September / October 1975, *4*(5), 217–326.

HOWARD, J. H. et al. Health patterns associated with Type A behavior: A managerial population. *Journal of Human Stress*, March 1976.

HOWE, G. *Employee physical fitness programs: Protecting the company's investment*. Unpublished master's thesis, Clemson University, April 1978.

HUMPHREY, R. D. Are you a stress carrier? *Training and Development Journal*, February 1978, *32*(2), 32–34.

HUNT, W. S. Change, stress and credit management. *Credit and Financial Management*, March 1981, *83*(3), 32–34.

HUSE, E. F. *Organizational development and change*. Boston: West, 1975.

IGLEHART, J. K. Health care and American business. *New England Journal of Medicine*, January 14, 1982, 120–124.

ILGEN, R., and HOLLENBACK, J. H. Role of job satisfaction in absence behavior. *Organizational Behavior and Human Performance*, June 1977.

INGELFINGER, F. J. Can you survive a medical diagnosis? *Human Behavior*, November 1980, 38–39.

International Management. Executive report: Shop-floor workers suffer most stress. January 1977, *32*(1), 4.

International Management. Executive fitness aids corporate health. February 1980, *35*(2), 19. (a)

International Management. The stresses that make managers ill. April 1980, 51–52. (b)

International Management. Stressing family life. May 1980, *35*(5), 37–38+.

International Management. Fitness counseling at work keeps executives trim. May 1981, *36*(5), 47.

IVANCEVICH, J. M., and MATTESON, M. T. Managing for a healthier heart. *Management Review,* October 1978, *67*(10), 14–19.

IVANCEVICH, J. M., and MATTESON, M. T. Optimizing human resources: A case for preventive health and stress management. *Organizational Dynamics,* Autumn 1980, *9*(2), 4–25.

JACOBS, J. Stay healthy, earn a reward. *San Francisco Sunday Examiner & Chronicle,* July 6, 1980, Section A, p. 1.

JACOBS, J. A profile of the workaholic: Addicted to work, not results. *San Francisco Sunday Examiner & Chronicle,* April 5, 1981, Section B, p. 2.

JACQUES, N., KOZLOWSKI, J. G., and MATHEUS, J. W. Personnel leadership in action. *Personnel Journal,* November 1979, *58*(11), 751, 757+.

JAFFE, D. *Healing from within.* New York: Alfred A. Knopf, 1980.

JANSSENS, L., and VANSINA-COBBAERT, M.-J. Closing a factory—managing termination. *Human Resource Management,* 1980, *4*(6), 2–5.

JENKINS, C. D. Social and epidemiologic factors in psychosomatic disease. *Psychiatric Annals,* 1972, *2*, 8–21.

JENNINGS, C., and TAGER, M. J. Good health is good business. *Medical Self-Care,* Summer 1981, 14–18.

JETTE, M. The participation of Canadian employees in physical activity. *Canadian Journal of Public Health,* 1980, No. 2, 109–111. (a)

JETTE, M. A regional analysis of physical fitness in a Canadian employee population. *Canadian Journal of Public Health,* 1980, *71*(4), 237–240. (b)

Johns Hopkins Medical Institutions. What do cost-benefit studies say about health education? *Physician's Patient Education Newsletter,* October 1979, *2*, 1–2.

JOHNSON, H. Are you the type to get a coronary? *International Management,* April 1979, *34*(4), 63.

JOHNSON, R. T., and OUCHI, W. G. Made in America (under Japanese management). *Harvard Business Review,* September / October 1974.

JOURARD, S. *The transparent self: Self-disclosure and well-being.* Princeton, N.J.: Van Nostrand, 1964.

JUDGE, J. F. Business moves, government lags. *Government Executive,* Washington, D.C., April 1974, *6*.

KAHN, R. L. Work, stress and health. *Industrial Relations Research Association Proceedings,* 1980, 257–265.

KAMIYA, J., and KAMIYA, J. Biofeedback. In Hastings, A. et al. (eds.), *Health for the whole person.* Boulder, Colo.: Westview Press, 1980.

KANTER, R. M. *Men and women of the corporation*. New York: Basic Books, 1979.

KARASEK, R. A., JR. Job demands, job decision latitude, and mental strain: Implications for job redesign. *Administrative Science Quarterly*, June 1979, *24*(2), 285–308.

KEEFER, R. D. Combating fraud and abuse—to your body. *Government Accountants Journal*, Winter 1979–80, *28*(4), 14–18.

KEELOR, R. O., Director of Program Development of the President's Council on Physical Fitness and Sports. Address to the 1976 Blue Shield Annual Program Conference, October 1976.

KEEN, S. Lovers vs. workers. *Quest / 81*, September 1981, 15–84.

KENNEDY, C. Maintaining top managers in good running order. *Director*, May 1976, *28*(11), 57.

KENTON, L., and PHILLIPS, C. Coping with stress. *Industrial Management*, November 1975, 32–35.

KETS DE VRIES, M. F. R. The midcareer conundrum. *Organizational Dynamics*, Autumn 1978, *7*(2), 45–62.

KETS DE VRIES, M. F. R. Organizational stress: A call for management action. *Sloan Management Review*, Fall 1979, *21*(1), 3–14.

KIEFHABER, A., WEINBERG, A., and GOLDBECK, W. *A survey of industry sponsored health promotion, prevention and education programs*. Washington, D.C.: Washington Business Group on Health, 1978.

KIEV, A., and KOHN, V. *Executive stress*. New York: AMACOM, 1979.

KIRITZ, S., and Moos, R. H. Physiological effects of social environments. *Psychosomatic Medicine*, March–April 1974, *36*(2), 96–114.

KLARMAN, H. E. *The economics of health*. New York: Columbia University Press, 1965.

KNOWLES, J. H. (ed.). *Doing better and feeling worse*. New York: Norton, 1977. (a)

KNOWLES, J. H. The responsibility of the individual. *Daedalus*, Winter 1977, 57–80. Adapted and reprinted in *Science*, December 16, 1977, *198*(4322). (b)

KOBASA, S. C. Stressful life events, personality, and health: An inquiry into hardiness. *Journal of Personality and Social Psychology*, 1979, *37*(1), 1–11.

KOBASA, S. C. The hardy personality: Toward a social psychology of stress and health. In J. Suls and G. Sanders (eds.), *Social psychology of health and illness*. Hillsdale, N.J.: Lawrence Erlbaum Associates, 1981.

KOBASA, S. C., HILKER, R. R., and MADDI, S. R. *Remaining healthy in the encounter with stress*. Presented to the 37th AMA Congress on Occupational Health, 1977.

KOBASA, S. C., HILKER, R. R., and MADDI, S. R. Who stays healthy under stress? *Journal of Occupational Medicine*, September 1979, *21*(9), 595–598.

KOERNER, D. R. Cardiovascular benefits from an industrial physical fitness program. *Journal of Occupational Medicine*, September 1973, 700–707.

KONDRASUK, J. Company physical fitness programs: Salvation or fad? *The Personnel Administrator*, November 1980, *25*(11), 47–50, 60.

KORNBERG, A. Genetic engineering—a revolution in medicine. *U.S. News & World Report*, March 16, 1981, 74.

KORNFELD, J. Hemodynamic anxiety ignoring Type A theory? *Medical Tribune,* May 27, 1981, 39.

KORNHAUSER, A. *Mental health of the industrial worker.* New York: Wiley, 1965.

KOTULAK, R. Prevention key to cutting doctor bills, hospital stays. *Chicago Tribune,* 1976.

KRAVETZ, D. J. Counseling strategies for involuntary terminations. *The Personnel Administrator,* October 1978, *23*(10), 49–54.

KREITNER, R. Employee physical fitness: Protecting an investment in human resources. *Personnel Journal,* July 1976, *55*(7), 340–344, 348.

KREITNER, R., WOOD, S. D., and FRIEDMAN, G. M. Warning: Your job may be killing you. *Business Week,* January / February 1981, *31*(1), 2–6.

KREVANS, J. R. Letter to UCSF campus community. August 4, 1982, 2.

KRISTEIN, M. Economic issues in prevention. *Preventive Medicine,* June 1977, *6.*

KRISTEIN, M. M., ARNOLD, C. B., and WYNDER, E. L. Health economics and preventive care. *Science,* February 4, 1977, *195,* 457–462.

KUNTZ, E. F. Businesses may be steady buyers of hospitals' wellness programs. *Modern Healthcare,* August 1981, *11*(8), 104, 106.

LALONDE, M. *A new prospective on the health of Canadians.* Ottawa: National Health and Welfare, 1974.

LAMBERSON, T. O. Realities of retirement point to need for corporate counseling programs. *Risk Management,* May 1978, *25*(8), 28–32.

LARSEN, R. *The Wausau story in good employee health.* President's Council on Physical Fitness and Sports. (Pamphlet)

LARSON, D. A. Labor supply adjustment over the business cycle. *Industrial and Labor Relations Review,* July 1981, *34*(4), 591–595.

LARSON, K. How companies can rein in their health care costs. *The Personnel Administrator,* November 1979, *24.*

LATACK, J. C. Person / role conflict: Holland's model extended to role-stress research, stress management, and career development. *Academy of Management Journal,* January 1981, *6*(1), 89–103.

LATTIME, E. C., and STRAUSSER, H. R. Arteriosclerosis: Is stress-induced immune suppression a risk factor? *Science,* October 21, 1977, *198,* 302–303.

LAZARUS, R. S. A strategy for research on psychological and social factors in hypertension. *Journal of Human Stress,* September 1978, 35–40.

LAZARUS, R. S. Little hassles can be hazardous to your health. *Psychology Today,* July 1981, 58–62.

LAZES, P. M. (ed.). *The handbook of health education.* Germantown, Md.: Aspen Systems, 1979.

Leading Edge. Aerospace employees network makes a difference. October 19, 1981, *2*(4), 1–2.

LEAVENWORTH, G. Building a mecca for executive fitness. *Venture,* June 1980, *2*(6), 78–79.

LECKER, S. Personality could be the key to business success. *International Management,* May 1981, *36*(5), 23–24.

LEFTON, D. Air controllers' stress debated. *American Medical News,* August 21–28, 1981, 1.

LEVEY, R. Fitness fever: Everybody into the company gym. *Dun's Review,* November 1980, *116*(5), 115–118.

LEVIN, A. S. *Protocol for immunologic assessment of cancer patients undergoing psychotherapy.* Grant Proposal. Oakland, Calif.: Western Laboratories Medical Group, 1979.

LEVIN, L. S., and IDLER, E. L. *The hidden health care system.* Cambridge, Mass.: Ballinger Publishing, 1981.

LEVIN, P. J., and WOLFSON, J. Health care and American business. *New England Journal of Medicine,* July 24, 1982, 320.

LEVINSON, H. *Emotional health in the world of work.* New York: Harper & Row, 1964.

LEVINSON, H. On executive suicide. *Harvard Business Review,* July–August 1975, *53*(4), 118–122.

LEWIS, C. My unprodigal sons. *Newsweek,* May 10, 1982, 11.

LIFF, S. Mental health of women factory workers. *Journal of Occupational Behavior,* April 1981, *2*(2), 139–146.

LIGHTBODY, J. A safety valve for employee stress. *International Management,* February 1981, *36*(2), 17–18.

LIPTON, M. Stress and the specter of the law. *Management World,* July 1981, *10*(7), 14–15, 44.

LOCKE, S. E. Stress, adaptation, and immunity: Studies in humans. *General Hospital Psychiatry,* 1982, *4,* 49–58.

LONDON, P., and SPIELBERGER, C. Job stress, hassles, and medical risk. *American Health,* March / April 1983, 58–63.

LOVE, J. R., and LOVE, L. B. Cost-benefit concepts in health: Examination of some prevention efforts. *Preventive Medicine,* September 1978, *7,* 414–423.

LOVE, K. G., and BEEHR, T. A. Social stressors on the job: Recommendations for a broadened perspective. *Group and Organization Studies,* June 1981, *6*(2), 190–198.

LUBLIN, J. S. Seeking a cure: Companies fight back against soaring cost of medical coverage. *The Wall Street Journal,* May 10, 1978 (front page).

LUBLIN, J. S. Stress research seeks clues to why children can't cope with life. *The Wall Street Journal,* April 10, 1979.

LUSTMAN, P., and O'HARA, D. J. Biofeedback—a new strategy for coping with stress. *Management World,* July 1981, *10*(7), 12–13.

LYNN, N. B., and VADEN, R. E. Role ambiguity and role conflict. *The Bureaucrat,* Winter 1978, *7*(4), 34–37.

MCALISTER, A., FARQUHAR, J., THORESEN, C., and MACCOBY, N. Behavioral science applied to cardiovascular health: Progress and research needs in the modification of risk-taking habits in the adult population. *Health Education Monographs,* 1976, *45*(4), 45–74.

MCCAMY, J. L., and PRESLEY, J. *Human life styling.* New York: Harper & Row, 1977.

MCCANN, J. P. A strategy to improve executive health. *SAM Advanced Management Journal,* Spring 1977, *42*(2), 33–37.

MCDONALD, C. A. Political-economic structures—approaches to traditional and modern medical systems. *Social Science & Medicine,* 1981, *15A,* 101–108.

McGaffey, T. N. New horizons in organizational stress prevention approaches. *The Personnel Administrator,* November 1978, *23*(11), 26–32.

McLean, A., *Occupational stress.* Springfield, Ill.: Charles C. Thomas, 1974.

McLean, A. A. Job stress and the psychosocial pressures of change. *Personnel,* February 1976.

McLean, A. A. (ed.). *Reducing occupational stress.* Cincinnati: DHEW (NIOSH) Publication No. 78–140, 1978.

McLean, A. A. *Work stress.* Reading, Mass.: Addison-Wesley, 1979.

Machlowitz, M. *Workaholics: Living with them, working with them.* Reading, Mass.: Addison-Wesley, 1980.

Maisel, A. Q. (ed.). *The health of people who work.* New York: The National Health Council, 1960.

Management Review. Staying in shape for the rigors of management. January 1975.

Management Review. Management stress: Sifting fact from myth. May 1979, *68*(5), 35.

Management Review. Managing employee health at Kimberly-Clark. August 1979, *68*(8), 42.

Management Review. One man's stress can be another man's challenge. September 1979, *68*(9), 36.

Management Review. Cooling the emotional climate. December 1979, *68*(12), 52.

Mandelblit, C. Personal communication, November 25, 1982.

Mann, G. V. *A proposal for a trial of the efficiency of fitness training for employed persons.* Nashville, Vanderbilt University, AAFDBI Abstract, 1979.

Manuso, J. Coping with job abolishment. *Journal of Occupational Medicine,* 1977, *19*(9), 598–602. (a)

Manuso, J. The use of biofeedback assisted hand warming training in the treatment of chronic eczematous dermatitis of the hands: A case study. *Journal of Behavior Therapy and Experimental Psychiatry,* 1977, *8,* 445–446. (b)

Manuso, J. Testimony to the President's Commission on Mental Health, Panel on Costs and Financing. *Report of the President's Commission on Mental Health* (Vol. 2, Appendix). Washington, D.C.: U.S. Superintendent of Documents, 1978, 512.

Manuso, J. Corporate mental health programs and policies. In L.K.Y. Ng, and D. Davis (eds.), *Strategies for public health.* New York: Van Nostrand Reinhold, 1981. (a)

Manuso, J. Executive stress management. *The Personnel Administrator,* November 1979, *24*(11), 23–26. (b)

Manuso, J. Staffing a corporate emotional health program. In Boston University–Washington Business Group on Health (eds.), *Employee mental wellness programs.* New York: Springer-Verlag, 1979. (c)

Manuso, J. *Affirmative action and corporate emotional health programs.* Presented at the American Psychiatric Association's Annual Convention, Chicago, Illinois, May 11–18, 1979. (d)

Marcus, A. M. Stress and choice: Making life decisions in mid-career. *Optimum,* 1979, *10*(2), 28–33.

Marcus, J. B. What the supervisor should know about transcendental meditation (Part 1). *Supervisory Management,* June 1978, *23*(6), 31–41.

MARGERISON, C., and FORDHAM, M. How to avoid the director's disease. *Director,* May 1976, *28*(11), 69–71.

MARSHALL, E. The politics of lead. *Science,* April 30, 1982, 496. (a)

MARSHALL, E. NRC must weigh psychic costs. *Science,* June 11, 1982, 1203–1204. (b)

MARSHALL, E. EPA's high risk carcinogen policy. *Science,* December 3, 1982, 975–978. (c)

MARSHALL, J. Job pressure, satisfaction and stress at executive levels: The implications for management development. *Proceedings of Academy of Management,* 38th Annual Meeting, August 1978, 33–37.

MARTIN, J. Corporate health: A result of employee fitness. *The Physician and Sportsmedicine,* March 1978.

MATTESON, M. T., and IVANCEVICH, J. M. Organizational stressors and heart disease: A research model. *Academy of Management Journal,* July 1979, *4*(3), 347–357. (a)

MATTESON, M. T., and IVANCEVICH, J. M. Straining under too much stress? *Management World,* July 1979, *8*(7), 4–7. (b)

MAULTSBY, M. Controlled study of effective psychotherapy on self-reported maladaptive traits, anxiety scores, and psychosomatic disease attitudes. *Journal of Psychiatric Research,* 1974, *10,* 121–132.

MAYER, L. A. That confounding enemy of sleep. *Fortune,* June 1975, *91*(6), 158–170.

MECHANIC, D. *Research and Analytic Report Series No. 14–74.* Madison: University of Wisconsin, Health Economics Research Center, 1974, 33.

Medical Economics. Patient visits down? Maybe they're seeing shrinks. November 9, 1981, 12.

Medical Tribune. CHD reactions to stress seem unrelated to either Type A or Type B personality. May 13, 1981, 1.

Medical World News. Companies urged to get more involved in health care. November 13, 1978, 85.

Medical World News. HMO's and NHI rate high on index of public ignorance. June 25, 1979, 52.

MEGLINO, B. M. Stress and performance: Implications for organizational policies. *Supervisory Management,* April 1977, *22*(4), 22–28. (a)

MEGLINO, B. M. The stress-performance controversy. *MSU Business Topics,* Autumn 1977, *25*(4), 53–59. (b)

MELHUISH, DR. A. Weighing the benefits of slimming. *International Management,* September 1979, *34*(9), 63.

MELHUISH, A. Keeping fit. *The Accountant,* August 21, 1980, *183*(5506), 302–304.

MELHUISH, A., and COOPER, G. The stresses that make managers ill. *International Management,* April 1980, *35*(4), 51–55.

MELSKI, B. *Body composition—its use in fitness programs.* Austin, Texas: AAFDBI Abstract, 1979.

Metropolitan Life Association. *National Newspaper Advertisement.* New York: Metropolitan Life Insurance Company, 1982.

MEYER, H. E. A fitness program for Canadian business. *Fortune,* January 14, 1980, *101*(1), 94–98.

MICKEL, F. B. Stress: Race to the bottom line. *Management Accounting.* April 1981, *62*(10), 15–20.

MILBOURN, G., JR. Alcohol and drugs: Poor remedies for stress. *Supervisory Management,* March 1981, *26*(3), 35–42.

MILES, R. H. Role requirements as sources of stress in R and D organizations. *Proceedings of Academy of Management,* August 1975, 191–193.

MILES, R. H. Individual differences in a model of organizational role stress: An empirical investigation. *Journal of Business Research,* May 1976, *4*(2), 87–102.

Ministry of National Health and Welfare and Recreation (Canada). *Proceedings of the National Conference on Employee Physical Fitness,* December 1975.

Minnesota Workers' Compensation Study Commission. *Who Pays?,* September 1977.

MIRKIN, G. How to cope with job stress. *Nation's Business,* January 1979, *67*(1), 69–72.

MOLANDER, C. The "mid-life crisis." *Journal of European Training,* 1976, *5*(1), 21–28.

MONAGAN, D. Auto industry seeks alcohol substitute. *Medical Tribune,* August 12, 1981, 12.

MOORE, W. C. Learning to live with stress. *Association Management,* June 1980, *32*(6), 113.

MORANO, R. A. How to manage change to reduce stress. *Management Review,* November 1977, *66*(11), 21–25.

MORRISON, D. E. Stress and the public administrator. *Public Administration Review,* July / August 1977, *37*(4), 407–414.

MORTON, W. E., and UNGS, T. J. Cancer mortality in the major cottage industry. *Medical Self-Care* (women and health issue), Winter 1979, *4*(4), 345–354.

MOSS, N. H., and MEYER, J. (eds.). *Food and nutrition in health and disease.* New York: New York Academy of Sciences, 1977.

MOUSTAFA, A. T., and SEARS, D. W. Feasibility of simulation of health maintenance organizations. *Inquiry,* June 1974, *11*(2), 143–150.

MUCHINSKY, P. M. Employee absenteeism—a review of the literature. *Journal of Vocational Behavior,* June 1977, *10*(3), 316–340.

The National Chamber Foundation. *How business can promote good health for employees and their families,* 1978.

The National Chamber Foundation. *A national health care strategy: How business interacts with the health care system,* 1978, pp. 17–18. (b)

Nation's Business. Staying trim, productive, and alive. December 1974, *62*(12), 26–28.

Nation's Business. How to succeed in fitness without really trying. January 1975, *63*(1), 45.

Nation's Business. A simple, cost-free and comfortable way to combat job tension. December 1976, *64*(12), 29–36.

NEHRBASS, R. G. Physical fitness pays off in productivity. *Personnel Journal,* December 1976, *55*(12), 600.

NELSON, H. U.S. medical cost: We're all to blame. *Los Angeles Times,* July 17, 1977.

NELSON, J. G. Health: A new personnel imperative. *The Personnel Administrator,* February 1980, *25*(2), 69–71.

New England Journal of Medicine. Detection and treatment of hypertension at the worksite, July 10, 1975, 65–68.

New England Journal of Medicine. Sounding board, September 28, 1977.

New York City Department for the Aging Newspaper. Pre-retirement resources, *Options,* February / May 1979, 6–7.

NEWMAN, J. E., and BEEHR, T. A. Personal and organizational strategies for handling job stress: A review of research and opinion. *Personnel Psychology,* Spring 1979, *32*(1), 1–43.

NEWMAN, J. W. The knack of learning to relax. *Marketing Times,* March / April 1979, *27*(2), 19–20.

Newsweek. Seeking cancer cures, August 31, 1970, *76,* 48.

Newsweek. Run for your life, April 19, 1976, 100.

NG, L.K.Y., and DAVIS, D. L. *Strategies for public health: Promoting health and preventing disease.* New York: Van Nostrand Reinhold, 1981.

NG, L.K.Y., DAVIS, D. L., and MANDERSCHEID, R. W. The health promotion organization: A practical intervention designed to promote healthy living. *Public Health Reports,* September / October 1978, *93*(5), 446–455.

NG, L.K.Y., DAVIS, D. L., and MANDERSCHEID, R. W. *Toward a conceptual formulation of health and well being.* Paper presented to AAAS, Houston, Texas, January 4, 1979.

NIEHOUSE, O. L., and MASSORI, K. B. Stress—an inevitable part of change. *SAM Advanced Management Journal,* Spring 1979, *44*(2), 17–25.

NOLAND, R. L. (ed.). *Industrial mental health and employee counseling.* New York: Human Sciences Press, 1973.

North American Rockwell and Phillips Petroleum Company. *Physical fitness—we support it* (pamphlet).

NOVACO, R. L. *Anger control: The development and evaluation of an experimental treatment.* Lexington, Mass.: D. C. Heath, 1975.

The Nutrition Foundation, Inc. *Present knowledge in nutrition* (4th ed.). Washington, D.C.: 1978.

ODE WAHN, C. A., and PETTY, M. M. A comparison of levels of job satisfaction, role stress, and personal competence between union members and nonmembers. *Academy of Management Journal,* March 1980, *23*(1), 150–155.

ODIORNE, G. S. Executives under siege: Strategies for survival. *Management Review,* April 1978, *67*(4), 7–12.

Office of Health Information and Health Promotion. *Proceedings of the National Conference on Health Promotion Programs in Occupational Settings,* State of the Art Papers. Washington, D.C.: Office of Health Information and Health Promotion, Public Health Service, Department of Health, Education, and Welfare, January 1979.

OGLIVIE, B. C., and PORTER, A. L. Business careers as treadmill to oblivion: The allure of cardiovascular death. *Human Resource Management,* Fall 1974, *13*(3), 14–18.

OLBRISCH, M. E. Psychotherapeutic interventions in physical health-effectiveness and economic efficiency. *American Psychologist,* September 1977, *32,* 761–775.

O'REGAN, B. Comparison of holistic and Western medical systems. *The Institute of Noetic Sciences Newsletter,* Fall / Winter 1978, 13.

ORGAN, D. W. The meanings of stress. *Business Horizons,* June 1979, *22*(3), 32–40.

ORTMEYER, C. F. Variations in mortality, morbidity, and health care by marital status. In C. L. Erhardt and J. E. Berlin (eds.), *Mortality and morbidity in the United States.* Cambridge, Mass.: Harvard University Press, 1974, pp. 159–588.

OUCHI, W. *Theory Z.* Boston: Addison-Wesley, 1981.

PALMORE, E. Predicting longevity: A follow-up controlling for age. *Gerontology,* Winter 1969, 14–20.

PAOLONE, A. M. et al. Results of two years of exercise training in middle-aged men and its effects on physical fitness. *American Journal of Public Health,* May 1974, 459–465.

PAOLONE, A. M. et al. Results of two years' exercise training in middle-aged men and its effects on physical fitness. *The Physician and Sportsmedicine,* December 1976, *4.*

PARASURAMAN, S., and ALUTTO, J. A. An initial multi-dimensional study of the causes and consequences of stress: Development of a predictive model. *Proceedings of Academy of Management,* 38th Annual Meeting, August 1978, 84–88.

PARASURAMAN, S., and ALUTTO, J. A. An examination of the organizational antecedents of stressors at work. *Academy of Management Journal,* March 1981, *24*(1), 48–67.

PARKES, C. M. *Bereavement: Studies of grief in adult life.* New York: International Universities Press, 1972.

PARKINGTON, J. J., and SCHNEIDER, B. Some correlates of experienced job stress: A boundary role study. *Academy of Management Journal,* June 1979, *22*(2), 270–281.

PARKINSON, R. S., and Associates (eds.). *Managing health promotion in the workplace: Guidelines for implementation and evaluation.* Palo Alto, Calif.: Mayfield Publishing Company, 1982.

PARSLOE, E. Developing the mind. *Management Today,* October 1978.

PASCALE, R. T., and ATHOS, A. G. *The Art of Japanese Management.* New York: Simon and Schuster, 1981.

PATCHIN, R. I., NOVAK, J., and DOTLICH, D. What happens when Americans try quality circles. *Boardroom Reports,* July 13, 1981, 5–6.

PATRINOS, D. Health pays industry dividends. *Milwaukee Sentinel,* April 19, 1977.

PATTERSON, W. P. Getting tanked up soothes body, mind. *Industry Week,* May 4, 1981, *209*(3), 102, 107.

PEARSON, C. E. *Educating for health in the workplace.* Presented at the 10th International Conference on Health Education, London, September 2–7, 1979. New York: Metropolitan Life Insurance Company.

PELLCANO, D. F. Overview of corporate pre-retirement counseling. *Personnel Journal,* May 1977, *56*(5), 235–237, 255.

PELLETIER, K. R. Biofeedback, In *Collier's Encyclopedia.* New York: Macmillan, 1977, 164–165. (a)

PELLETIER, K. R. *Mind as healer, mind as slayer: A holistic approach to preventing stress disorders.* New York: Delacorte and Delta, 1977. (b)

PELLETIER, K. R. Mind as healer, mind as slayer. *Psychology Today,* February 1977, 35–42 (c). Reprinted in C. F. Wilson and D. L. Hall (eds.), *Stress management for educators.* San Diego: Department of Education, 1980.

PELLETIER, K. R. Stress: Managing and overcoming it. In "Tools for transformation" section of *New Realities,* August 1978, 43–45.

PELLETIER, K. R. *Toward a science of consciousness.* New York: Delacorte and Delta, 1978.

PELLETIER, K. R. Holistic medicine: From pathology to prevention. *The Western Journal of Medicine,* December 1979, *13*(6), 481–483.

PELLETIER, K. R. *Holistic medicine: From stress to optimum health.* New York: Delacorte and Delta, 1979.

PELLETIER, K. R. Stress / unstress: A conversation with Kenneth R. Pelletier. *Medical Self-Care,* No. 5, 1979, 3–9.

PELLETIER, K. R. Holistic approaches to healing. In G. G. Meyer, K. Blum, and J. Cull (eds.), *Folk healing and herbal medicine.* Springfield, Ill.: Charles C. Thomas, 1980. (a)

PELLETIER, K. R. The mind is health and disease. In A. Hastings, J. Fadiman, and J. S. Gordon (eds.), *Holistic medicine: An annotated bibliography.* Rockville, Md.: National Institute of Mental Health, 1980. (b) Reprinted as *Health care for the whole person: A comprehensive guide to holistic medicine.* Boulder, Colo.: Westview Press, 1980. (c)

PELLETIER, K. R. *Longevity: Fulfilling our biological potential.* New York: Delacorte and Delta, 1981.

PELLETIER, K. R. *Corporate health promotion programs.* Ongoing study of the California NEXUS Foundation, San Francisco, 1983.

PELLETIER, K. R. Stress / unstress: A conversation with Kenneth R. Pelletier.

PELLETIER, K. R. "Stress: etiology, assessment, and management in holistic medicine." In *Selye's guide to stress research, vol. III.* New York: Van Nostrand Reinhold Company, Inc., 1983, 43–78.

PELLETIER, K. R. "Stress management: a positive approach to optimum health and longevity." *Generations: The Journal of the Western Gerontological Society,* Spring 1983, 26–30.

PELLETIER, K. R. "The longevity game: fulfilling our biological potential." *Healthline: The Journal of the Robert A. McNeil Foundation for Health Education,* August 1983, vol. II, no. 8, 1–3.

PELLIGRINO, J. F. Teaching stress management: Meeting individual and organizational needs. *SAM Advanced Management Journal,* Spring 1981, *46*(2), 27, 39+.

PENDLETON, B. Coping with managerial stress. *Management World,* January 1981, *10*(1), 25–27.

PENFIELD, W. *The mystery of the mind.* Princeton, N.J.: Princeton University Press, 1975.

The Perrier Study. *The Perrier Study: Fitness in America.* New York: Great Waters of France, January 1979.

The Personnel Administrator. Troubled employees: Whose responsibility? June 1979, *24*(6), entire issue.

Personnel Management. Strategies for relieving stress at work. June 1979, *11*(6), 28–31.

PETERS, J. M., PRESTON-MARTIN, S., and YU, M. C. Brain tumors in children and occupational exposure of parents. *Science,* July 10, 1981, *213*, 235–237.

PETERS, R. K., and BENSON, H. Time out from tension. *Harvard Business Review,* January / February 1978, *56*(1), 120–124.

PETERS, R. K., BENSON, H., and PORTER, D. Daily relaxation response breaks in a working population: I. Effects on self-reported measures of health, performance and well-being. II. Effects on blood pressure. *American Journal of Public Health,* October 1977, *67*, 946–953.

PETERSON, I. Stress can cause work "epidemics." *The New York Times,* Science Times section, May 29, 1979, 1.

PETERSON, I. Doubts surface on Love Canal study. *Science News,* August 14, 1982, *122*, 102.

PFEIFFER, G. Personal communication and packet of the Xerox Health Management Program, September 1983.

PHILLIPS, M. *The seven laws of money.* New York: Random House, 1974.

PILLER, C. Staying healthy at work. *Medical Self-Care,* Summer 1981, 6–11.

PINES, M. Psychological hardiness. *Psychology Today,* December 1980, 34–98.

POLLOCK, M. L., WILMORE, J. H., and FOX, S. M. *Health and fitness through physical activity: A volume of the American College of Medicine.* New York: Wiley, 1978.

PORTER, L. W. et al. *Behavior in organizations.* New York: McGraw-Hill, 1979.

PORTER, M. The loneliness of the long distance traveller. *Industrial Management Magazine,* July 1978, 20–23+.

A Practical guide for employee health promotion programs. Madison, Wis.: Health Planning Council, February 1979.

President's Council on Physical Fitness and Sports. *Fitness in the workplace.* Washington, D.C. 20201: 1982.

PRICE, B. Mental illness: A case for company concern. *Personnel Management,* December 1978, *10*(12), 39–43.

Private Practice. The great war in medicine, February 1981, 17–21.

Professional Reports. How to recognize and control stress that hurts your efficiency, April 1977, *7*(4), 12–14.

Professional Reports. How to reduce stress that threatens your well-being, July 1980, *10*(7), 9–12.

Professional Reports. Exercises to relieve tension and tone muscles when you're stuck at your desk, October 1980, *10*(10), 20–22.

PROVOSUDOV, V. *The effects of physical exercises on health and economic efficiency.* Paper presented at the University of Physical Culture, Leningrad, USSR.

PYLE, R. L. Corporate fitness programs—how do they shape up? *Personnel,* January / February 1979, *56*(1), 58–67. (a)

PYLE, R. L. Fitness development programs: Strengthening the corporate body. *Management World,* July 1979, *8*(7), 8–11. (b)

PYLE, R. L. Performance measures for a corporate fitness program. *Training and Development Journal,* August 1979, *33*(7), 32–38. (c)

PYLE, R. L. Performance measures for a corporate fitness program. *Human Resource Management,* Fall 1979, *18*(3), 26–30. (d)

PYLE, R. L. Trimming the corporate waist with fitness programs. *Business Horizons,* April 1980, *23*(2), 70–72.

QUICK, J. C. Dyadic goal setting and role stress. *Academy of Management Journal,* June 1979, *22*(2), 241–252.

QUICK, J. C., and QUICK, J. D. Reducing stress through preventive management. *Human Resource Management,* Fall 1979, *18*(3), 15–22.

QUINN, J. B. Do-it-yourself benefits. *Newsweek,* September 25, 1982, 17c–17g.

RABKIN, S. W., MATHEWSON, F. A., and TATE, R. B. Chronobiology of cardiac sudden death in men. *Journal of the American Medical Association,* September 1980, *244,* 1357–1358.

RADER, M. Suffering from information overload? *Management World,* December 1979, *8*(12), 9–11.

RAHE, R. H. Subjects' recent life changes and their near-future illness reports. *Annals of Clinical Research,* 1973, *4,* 1–16.

RAHE, R., and ARTHUR, R. Life change and illness studies: Past histories and future directions. *Journal of Human Stress,* March 1978.

RAHE, R. H., MAHAN, J. L., and ARTHUR, R. J. Prediction of near-future health change from subject's preceding life changes. *Journal of Psychosomatic Research,* 1970, *14,* 401–406.

RANDOLPH, T. Specific Adaptation. *Annals of Allergy,* Vol. 40, No. 5, May 1978, 333–345.

RASSMAN, W. R. Why health care is a costly disgrace. *Business Week,* January 26, 1981, 16.

RATKIN, I. D., and MERCHANT, R. K. Papanicolaou smear survey of a selected industrial population. *Journal of Occupational Medicine,* October 1968, *10,* 594–599.

Reader's Digest. Exercise is "plain good business." February 1976, 127–130.

RHOADS, J. M. *When is overwork not overwork?* Paper presented to Annual Meeting of the Academy of Psychosomatic Medicine, November 17, 1978. Adapted chart in J. I. Walker, Prescription for the stressed physician, *Behavioral Medicine,* September 1980, 12–17.

RHODES, E. C., and DUNWOODY, D. Physiological and attitudinal changes in those involved in an employee fitness program. *Canadian Journal of Public Health,* 1980, *71*(5), 331–336.

RICE, B. Can companies kill? *Psychology Today,* June 1981, 78–85.

RICE, D. *Estimating the cost of illness.* Washington, D.C.: National Center for Health Statistics, Public Health Service Publication 947-6.

RICHMOND, J. B. *Promoting health—preventing disease: Objectives for the nation.* U.S. Department of Health and Human Services. Washington, D.C.: U.S. Government Printing Office, 1980.

RIGGS, C. R. Working out at work. *Dun and Bradstreet Reports,* May / June 1980, *28*(3), 17–23.

ROESKE, N.C.A. Stress and the physician. *Psychiatric Annals,* July 1981, *11*(7), 10–31.

ROGERS, R. E. Executive stress. *Human Resource Management,* Fall 1975, *14*(3), 21–24.

ROMM, J. *Health promotion and disease prevention in the workplace.* Final report: Contract #233-79-3012. Bethesda, Md.: System Sciences, Inc., March 31, 1981.

ROSEN, G. *Preventive medicine in the United States 1900–1975.* New York: Science History Publications, 1975.

ROSENTHAL, S. Expressions of the emotions in the world of work. *Psychiatric Opinion,* December 1978, 24–28.

ROSS, G.H.B., and GOODFELLOW, J. L. A "fitness" approach to corporate survival. *Business Quarterly,* Autumn 1980, *45*(2), 19–25.

ROTENBERG, R. H., and SHRIER, E. Business travel; does it affect the marketing executive's performance? *Business Quarterly,* Winter 1979, *44*(4), 43–48.

ROUSSEY, L. E. Preventative maintenance for people, the hedge against stress cracks. *Personnel Journal,* May 1980, *59*(5), 354.

RUMMEL, R. M., and RADER, J. W. Coping with executive stress. *Personnel Journal,* June 1978, *57*(6), 305–307, 332.

RUSSEK, H. I., and RUSSEK, L. G. Is emotional stress an etiologic factor in coronary heart disease? *Psychosomatics,* 1976, *17*(2), 63.

RUTHERFORD, D. Alcoholic solutions. *The Accountant,* August 21, 1980, *183*(5506), 309–310.

SAGER, L. B. The corporation and the alcoholic. *Across the Board,* June 1979, *26*(6), 79–82.

SALK, J., and SALK, J. *World population and human values.* New York: Harper & Row, 1981.

SALMON, J. W., and BERLINER, H. S. Health policy implications from the holistic health movement. *Journal of Health Politics, Policy and Law,* Fall 1980, *5*(3), 1–47.

SALVENDY, G. Effects of job pacing on job satisfaction, psychophysiological stress and industrial productivity. *Proceedings of American Institute of Industrial Engineers,* Annual Conference, Spring 1980, 433–442.

San Francisco Chronicle. Medical care program developed by Mendocino city education department eyed. July 6, 1979, Section A, 1.

San Francisco Chronicle. Assistant superintendent of Mendocino schools views his health care plan. July 6, 1979, Section B, 5.

San Francisco Examiner. Study finds businesswomen hit more by stress than men. January 9, 1981, Section C–Business, 1.

San Francisco Chronicle. New health problem–longer lives. December 4, 1981, 1.

SAPOLSKY, H. M., ALTMAN, D., GREENE, R., and MOORE, J. D. Corporate attitudes toward health care costs. *Milbank Memorial Fund Quarterly, Health and Society,* 1981, *59*(4), 561–585.

SAPP, R. W., and SEILER, R. E. Accounting for performance: Stressful–but satisfying. *Management Accounting,* August 1980, *62*(2), 29–35.

SAUSER, W. I., ARAUX, C. G., and CHAMBERS, R. M. Exploring the relationship between level of office noise and salary recommendations: A preliminary research note. *Journal of Management Studies,* Spring 1978, *4*(1), 57–63.

SCHERER, G. Information packet of Scherer Brothers Lumber Company Program, 1983.

SCHRAMM, C. J. Measuring the return on program costs: Evaluation of a multiemployer alcoholism treatment program. *American Journal of Public Health,* January 1977, *67,* 50–51.

SCHULER, R. S. Effective use of communication to minimize employee stress. *The Personnel Administrator,* June 1979, *24*(6), 40–44. (a)

SCHULER, R. S. Managing stress means managing time. *Personnel Journal,* December 1979, *58*(12), 851–854. (b)

SCHUMACHER, E. F. *Small is beautiful.* New York: Harper & Row, 1973.

SCHWARTZ, G. E. *Stress management in occupational settings.* National Conference on Health Promotion Programs in Occupational Settings. Washington, D.C.: Department of Health, Education, and Welfare, January 17–19, 1979.

SCOTS, A. A., DUFF, J. I., and BERNSTEIN, J. E. *Health risk appraisal: The estimation of risk.* National Conference on Health Promotion Programs in Occupational Settings. Washington, D.C.: Department of Health, Education, and Welfare, January 17–19, 1979.

SEHNERT, K. W., and TILLOTSON, J. K. *A national health care strategy: How business can promote good health for employees and their families.* Washington, D.C.: The National Chamber Foundation, 1978.

SELIGMAN, M. E. *Helplessness: On depression, development, and death.* San Francisco: W. H. Freeman, 1975.

SELYE, H. *The stress of life.* New York: McGraw-Hill, 1956.

SELYE, H. On the benefits of eustress. *Psychology Today,* March 1978. (a)

SELYE, H. *The stress of life.* New York: McGraw-Hill, 1978. (b)

SHAY, P. E. The west—is it in a fatal tailspin? *San Francisco Chronicle,* March 3, 1981, 17.

SHEA, G. F. Cost effective stress management training. *Training and Development Journal,* July 1980, *34*(7), 25–26, 28–33.

SHEEHAN, D. W. Psychiatry in medicine. *Science News,* August 22, 1981, *11*(2), 119 (cited).

SHIMER, P. (ed.). Life insurance companies offer discounts for the fit. *Executive Fitness Newsletter,* 1978, *9*(21), 1–2.

SHOSTAK, A. B. Blue-collar stressors—workplace stress, reforms and prospects. *Reducing Occupational Stress,* Conference Proceedings of Center for Occupational Mental Health, Cornell College, and the National Institute for Occupational Safety and Health, U.S. Department of Health, Education, and Welfare, April 1978, 73–85.

SIEGENER, R. The thrill of victory, the agony of the feet. *Sales & Marketing Management,* December 1978, *121*(8), 42–43.

SIMPSON, D. *Analysis of the rationale for employee fitness.* Waterloo: Mutual Life Assurance Company of Canada, AAFDBI Abstract, August 1979.

SMALL, G. W., and BORUS, J. F. Outbreak of illness in a school chorus. *New England Journal of Medicine,* March 17, 1983, 632–635.

SMITH, H. P. Misconceptions about motivation. *Training,* March 1979, *16*(3), 54–56.

SMITH, L. Fighting stress. *Dun's Review*, January 1977, *109*(1), 59–61.

SMITH, R. D., and SHERMAN, C. Change of heart . . . change of mind. *American Health*, July / August 1982, 52–54.

Society of Prospective Medicine. New concepts in health: A new horizon. *Proceedings of 12th Annual Meeting of Society of Prospective Medicine*, San Diego, California, October 1976.

Society of Prospective Medicine. Let's all join the lucky people. *Proceedings of the 13th Annual Meeting of Society of Prospective Medicine*, San Diego, California, September 29–October 2, 1977.

SPERRY, ROGER W. Mental phenomena as causal determinants in brain function. In G. G. Globus (ed.), *Consciousness and the brain*. New York: Plenum Publishing, 1976, *5*, 195–206.

SPERRYN, D. Executive fitness. *The Accountant*, July 3, 1980, *183*(5499), 8–10.

SQUYRES, W. *Employee health promotion demonstration project*. Kaiser-Permanente Medical Group, Oakland, California, 1983.

STACEY, J. Business taking new look at care costs. *American Medical News*, October 3, 1980, 1–9.

STACEY, J. Business speaking up about health concerns. *American Medical News*, March 6, 1981, 20.

STAMLER, J. Primary prevention in mass community efforts to control the major coronary risk factors. *Journal of Occupational Medicine*, January 1973, *15*(1).

STAMLER, R. et al. A hypertension control program based on the workplace: A report on the Chicago Center. *Journal of Occupational Medicine*, September 1978, *20*, 618–625.

STANDKE, L. The advanages of training people to handle stress. *Training*, February 1979, *16*(2), 23–26. (a)

STANDKE, L. How to make sure the anti-stress training you get is what you need. *Training*, February 1979, *16*(2), 26. (b)

STARR, P. *The social transformation of American medicine*. New York: Basic Books, 1982.

Statistical Bulletin. Longevity of corporate executives. Metropolitan Life Insurance Company, February 1974.

STAVER, S. Physician teaches workaholics how to play again. *American Medical News*, February 20, 1981, 15.

STELLMAN, J. M., and DAUM, S. M. *Work is dangerous to your health*. New York: Pantheon, 1973.

STERN, F. M., and ZEMKE, R. First aid for stress. *Sales & Marketing Management*, May 18, 1981, *126*(7), 80–81.

STEWART, P. Healthy worker wins two tickets to Hawaii. *San Francisco Chronicle*, September 1, 1981, 5.

STOKES, B. Self-care: A nation's best health insurance. *Science*, August 10, 1979, *205*(4406), editorial page.

STOKES, J. Why not rate health and life insurance premiums by risks? *New England Journal of Medicine*, February 17, 1983, *38*(7), 393–395.

STONE, J. L., and CROWTHERS, V. Innovations in program and funding of mental health service for blue-collar families. *American Journal of Psychiatry*, May 1972, *128*(11).

STUDENT, K. Coping with psychological responsibility. *Conference Board Record,* July 1975, *12*(7), 61–64.

STUDENT, K. R. Changing values and management stress. *Personnel,* January / February 1977, *54*(1), 48–55. (a)

STUDENT, K. R. Coping with psychological responsibility. *The Personnel Administrator,* February 1977, *22*(2), 43–46. (b)

STUDENT, K. R. Managing change: A psychologist's perspective. *Business Horizons,* December 1978, *21*(1–6), 28–33. (a)

STUDENT, K. R. Personnel's newest challenge: Helping to cope with greater stress. *The Personnel Administrator,* November 1978, *23*(11), 20–24. (b)

STYBEL, L. J. Getting over getting fired. *Business Week,* January / February 1981, *31*(1), 48–51.

SUMNER, S. How 4 women executives in Solano County handle stress. *Vallejo Times Herald,* January 18, 1981.

SUN, M. Preventive research office suggested. *Science,* March 26, 1982, *215*, 1599.

SUOJANEN, W., and HUDSON, D. Coping with stress and addictive work behavior. *Atlanta Economic Review,* March / April 1977, *27*(2), 4–9.

SUOJANEN, W. W., and HUDSON, D. R. Coping with stress and addictive work behavior. *Business,* January / February 1981, *31*(1), 7–14.

SUTTERLY, D. C. Stress and health: A survey of self-regulation modalities. *Topics in Clinical Nursing,* April 1979, *1*(1), 1–30.

SYME, S. L., and BERKMAN, L. F. Social class, susceptibility, and sickness. *American Journal of Epidemiology,* 1976, *104*(1), 1–8.

SYME, S. L., and TORFS, C. P. Epidemiologic research in hypertension: A critical appraisal. *Journal of Human Stress,* March 1978, 43–48.

SZENT-GYORGYI, A. *Electronic biology and cancer: A new theory of cancer.* New York: Marcel Dekker, 1976.

TARDY, W. Ten ways to cope with stress in your working environment. *Black Enterprise,* November 1977, *8*(4), 39–42.

TAVERNIER, G. How to cope with the middle-age crisis. *International Management,* April 1977, *32*(4), 24–26.

TAVERNIER, G. Twilight world of the night-shift. *International Management,* November 1978, *33*(11), 18–26.

TAYLOR, G. R. People pollution. *Ladies' Home Journal,* October 1970, 74–79.

TAYLOR, H. M. Occupational health management—by objectives. *Personnel,* January / February 1980, *57*(1), 58–64.

TAYLOR, R. L. The widowed: Risks and interventions. *Wellness Resource Bulletin,* California Department of Mental Health, Mental Health Promotion Branch, Winter 1981, *2*(1).

TAYLOR, T. G. *Importance of vitamins to human health nutrition.* Baltimore: University Park Press, 1979.

TEAS, R. K., WACKER, J. G., and HUGHES, R. E. A path analysis of causes and consequences of salespeople's perceptions of role clarity. *Journal of Marketing Research,* August 1979, *16*(3), 355–369.

TERKEL, S. *Hard times.* New York: Washington Square Press (Simon and Schuster), 1978.

THOMAS, L. Cancer viewpoint. *Medical Tribune,* November 19, 1980, 8.

THORESEN, C. E., TELCH, M. J., and EAGLESTON, J. R. Approaches to altering the Type A behavior pattern. *Psychosomatics,* June 1981, *22*(6), 472–481.

Time. Stunning turnaround at Tarrytown, May 5, 1980, 87.

Time. America shapes up, November 2, 1981, 94–106.

TIMMINS, W. Public-employee physical fitness programs. *Public Personnel Management,* 1981, *10*(2), 217–222.

Training. Helping your people manage stress. June 1977, *14*(6), 8.

Training. MBO can improve quality of working life. May 1979, *16*(5), 6–8. (a)

Training. Teaching employees to be physically fit. February 1979, *16*(2), 30–31. (b)

Training. Training salespeople to deal with stress: An interview with Francis Meritt Stern. August 1979, *16*(8), 26–28. (c)

Training. Study tracking stress responses. June 1981, *18*(6), 21, 87.

TUBBS, S. L. How physician and therapist team up in a company setting. *Occupational Health & Safety,* April 1979, 63–67.

TUBBS, S. L. Effective stress management. *Proceedings of American Institute of Industrial Engineers,* Spring Annual Conference, 1980, 227–229.

TULKU, T. *Time, space and knowledge.* Berkeley, Calif.: Dharma Publishing, 1977.

TULLOH, B. High pressure man. *Director,* July 1977, *30*(1), 34–35.

University of Michigan Press. *The economics of health and medical care.* Ann Arbor, 1974.

U.S. Department of Health, Education, and Welfare. *Healthy People: The Surgeon General's report on health promotion and disease prevention.* Department of Health, Education, and Welfare (PHS), Pub. #79-55071. Washington, D.C.: U.S. Government Printing Office, 1979.

U.S. Department of Health, Education, and Welfare. *National conference on health promotion programs in occupational settings.* Washington, D.C.: U.S. Government Printing Office, January 17–19, 1979.

U.S. Department of Health, Education, and Welfare. *Proceedings of the National Conference of Health Promotion Programs in Occupational Settings.* Washington, D.C.: U.S. Government Printing Office, 1979.

U.S. Department of Health and Human Services, Public Health Service, Office of Health Information and Health Promotion. *Toward a healthy community (organizing events for community health promotion).* Publication #DHHS (PHS) 80-50113. Washington, D.C.: U.S. Government Printing Office, 1980.

U.S. Department of Labor. *OSHA safety and health standards: General industry digest.* OSHA #2201. Washington, D.C.: U.S. Government Printing Office, 1975.

U.S. News & World Report. Why 60 million Americans are on a fitness kick. January 14, 1974.

U.S. News & World Report. How to deal with stress on the job. March 13, 1978, 80–81.

U.S. News & World Report. As companies jump on fitness bandwagon. January 28, 1980, 36–39.

U.S. News & World Report. Medicine and profits—unhealthy mixture? August 17, 1981, 50–54.

VAILLANT, G. E. *Adaptation to life: How the best and brightest came of age.* Boston: Little, Brown, 1977.

VICKERY, D. M., and FRIES, J. F. *Take care of yourself: A consumer's guide to medical care.* Reading, Mass.: Addison-Wesley, 1976, Revised Ed., 1981.

VISINTAINER, M. A., VOLPICELLI, J. R., and SELIGMAN, M. E. Tumor rejection in rats after inescapable or escapable shock. *Science,* April 23, 1982, *216,* 437–439.

VOGEL, E. *Japan as number one.* Cambridge, Mass.: Harvard University Press, 1979. See chapter, The large company: Identification and performance.

WALDRON, I. et al. The coronary-prone behavior patterns in employed men and women. *Journal of Human Stress,* December 1977, 2–18.

WALKER, J. I. Prescription for the stressed physician. *Behavioral Medicine,* September 1980, 12–17.

The Wall Street Journal. Age of anxiety: Stress and how it affects our lives, April 2, 5, 10, 16, 1979, 1 et seq.

WANZEL, R. S. *Determination of attitudes of employees and management of Canadian corporations toward company sponsored physical activity facilities and programs.* Unpublished doctoral dissertation, Edmonton, Alberta, 1974.

WARRICK, D. D. Managing the stress of organization development. *Training and Development Journal,* April 1981, *35*(4), 37–41.

WARSHAW, L. J. *Managing stress.* Reading, Mass.: Addison-Wesley, 1979.

WEBER, S. *How OSHA enforces the law.* New York: INFORM, 25 Broad Street, 10004, 1981.

WEGMAN, D. H., and PETERS, J. M. Oat cell lung cancer in selected occupations. *Journal of Occupational Medicine,* December 1978, *20*(12), 793–796.

WEICK, K. E. The management of stress. *Masters in Business Administration,* October 1975, *9*(9), 37–40.

WEINBERG, S., KIEFHABER, A., and GOLDBECK, W. Health Promotion in the Community: A Guide to Working with Employers. Report prepared by the staff of the Washington Business Group on Health. Fall 1980.

WEISS, S. M. et al. Coronary-prone behavior and coronary heart disease: A critical review. *Circulation,* June 1981, *63*(6), 1199–1215.

WELCH, R. Ontario strives for fitness. *Municipal Recreation Pools, Rinks, & Parks,* Summer 1977, 8–14.

WHITELY, W. T. Nature of managerial work revisited. *Proceedings of Academy of Management,* 38th Annual Meeting, August 1978, 195–199.

WIDNER, P. *Behavior modification weight control groups for employees.* Boston: Peter Bent Brigham Hospital, AAFDBI Abstract, 1979.

WILL, G. F. Run for your life. *Newsweek,* April 19, 1976.

WILL, G. F. A right to health? *Newsweek,* August 7, 1978, 88.

WILLARD, H. S., and SPACKMAN, C. S. (eds.). *Occupational therapy.* Philadelphia: Lippincott, 1974.

WILLIAMS, R. B., JR., et al. Type A behavior and elevated physiological and neuroendocrine responses to cognitive tasks. *Science,* October 29, 1982, *218,* 483–485.

WILSON, C. F., and HALL, D. L. *Preventing burnout in education.* La Mesa, Calif.: The Wright Group, 1981.

WILSON, L. *The wellness phenomenon.* Minneapolis, Minn.: Wilson Learning Corporation, 1980.

WILSON, P. *Industrial fitness programs in the United States: A 1979 status study.* La Crosse, Wis.: University of Wisconsin at La Crosse, AAFDBI Abstract, August 1979.

WITTE, R., and CANNON, M. Employee assistance programs: Getting to management's support. *The Personnel Administrator,* June 1979, *24*(6), 23–26+.

WITZENBURG, G. A management philosophy for the eighties. *Mainliner,* November 1981, 111–118.

WOELFEL, C. J. Stress in public accounting. *National Public Accountant,* July 1979, *24*(7), 8–10.

WOMACK, W. M., MUNDT, J. W., and REINKING, R. What you should know about stress. *Management World,* July 1981, *10*(7), 8–11, 44.

WONKEL, M. L. *Involvement in vigorous physical activity: Considerations for enhancing self-motivation fitness motivation.* Workshop, Geneva Park, Ontario, March 26–28, 1980.

WRICH, J. T. *The employee assistance program.* Center City, Minn.: Hazelden Foundation, 1974.

WRIGHT, H. B. Multinationals—the stress problem. *Director,* April 1977, *29*(10), 24.

WRIGHT, H. B. Executive health: Health maintenance. *The Accountant,* June 22, 1978, *178*(5396), 841.

WRIGHT, H. F. *Physiological changes in a large employee population.* Fairfax, Va.: Institute of Human Performance, AAFDBI Abstract, August 1979.

YANKELOVICH, D. The new job values. *Psychology Today,* May 1978, 46–50.

YANKELOVICH, D. The work ethic is underemployed. *Psychology Today,* May 1982, 5–8.

YARVOTE, P. M. *Management and organizational development.* New York: McGraw-Hill, 1971.

YARVOTE, P. M. et al. Organization and evaluation of a physical fitness program in industry. *Journal of Occupational Medicine,* September 1974, *16*(9), 589–598.

YOUNG, R. Sweat equity. *Next,* May 1981, 34–43. (a)

YOUNG, R. Working out at work, or how corporations intend to trim the fat. *Next,* March / April 1981, 75–83. (b)

YUHASZ, M. Western's Business School a pioneer in fitness program for managers attending management courses. *Business Quarterly,* Summer 1978, *43*(2), 82–85.

YUHASZ, M. Physical fitness in Canadian business and industry. *Business Quarterly,* Spring 1979, *44*(1), 72–75.

ZALESKI, H. K. Shaping your in-house physical fitness program. *Industry Week*, September 18, 1978, *198*(6), 121–144.

ZALEZNIK, A. et al. Stress reactions in organizations: Syndrome, causes and consequences. *Behavioral Science, 22,* 1977.

ZEMKE, R. Try behavioral contracts and feedback. *Training,* November 1979, *16*(11), 32.

ZEMKE, R. Quality circles: Using pooled effort to promote excellence. *Training,* January 1980, 30–31.

ZEMKE, R., STERN, F., and SCHWARTZ, C. Stress: A convincing argument for increasing sales training during the coming recession. *Training,* December 1979, *16*(12), 31.

ZION, L. Keeping fit in the company gym. *Fortune,* October 1975, 136–143.

ZION, L. Exercise in plain good business. *Reader's Digest,* February 1976, 127–130.

ZION, L. A layman's guide to cardiovascular disease. *Bostonia* (Boston University), Winter 1978. (a)

ZION, L. The new business boom—employee fitness. *Nation's Business,* February 1978, 68–73. (b)

ZION, L. From board to locker room. *Time,* January 22, 1979.

ZOHMAN, L. *Run for life.* Hartford: Connecticut Mutual Life Insurance Company, 1978.

ZOOK, C. J., and MOORE, F. D. High cost users of medical care. *New England Journal of Medicine,* May 1, 1980, 996–1002.

Index

KENNETH R. PELLETIER, PH.D., is an assistant clinical professor in the Department of Medicine—Division of General Internal Medicine, the Department of Psychiatry, and the Langley Porter Psychiatric Institute, University of California School of Medicine, San Francisco; also assistant professor, Department of Public Health, University of California, Berkeley; and director of the California Health and Medical Foundation in San Francisco. Dr. Pelletier was a Woodrow Wilson Fellow and studied at the C. G. Jung Institute in Zurich, Switzerland. He has published over 100 professional journal articles in behavioral medicine, clinical biofeedback, and neurophysiology. Dr. Pelletier has been an advisor to the Department of Health and Human Services, the National Institute of Mental Health, the Institute for the Advancement of Health, the Canadian Ministry of Health, and the World Health Organization. During the development of health promotion programs, Dr. Pelletier has been a consultant to the Washington Business Group on Health and many major corporations including Xerox, IBM, Wells Fargo Bank, Del Monte, Lawrence Livermore Laboratories, and Bank of America. He was appointed by former Governor Jerry Brown to the California Governor's Council on Wellness and Physical Fitness. Dr. Pelletier is co-author of *Consciousness: East and West,* author of the international best seller *Mind as Healer, Mind as Slayer: A Holistic Approach to Preventing Stress Disorders; Toward a Science of Consciousness; Holistic Medicine: From Stress to Optimum Health;* and *Longevity: Fulfilling Our Biological Potential.*